THE POLITICAL ECONOMY
OF BIG BUSINESS

THE POLITICAL ECONOMY OF BIG BUSINESS

M. A. Utton

St. Martin's Press · New York

St. Martin's Press, Inc., 175 Fifth Avenue, New York, NY 10010
Printed in Great Britain
First published in the United States of America in 1982
ISBN 0-312-62255-4

Library of Congress Cataloging in Publication Data

Utton, M.A. (Michael A.), 1939 –
The political economy of big business

1. Big business – Great Britain.
2. Industrial Concentration – Great Britain.
3. Industry and State – Great Britain.
I. Title
HD2356. G7U87   1982   338.8'0941 82-10739

ISBN 0-312-62255-4

For VERA
and also for
RALPH, OLIVER and TIM

Contents

Preface

During the last thirty years there has been an enormous growth in the largest private sector enterprises in the UK. Big business has thus become even bigger and the doubts and ambiguities that have always surrounded its activities have multiplied. To the traditional concerns about the relationship between size and efficiency and the effectiveness of competition in oligopoly have been added those of consumer sovereignty and protection, conglomerate growth, pollution and deterioration of the environment, and political influence.

The development places governments in a quandary. If macroeconomic policies are to be successful, big business has to thrive but precisely which micro-policies will bring the most satisfactory economic performance are still the subject of a great deal of controversy. One view, which I largely share, is that an invigorated antitrust policy, supplemented by discriminatory taxes, is likely to produce the best long-run results. Alternatively some argue that the private sector should be left to its own devices with a minimum of government intervention, while there is still considerable support for a third approach which involves a tripartite agreement between government, trade unions and business to achieve national economic objectives. Other observers, of course, regard the whole edifice of the mixed economy as so bad as not to be worth saving in anything like its present form.

The aim of the book is first to discuss the economics of big business, drawing on the empirical evidence that is now available on a number of the central issues (Part two) and then to use this as the framework for an examination of several different policy approaches (Part three). Some of the material I have used recently in a course on Industrial Economics given at Reading and I am grateful to the many students whose perceptive comments have been of great value while the book was being written.

I would especially like to thank Margaret Lewis and Beryl Jones who prepared speedily and with great efficiency the final typescript.

Michael Utton
University of Reading
July 1981

Part One: Introduction

Part One: Introduction

1

The Ambiguities of Size

INTRODUCTION

Most people writing about large companies tend to be either iconoclasts or apologists. Extreme views are not difficult to understand when a small group of massive companies, privately owned and operated, seem to impose themselves on more and more aspects of everyone's lives. The absolute size of the largest private[1] companies seems, to many people, to free them from the kinds of constraints to which all institutions in a democracy are supposed to be subject and makes it almost inevitable that they will be the centre of intense controversy. Furthermore, the controversy does not vary with the general economic climate. Whether or not most macroeconomic policy objectives are being achieved, the obtrusiveness of the largest companies will still generate a lot of opposition. For example, when things are going well, since their investments are likely to be very large and frequently in industries of advanced technology the spillover or external effects may be especially dramatic. As a result in many people's minds the problems of pollution are inextricably bound up with the development of the largest companies.

On the other hand, when things are going badly the obtrusiveness of the largest companies shows itself in a different way. It is not long ago that various writers were able to claim that the largest companies had found the secret of eternal life. No longer dependent on the fortunes and energies of the members of a single family, it appeared for a time that nothing could interrupt the consolidation and growth of those mature companies whose reputation made their names household words. Starting, however, with the recession in the late sixties and then regularly ever since, a steady procession of these companies, on the point of extinction, has sought assistance from the state. While the last

3

rites may be uttered over the all but lifeless bodies of its human citizens, illustrious corporate citizens *in extremis* have been able to regenerate themselves by a transfusion of public money. Again the sheer size of some of these companies goes a long way to explain this policy of successive governments. They quickly recognized that the direct and indirect effects of the complete collapse of these firms would have such a profound effect on employment, output and exports that, whatever their election manifesto may have proclaimed about the need for private industry to be independently viable, direct assistance has to be given if their other economic policies are to succeed (and their chances of eventual re-election kept alive).

Thus whatever the overall condition of the economy the largest companies pose a number of serious political and economic problems which the mixed economies of Western Europe and North America are still trying to resolve.

There are many observers, quite apart from those of the revolutionary left, who are highly critical of the economic power of large companies, including groups who would regard themselves as strongly wedded to a society organized along 'liberal-capitalist' lines. In the remainder of this chapter, therefore, we describe some of the main economic objections to the size and power of the largest companies, followed by the counter arguments that can be made in their defence.

THE CASE AGAINST LARGE COMPANIES

One argument which has always found some support, is that many of the largest companies have either made no gains in their efficiency by increasing their size or have actually had their efficiency diminished by growing too large. In its present form the argument has a number of separate strands which are mentioned here and developed in chapter 3.

The first point is that used by Marshall to explain why firms are likely to suffer eventually from decreasing returns to scale. Long-run unit costs will rise, on this view, because of the growing problems of co-ordination created by the complexity of large organizations. The input of entrepreneurial skills will grow less than in proportion to the growth of output and even if production costs are lower for larger firms these will be more than outweighed by managerial diseconomies in such areas as input procurement and scheduling, distribution of the final product and flexibility of response to changes in demand. Furthermore, even though large-scale production techniques may on paper suggest lower unit costs, because of the difficulties of ensuring good labour relations in the very large plants that these methods may often require, in practice actual output per time period may fall far short of what is theoretically possible.

Secondly, very large firms are likely to encounter problems of X-inefficiency. Where they have some measure of market power and where the pressures of competition on profit margins are therefore diminished, managements may find it increasingly difficult to keep costs to a minimum. Indeed they may themselves pursue policies that are incompatible with cost minimization. Clearly there is a distinction between decreasing returns to scale, shown traditionally by the rising section of a long-run average cost curve and X-inefficiency which implies that the firm is operating above both the long-run curve and the relevant portion of the appropriate short-run average cost curve.

Market power is usually seen as a necessary condition for the emergence of X-inefficiency. But it also suggests the presence of another kind of inefficiency. Where firms are able persistently to keep prices above long-run marginal costs (a standard definition of market power), one inference is that output is being restricted below the level compatible with a socially optimum allocation of resources. Furthermore not only is a regime of very large firms going to produce these static inefficiencies in allocating a given bundle of resources, but they are also likely to produce an inferior growth performance. Lacking the incentives provided by competition and weighed down by a bureaucracy which may be over cautious and cumbersome in making vital decisions, the largest companies, it is claimed, will stifle innovation not from conspiracy but through sloth.

The indictment, then, of very large firms for inefficiency rests on four grounds, (a) they will suffer from decreasing returns to scale, (b) they will be unable to control their cost levels, even if they really want to, (c) they generate a socially suboptimal allocation of resources, and (d) their innovation performance will be poor.

The next part of the case against large companies concerns their effect on competition. Some of the staunchest supporters of competitive markets for the allocation of resources may be found on the boards of the largest companies. Yet some of their policies are often seen as a major force in the destruction of competition. A special place in this part of the argument is reserved for diversification, or in its more recent and sinister sounding guise, 'conglomeration'. As we shall see in chapter 5, this feature of the recent rapid growth of the largest companies (their tendency to spread their activities across a wide range of industries, especially, in the first instance, by acquisition), has received a great deal of attention, yet the systematic evidence both on the extent of this development and more important on its effects, is still rather scanty. First, it is argued that large firms will be able to subsidize losses in some markets into which they are diversifying from profits in other markets where they have an established (and possibly monopolistic) position. Such losses will go beyond those normally anticipated by the owners of risk capital entering a new field, and have the specific aim of eliminating or at least curbing more specialized rivals in order that eventually they may make a high return. In a comparatively short time, therefore, on this view, competitive markets will be reshaped into semi-monopolistic ones. As the large companies grow more diversified they will be able to negotiate reciprocal agreements with suppliers and customers on terms favourable to themselves. Indeed the use of the term 'reciprocal', implying mutual benefit, is simply a cynical gloss on arrangements which serve to undermine the independence of smaller, more vulnerable firms. Finally, once the level of aggregate concentration has reached a certain level (something like half the output produced by the hundred largest firms is a reasonable rule of thumb), the largest firms will encounter each other in so many different markets where they have shares of varying sizes, that they will find it mutually beneficial to compete in only muted ways. The forms of competition associated with oligopoly may thus find their way into markets hitherto regarded as competitive, even though the market shares of the largest companies may be quite modest. In order to avoid the danger of upsetting tacit agreements in other markets where they also compete with the largest firms they will arrive at similar arrangements in all the new markets they enter. The opportunities for enterprising and efficient smaller firms to increase their market shares will thus be undermined by the long reach of the conglomerates.

Ultimately all of these effects will mean that in most industries the only feasible new entry, customarily regarded as an important source of revitalization for competition, will be from the subsidiaries of existing giants which, as we have just seen, will be more interested in reaching a *modus vivendi* with established rivals than pursuing an independent policy. To the critics, there-fore, diversification by the largest firms will have important and adverse effects on competition.

On a number of grounds they also take strong exception to competition by varying selling costs (see chapter 4). Advertising in particular has always had an uneasy place in economic analysis but Professor Galbraith has no qualms in asserting that it is the primary means by which consumer sovereignty has been under-mined in order to ensure that consumption becomes a mere adjunct to the production process, thus assisting management in its planning objectives. On this view since advertising in effect creates demand there is no reason any longer to accept that satis-faction of these wants in any way enhances consumer welfare. In Galbraith's words 'Producers proceed actively to create wants through advertising and salesmanship. Wants thus come on depend on output. In technical terms it can no longer be assumed that welfare is greater at an all round higher level of consumption than at a lower one' (Galbraith, 1976). Thus, if you share this view, a case can be made that the resources devoted both to the want creation and consequent production are being used in a socially wasteful way and should, therefore, be reallocated to a more socially useful purpose. A rather milder view which nevertheless is in the same vein as Galbraith's thesis, is that con-sumers (at least American consumers at whom the remarks were primarily aimed) have abdicated their position in the face of advertising and are prepared to accept passively whatever man-ufacturers wish to produce for them which may better suit large-scale production techniques than a discriminating taste. The in-ference is again that consumers' satisfaction is less than it might be with the same level of resources but differently deployed.

A subtler variation on this theme is that advertising may actu-ally help to destroy consumer satisfaction. The images and ways of life portrayed in advertisements tend to create dissatisfactions amongst observers who measure their own standard of living adversely against that created in the synthetic world on the tele-vision screen or roadside hoarding. If some of the products shown in the advertisements are actually purchased by friends and neighbours the effect becomes many times stronger. The satisfac-tion or utility that a consumer obtained from his Mini declines when his neighbour buys a Jaguar. In this case the level of his utility does not depend solely on the bundle of goods (including money) that he has but also on the bundle of goods that his neighbour has. Under these circumstances it is again no longer necessarily true that if his bundle of goods increases he is in any sense 'better off' because his neighbour may have had an even greater increase in his bundle of goods: he not only acquires a Jaguar but a swimming pool and a cottage in the country. Thus by helping to generate these interdependencies between consumers' utility functions, advertising undermines consumer satisfaction.

Those who hold these views, however, would be quick to point out that this is only one side of the case against advertising and the large firm. The points made so far concentrate on the side of consumption. On the production side an equally strong case can be made against the inherent waste and damage to competition from large-scale advertising.

One view is that advertising leads to a proliferation of brands of a product which are basically all the same but which have superficial differences of packaging, colouring or presentation. If the products could somehow be standardized scarce resources could be released for more pressing economic needs. In addition the nature of competition in many consumer goods industries where firms are few, strengthens the argument that advertising leads to waste. Direct price competition is rare in such industries and any fundamental changes in supply or demand conditions calling for a change in prices is administered by the price leader. The major part of the competitive effort is, therefore, channelled into various forms of non-price competition, especially advertising. For the firms themselves the problem is then one of deciding exactly what level of expenditure on advertising and related sales promotion will just meet their explicit objectives. Unfortunately because of the interdependence of the behaviour of the leading firms a large part of the advertising budget may have to be based on conjectures about the likely policies that rivals are going to adopt. On top of this is a degree of uncertainty about the impact a particular campaign: similar expenditures in successive periods may have quite different effects on sales. Unlike a price cut whose effect may be rapid and fairly predictable the outcome of an increased advertising budget is likely to be much less certain. For these reasons, just as a nuclear arms race may be set in motion by one country attempting to gain an advantage over another with a new weapon but then finding that all that has happened is both countries have doubled their stockpiles, so increased advertising expenditures by one oligopolistic firm may be largely neutralized by the response of this closest rival. Neither may then find it possible to reduce their expenditures. Advertising agents, television tycoons and newspaper proprietors may rejoice but many others will feel that 'competition' is far from producing an optimum allocation of resources.

What is more the cumulative effect of such expenditures may be especially harmful to the entry of new competition which is supposed to play an important part in regulating the performance of industry. The amount of brand preference built up by advertising over a number of years may mean that any newcomer to the industry will either have to incur higher selling expenses per unit of sales or similar selling expenses but at a lower unit price than established firms. In either case the entrant would be at a cost disadvantage and this may be sufficient to deter him altogether from entering the industry. The cost disadvantage will apply whether the potential entrant is well established in other industries and already of substantial size or whether it is an entirely new firm without other interests, although clearly in the latter case other difficulties, like raising adequate capital may also act as a deterrent. If the barriers to entry are important enough, little or no fresh competition will emerge and there may be few constraints on the prices charged by existing firms. So a further charge against the largest companies may be that they can earn high profits due to the effects of their past and present advertising expenses (amongst other factors) which shield them from the rigours of actual or potential competition.

More recently opponents of big business have turned their attention to externalities and in particular to pollution. They argue that just as such firms can control price and advertising levels to meet their private profit maximizing objectives, so too the choice of inputs and composition of output will be chosen without regard to the spillover effects. They are frequently using technologies whose long-run effects may be potentially devastating or at the very least highly uncertain. While at the simplest, therefore, their activities lead to a further misallocation of resources, more fundamentally they can result in the serious ill-health of workers, consumers or outsiders not to mention, in some instances, an irreversible degradation of the environment.

Furthermore, attempts by the government to control various forms of pollution by, for example, imposing restrictions on production methods or setting standards for the quality of discharges into the environment, are likely to be hampered by the collusion of the large firms who have a joint interest in ensuring that the cost increases that they will have to incur as a result of the policies, are minimized. They may either not disclose information about particular products or processes to which in the nature of the case they have greater access or they may deliberately exaggerate the private costs of installing pollution control equipment. There is no guarantee, as a result, that the controls imposed or the standards set are the socially most efficient and desirable.

The list of points mentioned in the case against big business is not intended to be exhaustive but it does contain the main elements of the usual lines of attack, embellished as they frequently have been in recent years by additional emphasis on multinational operations.

THE DEFENCE OF LARGE COMPANIES

In simply *meeting* the criticisms made above, it might appear that the case for large companies is simply a defensive or apologetic one rather than one of positive advantages. But the ambiguity surrounding such companies is due precisely to the reasoned reply that can be made to the critics. First, on the question of efficiency it may have been true at the time that Marshall was writing that diminishing returns to scale set an upper limit to the size of efficient companies but two recent developments have either nullified the argument altogether or in effect pushed further out the point where diminishing returns become important. The first of these developments has been the advances made in management science, especially in methods of co-ordinating very large operations even where these may be spread across many different industries. An example of this development is the adoption by many of the largest companies of a multi-divisional form of internal organization in place of the former, more monolithic, unitary form. This change, it is claimed, allows very large organizations to retain the flexibility and performance usually associated with much smaller companies. The second development is the use of high-speed computers which can process very rapidly the large volume of information on many aspects of the firm's operations and thus ensure that channels of communication stretching from the lowest to the highest levels can remain efficient. It is thus quite possible for even the largest companies to remain highly sensitive to factor price movements, changes in tastes and final demands, as well as labour relations on the shop floor.

Two of the other criticisms of the efficiency of the largest companies result, it might be argued, from a basic misunderstanding of the pressures of competition. The notion that managements in these firms will either have little interest in or be unable to minimize costs and thus tolerate X-inefficiency takes no account of the dynamics of the competitive process and probably stems from a misuse of the perfectly competitive model. Simply because there may be very few firms in an industry each with a large market share does not mean that they lose all interest in cost minimization. A firm which allowed its profit margins to fall because of its inability to control costs would soon find itself in difficulties. With profits out of line with comparable firms, funds for investment from internal sources would dry up and from external sources only be available on progressively worsening terms, as investors turned to more likely prospects. The need for very large organizations to monitor carefully the cost and profit performance of their separate components is one of the primary motives for their switch to the multi-divisional form of organization already mentioned.

The charge of X-inefficiency would, therefore, be denied. So too, the view that the largest companies cause social inefficiency by restricting output. Indeed the case may be stronger here because the original point depended on the assumption that a change in organization of industries from small-scale methods to large-scale, administered by relatively few firms, would leave the industry supply function unchanged. In many cases it is precisely because of the dramatic cost savings possible through large-scale production methods that led to the emergence of the large firms. In other words through important internal economies of scale the supply function for the industry shifts to the right giving lower costs of production than could be achieved by using small-scale methods. These savings would be sacrificed if the organization of such industries was fundamentally changed. Furthermore, although prices may be in excess of marginal cost, the difference (or net profit margin) will be kept to moderate levels not only by the form of competition described briefly above, but by competition from imports which for an economy like the UK may be the most important check on any monopolistic developments.

As far as the innovation performance of the largest companies is concerned their defenders may be content to rest their case on the recent experience in many industries. They may, however, add the following points. In many industrialized countries it has been the case for some time that the largest companies are responsible for a disproportionate share of all resources devoted to research and development. This is hardly surprizing since these companies are the best able to underwrite the potential losses that some research projects will undoubtedly incur. Similarly they are in the best position to afford large pieces of experimental equipment which may only show positive returns years after their construction. No-one denies that the brilliant, initial idea for a product or process may often come from an outstanding individual, but this is simply to say that fortunately men rather than machines are still the source of ideas. To ensure that those ideas do not languish and die, modern applied scientists need the resources of a large company especially during the most expensive, development stage. Unfortunately history does not record how many brilliant ideas in the past have been forgotten because the inventor ran out of funds at a crucial stage. But recent history does record the number of successes nourished by the support of the largest companies.

Furthermore, it may be argued, since the largest companies do tend to be more diversified than others, there is a higher chance that more discoveries will find fruitful applications in a shorter space of time than in an economy where smaller specialists predominate. The outcome of research is inherently unpredictable and frequently new possibilities may arise which the wide experience of a large diversified company may be able to take up but which a more specialized firm may either overlook or take much longer to develop simply because of its comparatively narrow range of knowledge. In other words this may be an important 'economy of diversification'.

As for the earlier point that large firm diversification tends to undermine competition, it can be argued that this is out of touch with industrial experience. The internal organization of the largest companies is designed precisely to ensure that each product division can be responsible for its own profit performance for which targets will have been set. The management of each division will be judged on its performance. Under these conditions to argue that one division may be used to subsidize the losses of another which is engaged in a predatory price war is to endow managers with a degree of altruism more likely in a charity than in a conglomerate. Quite apart from this, however, is the very strong possibility that cross subsidization will fail to gain a large market share in a newly entered industry. Even if the uneconomically low prices of the diversified company do drive specialized competitors from the industry (and this seems implausible, as we shall see below) they will only be able to make abnormally high profits thereafter if they can prevent the emergence of new competition, including that of other large firms.

A more likely prospect is for the entry of large diversifying firms to act as a pro-competitive force in industries which have had sheltered and cosy lives for some time. Far from undermining competition, therefore, as the critics allege, under modern conditions the diversification of large firms actually enhances the process.

Similarly, it can be argued that Galbraith's view of the 'dependence effect' misses the main point about consumer demand. Only in the most primitive and backward societies are the demands for goods based on innate needs for food, warmth and shelter. In any other society, including our own, individuals either learn by observing others or are told by word of mouth or some other means of the availability of goods which perform certain tasks. The desire neither for washing machines, nor Mozart operas, nor farmhouses in Vermont can by any stretch of the imagination be regarded as inborn but will be the result of a process of learning. An important role in this process is played by advertising. There seems to be no reason for regarding the post-advertising pattern of demands as any less urgent, virtuous or innate than pre-advertising demands. They are simply different. Furthermore, to blame advertising for the presence of interdependent utility functions is rather like blaming the meteorological office for bad weather. Envy has been with us considerably longer than Madison Avenue and will continue for long after it has returned to the wilderness.

The essence of the case for advertising is that it provides the essential function of informing consumers about the characteristics and availability of new and existing products. It thus helps to bridge the gap between production and final sale. In the absence of knowledge very few or no sales will be made and however efficient production is, a waste of resources will result. In the real world, rather than in the abstract world of economic models, information is not free and consumers do not all instantaneously have perfect knowledge of all the goods and services available to them. Consequently it is quite reasonable that information costs should be included in the final selling price.

As far as advertising and competition are concerned, economic analysis of this issue seems to have got off on the wrong foot about 1933 and has never properly corrected its early mistakes. As a result, the orthodox view is that in the absence of advertising the demand curves of individual firms are perfectly elastic. The introduction of advertising and recognizable brand names then has the effect of making demand curves relatively inelastic, or at any rate less than perfectly elastic. Consequently firms attain some degree of monopoly power over the market. In the Chamberlinian large group case this leads to the famous 'excess capacity' theorem of a long-run equilibrium where all firms make normal returns but produce at less than minimum unit cost.

If the world is viewed initially, however, as one of monopolies rather than as one of many competing firms in each industry, then the introduction of advertising has the effect of breaking up the market of the established monopolists and helping to produce a more competitive performance. In other words, on this view, advertising is seen as a means of making individual firm demand curves *more* not less elastic. The view is thus in line with the notion of the informative role of advertising. Furthermore the facts on this issue, it is claimed, tend to bear out this pro-competitive role of advertising rather than that mentioned in the previous section which saw advertising as the bulwark of monopoly.

Finally, as far as pollution is concerned, the problems would have arisen even if the concentration of industry had remained at the same level as it was at the turn of the century. They are the result of the growth of population, technical knowledge and output. By definition 'external' effects are not taken into account in market transactions. If they were they would no longer be external and there would be no problem. It is therefore illogical to attack firms for pursuing a private rather than a social objective. As is usual in economics the question is not one of all or nothing, but of deciding what is the optimal use of resources and, in the case mentioned, the optimal level of pollution.

Large companies operating in sensitive areas have been quick to recognize the need for co-operation with the government, if only because it is in their own long-run interest. By focusing mainly on the large size of the companies involved, critics tend to distract attention from the complexity of the problem which arises as much from final consumption as from production, as well as in economies with totally different social organizations.

CONCLUSION

The justice of these claims and counter-claims is examined in more detail in the successive chapters of Part two of this study (chapters 2–6), although for reasons of space we have had to be selective rather than encyclopaedic. The pretensions of economics to be a science implies that competing hypotheses on a particular issue can be tested against the facts: those that stand up to the test are accepted, at least temporarily, and those that do not are revised or rejected. Unfortunately, as we shall see, the evidence is not usually so easy to interpret or of a sufficiently high quality to give clearcut answers. Despite undoubted advances in empirical research there are still, therefore, many unresolved questions and differences of interpretation. As a consequence quite a wide spectrum of different policy proposals can be made by observers who are, by and large, all broadly in favour of the basic political and economic organization of western societies (chapters 7–9).

One group, however, does not share this common ground. They anticipate quite fundamental and revolutionary changes in society to correct the evils of advanced capitalism, some of whose main features were predicted long ago by Marx. Three points may be briefly mentioned. First, and most important, Marx envisaged the absolute and relative growth in size of some companies in capitalist economies which would bring very high levels of industrial concentration as the inevitable outcome of the competitive process. Secondly, he foresaw that the control of the largest companies would increasingly pass to specially trained managers who would not own a large part of the enterprise but who nevertheless would wield considerable power and influence because of the size of the resources over which they would preside. In its turn, this would mean, thirdly, that owners of capital would become to all intents and purposes simply rentiers without any positive role in the administration of resources. It is remarkable the way in which Marx foresaw these developments which now play a central part in the discussion of modern capitalism. In chapter 10, therefore,

we discuss more fully the interpretation put on these developments by some modern followers of Marx.

The final chapter summarizes those policies which, if adopted,
might serve to halt or even reverse the trend of increasing concentration while retaining a largely decentralized economy.

Part Two: Problems

2

The Anatomy of the Corporate Giants

INTRODUCTION

Serious concern amongst economists over the growth and size of the largest enterprises is of comparatively recent origin but it is true that they have been interested in the variable rates of growth of firms for some time. Marshall's analogy between firms and trees in the forest is one of the best known in economics and first made its appearance in the original edition of *Principles of Economics* in 1890. The purpose of that analogy was to explain the reassuring process by which firms grew to maturity, due largely to the skill and energy of one man, and then declined under the less robust guidance of the founder's more effete descendants. By the sixth edition of his book in 1910, Marshall was, with characteristic caution, hedging his bets. The analogy between firms and trees in the forest held 'only before the great recent development of vast joint-stock companies which often stagnate but do not readily die' (Marshall, 1961).

But for most who accepted the almost universal validity of the principle of diminishing returns to scale, the growth of firms could be viewed with equanimity. Thus, while a host of spectacular mergers and acquisitions were transforming the structure of American industry in the last part of the nineteenth century, economists were mainly wrestling with other problems, so that it was left largely to populists to stir Congress into passing the first antitrust laws. There was also a merger movement in the UK at the turn of the century and while it included a great many individual firms, it is generally agreed that the effect on the structure of industry was far less profound than in the USA and it provoked no direct policy response.

In the inter-war period the central concern was to mitigate the worst effects of the Depression and adopt policies which would

'rationalize' out-dated parts of the industrial structure by amal-
gamation to eliminate surplus capacity and by encouraging cartels
in the hope of maintaining employment. Only during the long
period of growth and full employment after the Second World
War have economists been prominent in questioning the wisdom
of the apparently relentless growth of the largest companies. Certainly the statistical materials available for analysing the dominance of the giants have improved enormously and some of these
are analysed in the present chapter. We can determine, for example, just how large the biggest companies are, and in which sectors of the economy they are mostly found. We can also trace the
relative growth of these companies in the UK in the last fifty
years and make some tentative comparisons with the largest
companies in other Western economies.

The growth and size of the largest companies reveals only one
side of the coin. To understand the significance of their growth we
need also to look at the other side, at who now owns and controls
the companies. The last few years have seen important shifts in
ownership away from a multitude of individual investors, each
holding only a minute fraction of the equity, towards an institutional ownership which owns large blocks of shares but which has
hitherto been loath to exercise anything other than the very negative power of selling holdings when they think appropriate.
Recent research also allows us to examine the present extent of
the divorce of ownership from control in these companies and to
determine the importance of internal compared with external
sources of finance for their growth.

These questions are the concern of the next two sections of this
chapter. In the fourth section we consider some more general
doubts about the continued viability and rationale of the corporate sector.

THE SIZE AND GROWTH OF THE GIANTS

The increasing concern at the growth of the largest companies in
the UK and elsewhere has ironically gone hand in hand with
unprecedented rises in real output and incomes. In the UK, for
example, gross domestic product per head at constant prices practically doubled between 1930 and 1965 compared with the
increase of rather more than one-fifth that occurred in the previous thirty-five years.[1] In view of such improvements representa-

Table 2.1 *Manufacturing enterprises[a] employing over 40 000 people: UK compared with other countries 1972*

	Size of country		Large enterprises		Importance of large enterprises relative to[c]	
	Population (millions)	Manufacturing employment (millions)	Number	Employment[b] (millions)	Population (indices, UK = 100)	Manufacturing employment (indices, UK = 100)
UK	55.8	7.78	30	2.67	100	100
USA	208.8	18.93	89	8.05	81	124
France	51.7	5.93	12	1.15	46	56
Germany	61.7	10.53	12	1.59	54	44
Italy	54.4	5.83	6	0.64	24	32
Benelux	23.4	2.47	5	0.80	72	95

Source: Prais (1981), p. 156

a Excluding iron and steel.
b World employment by parent and subsidiary companies (also used to determine which enterprises employ over 40 000).
c Ratios of employment in large enterprises to national population and to manufacturing employment converted to indices.

employment per plant therefore fell from 750 to 430 in the same period. This implies, secondly, that an important part of their growth was by acquisition and merger: different estimates put this at between one quarter and one third in the period 1960–72. Estimates of the effect of mergers on the increase in concentration in manufacturing have ranged from about 40 per cent to more than 100 per cent of the total (in the latter case, concentration would actually have fallen in the absence of mergers, see in particular Hannah and Kay (1977)). The multiplicity of their plants and the importance of their acquisitions suggests, thirdly, that concentration in individual industries as well as the spread of the largest firms' activities across different industries (that is diversification) has probably increased.

In fact there are clear indications that diversification and concentration in individual industries have both increased. Taking diversification first, and measuring it by the extent to which firms' output was in industries other than their primary (that is most important) industry, then diversification increased, on average, from 23 per cent in 1958 to 33 per cent in 1968. In other words by 1968 one third of firms' output came, on average, from their plants operating in industries away from their primary industry. For enterprises in a sample of forty-three industry groups this index of diversification increased in thirty-five cases between 1958 and 1968 and declined in only eight cases (Utton, 1979, Table 6.4).

Diversification, however, is an intrinsically slippery concept to measure and analyse. For example the percentage of firms' operations outside their most important industry (the measure we have just used) takes no account of the number of different activities undertaken whereas the simple number of industries in which firms operate gives no weighting to their respective importance. To overcome these difficulties measures have been developed which can be interpreted as a 'numbers equivalent'. A firm which has its activities spread *equally* among say, four industries is clearly more diversified than one operating equally in only three industries. An index which tells you, therefore, that the extent of diversification is the *equivalent* of a firm operating equally in four industries can be used for direct comparisons between firms. In fact measures of this kind for the UK and USA suggest that on the whole despite recent increases the largest firms are rather less diversified than some commentators, carried away perhaps by the conglomerate merger boom of the late

1960s and early 1970s, have proclaimed. For the largest 200 UK manufacturing companies the 'numbers equivalent' diversification index works out at between three and four: i.e. the largest firms were diversified to the equivalent of operating equally in three or four industries.[6] The figure for the largest 460 USA firms is rather less than this but since size and diversification are related, the index for the top 200 firms may be very close to that for the UK.

There are undoubtedly some highly diversified companies in both countries but even amongst the largest firms the statistics suggest that for many their most important two or three activities still play a dominant part in their overall strategy. On the other hand they do frequently have a large number of peripheral activities which may be quite remote from their 'home-base technology' or manufacturing skills but which account for only a small part of their total sales. It is this characteristic that accounts for our finding plants owned by one or other of the largest 200 manufacturing firms in every one of the 120 or so separate industries within manufacturing. The chances are also high that at least one of the leaders in these individual industries (and possibly two or three) also come from the largest firms. In each industry where one of the giants has its main operations there will now usually be the subsidiaries of between five and six other giants whose main activities are elsewhere (Utton, 1979). A similar pattern has been documented for the USA (Blair, 1972).

The picture, therefore, is one in which the largest firms have an increasing share of the manufacturing sector as a whole and an important part of this increase is accounted for by the spread of their activities across a number of different industries. The consequences for competition and the performance of industry of this web of relationships between the largest firms has recently been the subject of a great deal of speculation. The siren voice that has probably been heard longest in this respect is that of Corwin Edwards who has argued that oligopolistic interdependence may now depend on the firms' overall size and the multiplicity of their encounters in different industries rather than simply on a large market share in a particular industry (Edwards, 1964).

We return to this question in chapter 5 but for the present we look at what has been happening to the structure of individual manufacturing industries while the largest firms have been growing so rapidly. In theory at least the level of concentration in individual industries could have remained stable if the relative growth of the largest companies overall was entirely taken up with diversification. Thus, for example, although say, ICI may have increased its share of manufacturing output taken as a whole, this may have been achieved by diversifying into industries like paper, plastic products and man-made fibres without necessarily increasing its share in its more traditional chemical markets. In practice, of course, the increase in aggregate concentration has been so great and swift that a sharp increase in product concentration has also occurred. Over the period 1958–68, for example, Hart and Clarke recorded an increase in the average percentage of sales accounted for by the five largest firms for a sample of 144 products[7] from 55 per cent to 63 per cent. Between 1968 and 1975 for a larger sample, the average five-firm concentration ratio increased further from 63 to 65 per cent (Hart and Clarke, 1980; pp. 4–5). Their detailed analysis suggested that the rate of increase had slowed in the first half of the 1970s (just as the rate of growth of aggregate concentration has also slackened). A corollary of this increase in the average level of product concentration has been an increase in the number of products which can be classified as 'highly concentrated'. In one sample of 121 products, for example, the number having a concentration ratio of 75 per cent or above rose from thirty-five to fifty-five between 1958 and 1975 (Utton, 1981).

As a first approximation it is these industries where a few firms have large shares that we might expect oligopolistic collusion to be most successful, simply because it is likely to be easier for the leaders to monitor the behaviour of each other and trace and respond to any serious attempt to disrupt the prevailing price structure.[8] Not surprisingly where members of the largest hundred manufacturers are also market leaders for a particular product, concentration tends to be a lot higher than for other products (Utton, 1979).

One qualification to the above remarks on the growth and level of product concentration should be noted. The concentration data are collected in such a way that no allowance is made for imports while exported goods are included. In the present context if we are mainly concerned with the possible relationship between product concentration and market power, obviously imports are likely in many cases to be of great importance and should, therefore, be taken into account. There is some preliminary evidence that suggests that if imports are treated as in competition with domestic output, then the average level of product concentration is considerably lower than that suggested by the above figures. On this basis the average five-firm concentration level may have been nearer to 56 per cent than the 65 per cent in 1975 recorded by the official figures (Utton, 1981a).

The main points coming out of this brief discussion of the present structure of manufacturing industry in the UK are the following. First, a small group of very large enterprises are now responsible for more than two-fifths of sales in manufacturing, having practically doubled their share in the last thirty years. Secondly, members of this select group will encounter each other in a large number of different manufacturing industries through their subsidiaries (a reflection of the enormous growth in the number of separate plants operated by these companies). Thirdly, individual markets within manufacturing are increasingly dominated by firms with large market shares. The leaders will not always be from the group of the hundred largest overall but in many markets they will be and these tend to be more heavily concentrated. Fourthly, to the extent that imports compete directly with the domestic output of a particular product, the official figures will overstate the effective concentration level.

In other sectors, for which there are generally far less systematic data, the pattern is more varied.[9] At one extreme is the nationalized sector which now accounts for approximately 9 per cent of total employment. Thus in gas, electricity, railways, coal mines, postal services and telecommunications, steel and shipbuilding the single state-owned corporation rules in almost complete isolation. But in many of their markets the availability of close substitutes circumscribes the market power of the corporations. The creation of a nationalized enterprise for the production of electricity only establishes a 'monopoly' over those parts of its total output for which there are no close substitutes, namely lighting. Where other sources of energy are close substitutes for particular purposes, especially heating and power for appliances, the monopoly is limited. Thus in the UK there is the rather bizarre spectacle of two state-owned enterprises – electricity and gas – hiring prime time on the commercial television channel (they cannot advertise on the publicly owned BBC) to promote the merits of their respective products which for some purposes are in direct competition.[10]

At the other extreme are industries like agriculture, construction and some sections of the retail trade and personal services sector where entry is comparatively easy and any monopoly is highly localized and probably short lived. Even here, however, the last twenty-five years or so have seen some dramatic changes, especially in those areas of retailing which have switched to self-service methods. In practice this has meant, for example, that in many localities a large proportion of the food sales are made by the branches of perhaps four or five sizeable chain stores. On the other hand, only two companies in food retailing appear in a listing of the hundred largest 'industrial' companies.[11] But if retail distribution as a whole is taken as the frame of reference, including entertainments and mail order firms, then the number rises to about twelve and to about twenty-five in the largest 200.[12] Considering then, that the retailing, wholesaling and entertainment industries account for about 10 per cent of GNP compared with 29 per cent for the manufacturing sector these industries are still under-represented among the country's industrial giants.

As far as the financial sector is concerned commercial banking is now largely the province of the 'Big 4' following the realignments which took place in 1969 when the National Provincial merged with the Westminster and Barclays acquired Martins. The Monopolies Commission had in the previous year, however, recommended against the proposed merger between Barclays and Lloyds, then ranked first and third amongst London Clearing Banks. In insurance the structure is not quite as concentrated but in both the life and non-life parts of the industry the biggest company is much larger than its nearest rival and in each case perhaps four or five companies account for about 30–40 per cent of the total business.

Concentration amongst those institutions which have specialized in mobilizing the funds of small savers, unit trusts and building societies, was moderate in the middle 1970s. The largest five building societies were responsible for about half of all building society deposits and the largest four unit trusts accounted for about 43 per cent of all funds managed. The specialist institutions providing funds for private industry, finance and acceptance houses, were more heavily concentrated. In each, the largest five firms were responsible for about two-thirds of the total business (Aaronovitch and Sawyer, 1975; p. 111).

In the non-manufacturing sectors, therefore, and leaving aside the nationalized enterprises where entry is often prevented by law, there is nearly always a small number of very large concerns which would appear on any list of the country's largest commercial and industrial undertakings. We have to search very hard to find industries where this is not now the case: agriculture, parts of the construction, retail and personal services sectors are probably the best examples. If the home of 'big business' was once the public utilities and manufacturing it now seems to be equally comfortable in any environment.

OWNERSHIP, CONTROL AND FINANCE

The enormous growth in the size of the largest companies this century has meant that for most of them ownership has passed well beyond the reach of the original founders to a number of outside investors whose interest is almost purely financial. These owners may feel no continuous identity with the fortunes of the companies in which they hold shares and if company performance does not come up to scratch, then they can sell out. Control of the companies and responsibility for their destiny is now largely in the hands of professional managers who, for the most part, have probably attained their elevated position through ability and merit. Thus 'the managerial revolution' is an approximate counterpart in the private sector of industry to the reform of the civil service which took place in the latter part of the nineteenth century.

The broad outline of the changed pattern of ownership and control is well known. The main purpose of this section is to provide brief answers to three questions related to this change. First, who now owns the largest companies? Secondly, what stake do directors have in companies they control? Thirdly, what are the main sources of finance for the largest companies?

The answer to the first question would probably have been not so long ago that the 'new' owners of the largest companies[13] consisted usually of a very great number of not especially wealthy individuals. Indeed this view led certain commentators to argue that the traditional assumption of profit maximization as the prime motivation of firms should be replaced by some alternative that better reflected the preferences of managers who could, for the most part,[14] run the concern unhampered by irksome responsibilities to shareholders. As long as distributed profits were comparable with other companies encountering similar risks, then managers were free to run the companies in whatever way they pleased because the dispersal of share ownership made it very unlikely that they could be replaced.

The position now, however, is rather different. In the same period that the largest companies were, as we have seen, practically doubling their share of manufacturing sector output, the ownership of all quoted companies was passing rapidly into the hands of a comparatively small group of financial institutions. A detailed analysis of the recent changes in the financial environment of large companies has been published by Prais (1981). In this section we draw extensively on chapter 5 of this definitive study.

The financial institutions comprising insurance companies, pension funds, investment companies and unit trusts became, for a variety of reasons, so popular as a means of mobilizing personal savings, that by 1972 they held resources greater than the value of *all* commercial and industrial companies[15] in the UK. In the 1960s and early 1970s, the group's resources were growing at the rate of about 6 per cent per year and their funds requiring an investment home exceeded many times the total amount of new issues. The balance was made up by personal sales. If this trend were to continue unchanged, personal portfolios of shares would soon have disappeared entirely. In the sixteen-year period 1957–73 the percentage of all quoted ordinary shares in the UK held by these institutions more than doubled from approximately 18 per cent to just over 40 per cent.[16] There is no reason to think that this trend will be halted, let alone reversed, even given the increased uncertainty that has accompanied the economic recession of recent years. It therefore seems highly likely that by the mid or late 1980s the financial institutions will hold in the region of two-thirds of all ordinary shares of UK quoted companies.

So far the managers of these companies have shown little inclination to play any direct part in the running of the commercial companies in which they may have a large holding. But as their total holdings get larger they may decide to play a more positive role. Furthermore, as Prais clearly shows, for a number of perfectly good private reasons, the large financial institutions not surprisingly favour holdings in large quoted companies.[17] In particular as they wish to deal in large blocks of shares (to spread the administrative and fixed costs) obviously they will wish to do this without affecting the price of the shares concerned. Such operations are only possible for dealings in very large companies. One important consequence, therefore, of the concentration of ordinary share ownership in the hands of the financial institutions has been to worsen the prospects of small- and medium-sized companies seeking to raise new long-term capital.[18]

The argument is sometimes made that unit trusts are ensuring a much wider share ownership than would otherwise occur. The small investor obtains all the benefits usually associated with a large diversified portfolio, especially stability in earnings, and can therefore risk equity holdings, albeit at one remove. No doubt this accounts a great deal for their popularity but it does not alter the fact that *control* of a very large volume of shares is in the hands of a comparatively small number of people.

It is interesting to contrast this position with that of the directors of large industrial companies. The answer to the second question posed at the beginning of this section is that the directors of the largest companies own a very small share indeed of their companies' equity. Relying on Prais again, he estimated that in 1972 the median holding of the boards of the hundred largest manufacturing companies was a little under one-half of one per cent. There was considerable variation amongst the companies: in eleven, for example, the directors held more than 10 per cent and this helped to push the arithmetic mean holding to 4.2 per cent. The time is thus well passed when a substantial minority holding was thought necessary for those in control of a company.

A related aspect of this question concerns the extent of multiple directorships: in particular how many directors of the largest companies sit on more than one board? In Table 2.2 we show the number of directors from the largest fifty manufacturing companies who also had other directorships in that group as well as in large companies from other sectors, especially banking and finance, and insurance.[19] In all, ninety-two directors from the largest fifty manufacturing companies held a total of 150 other directorships in other large companies from the sectors shown. Especially striking are the number of links between the largest manufacturers and the clearing banks and financial companies (accepting houses). These two groups alone accounted for two-thirds of the inter-locking directorships. One of the main conclusions of a recent study of the long term trend of interlocking directorship amongst the largest companies in the UK was the increasing importance of the links between the banking-financial sector and manufacturing (Stanworth and Giddens, 1975). In view of the large equity holdings of manufacturers that insurance companies now have, the large number of interlocking directorships (forty shown in Table 2.2) is hardly surprising.

The figure which may surprise American readers is the first one in the table. This shows that directors from the largest manufacturing companies held a further thirty-eight directorships in other manufacturers in the sample. Under American anti-trust law it is illegal for a director of one company to hold a directorship in any other company which may be in direct competition with the first. In the UK there is no such restriction. The rationale of the American law is, of course, to prevent the possibility of collusion between companies ostensibly in competition. Since most forms of overt collusion between companies in the UK have in effect become illegal since the early 1960s[20] it is perhaps surprising that

Table 2.2 *Interlocking directorships by the fifty largest manufacturing companies, 1976*

Largest companies in:	Numbers of the ninety-two directors of the largest fifty companies also holding directorships in the following:
Manufacturing (50)[a]	38
Retailing/wholesaling/services (25)	4
Shipping (10)	5
Clearing banks (6)	32
Finance (17)	24
Insurance companies (50)[b]	40
Other[c]	7
Total	150

Source: Utton (1979), p. 102.

[a]Numbers in parentheses refer to the number of companies in each category included in the compilation of the table.

[b]Includes one directorship in a large building society.

[c]This category includes four directorships in the largest construction companies, two in property companies and one in an international merchant company.

the possible co-ordination of price and related policies by rival firms through interlocking directorships remains acceptable. In fact a closer examination of the thirty-eight interlocking director-ships in Table 2.2 suggests that there is unlikely to be much direct competition between the companies involved (see Utton, 1979; pp. 99–103). But with the growing diversification of the largest companies the likelihood of overlaps clearly increases.

The third question posed at the beginning of this section con-cerned the sources of finance available to the largest companies, and especially those sources that they have used to float their enormous growth of the last thirty years. The conventional wisdom on this issue has usually gone something like this: the very large size of the biggest companies allied to the divorce of ownership from control has meant that managements of such companies have been placed in an even stronger position than might at first be appreciated. They are now largely freed from the constraints and disciplines of the capital market by relying mainly on retained profits to finance their growth. On this view, therefore, managers are not only free of the sanction of disgruntled shareholders who in practice cannot unseat them because of dispersed share ownership but they are also free of the sanction of potential shareholders because they only have recourse to the capital market for an insignificant portion of their funds.

Actual experience in the UK since 1950 has been much more complex than this simple analysis implies but the facts also tend to refute the general point that large companies no longer rely on the capital market to finance their growth. In his analysis of the role of financial factors in the growth of aggregate concentration in the UK Prais (1981) distinguishes three components of the additions to firms' resources that may take place in any year: retentions from profits (funds generated internally); cash raised by the issue of new securities, such as ordinary shares or debentures (funds raised externally); and acquisitions of other companies involving an exchange of shares or other securities (external). The record of the last twenty-five years clearly shows that internally generated funds have been increasingly the junior partner in financing the growth of quoted companies. In the period 1950–54, for example, retentions expressed as a percentage of the increase in net assets amounted to more than 57 per cent. By 1970–73 the figure had dropped to 29 per cent. On the other hand, for 1976 a typical year for new issues, Prais found that as many as half of the hundred largest companies issued new shares for cash, and many of the remainder were involved with some adjustment to their capital structure, such as a reduction of a debenture or a preference issue (often associated with a capital issue in another year). He concludes: 'Comparing this result with a study for 1949–53, one may infer that the proportion of new companies going to the new issues market each year has perhaps about doubled in the intervening period' (Prais, 1981; p. 129). Furthermore, the growing importance of mergers in the 1960s and early 1970s meant that a large part of the new issues were made to acquire other companies. Nearly two-thirds of all issues in the period 1969–73 compared with about one-tenth in the period 1949–53.

In his final assessment of the relative importance of the three components to company growth Prais assigns them all approximately equal weight which means, in effect, that contrary to the popular view, the largest companies have recently relied for two-thirds of their growth on external sources. If the importance of mergers subsides more or less permanently, then this may mean that retained profits again play a more important part in financing growth. There is some evidence that merger activity proceeds in waves, so that the frantic levels reached in the late 1960s and early 1970s may not be repeated for some time. However, there is also evidence that positively associates mergers with stock exchange prices so the revival of the latter, as the economy emerges from the recession, may be accompanied by more acquisitions and the new issues to finance them.

The most striking point mentioned in this section has been the rapidity with which ownership of the ordinary shares of the private sector has been passing into the hands of a comparatively small group of financial institutions. This increasing concentration of financial control is the counterpart of the growth of concentration in manufacturing *output* referred to above. Not unexpectedly, therefore, the average shareholding of the board of directors in the largest companies is miniscule. While directors may have only a nominal holding of the companies ordinary capital, however, quite a number of them also hold directorships in other giant companies, most frequently a clearing or merchant bank. Finally, the recent evidence for the UK shows clearly that the largest companies are heavily and increasingly dependent on external sources to finance their growth, so the argument that they are effectively independent of the capital market must be consigned to that limbo reserved for all masterly but erroneous simplifications.

THE RATIONALE OF BIG BUSINESS

The developments surveyed above have led to renewed doubts about the whole rationale of the private industrial sector, especially manufacturing which is at the heart of the economy and in the forefront of the changes. Quite apart from certain uneasy feelings that the enormous size of the largest companies makes them a potential threat to the continued existence of democratic government, the following points are frequently made. First, the overall size of the giant companies and their relative position in many separate industries in which they operate, means that they usually have considerable market power. Even if they are not monopolists in the classical sense they may, with the tacit agreement of their rivals, manipulate the market to their advantage. They may well, for example, prevent the entry of new firms to the industry and thus maintain their dominance. Consequently, that part of the rationale of the private sector that depends on the efficient working of competitive markets may no longer hold. The competition of the many may have given way to the collusion of the few and this is likely to hinder improvements in the allocation of resources that the market mechanism is supposed to achieve. Secondly, the men who run the largest companies are in effect responsible to no-one. In law, of course, they are the servants of the company, appointed by the shareholders to administer the capital that they have invested. In practice the likelihood of their being removed by a shareholders' revolt is extremely slight, even though large blocks of shares are not now held by individuals but by the financial institutions. Ironically some of the managers themselves now see their responsibilities as much wider than those laid down by the law. Shareholders are only one group amongst the many who have apparently entrusted their interests to company directors. The others include customers, employees, suppliers, and the government. This 'managerial' view of the function of the large company was summed up recently as follows:

> The chief executive of a large corporation has the problem of reconciling the demands of employees for more wages and improved benefit plans, customers for lower prices and greater values, vendors for higher prices, government for more taxes, stockholders for higher dividends and greater capital appreciation–all within a framework that will be constructive and acceptable to society. (Preston and Post (1975), quoting a publication of the US Committee for Economic Development)

Under the weight of such responsibilities it is perhaps remarkable that any directors ever reach retiring age. But by taking on such all-embracing duties they may see some chance of overcoming the disability that rich men apparently have in being promoted to the Kingdom of Heaven. (At least British executives may have the second best compensation of elevation to the House of Lords, a reward not open to their American counterparts.)

The argument that directors of large companies now have 'social' as well as 'private' responsibilities plays into their opponents' hands. For if directors really do behave as if they have a duty to safeguard the often conflicting interests of these different groups, who has given them this authority? If directors fail in their apparent duty to employees or consumers do members of these groups have any sanction against them, to ensure that their performance improves in future? These kinds of question have recently led to a large number of proposals for the reform of the control structure of large companies. The most widely discussed has been provision for employees (through their trades unions) to appoint directors. But there is logically no reason why customer interests should not be represented in the same way.[21]

Thirdly, it is argued that investment in the largest companies in the private sector is now to all intents and purposes the same as investing in gilt-edged securities. Although the financial textbooks may still refer to 'raising risk capital in the market-place', for most large companies their sheer size and diversity makes the risk of loss negligible and even interruption to the flow of dividends low enough for most investors to treat them like government issues. In this case, it is argued, why not 'institutionalize' the companies completely and exchange their shares for government stock? This move would merely given legal recognition to what many people have long regarded as the true state of affairs.

Some of the severest critics of the giant companies are found in those wealthy Western nations which have probably benefitted most from their contribution to economic growth. They are criticized because their original rationale has been undermined by their very success and yet they have found no substitute which takes full account of their predominance. According to one distinguished American observer the criticism now amounts to a crusade which in America has been immensely effective.

> It will continue to be effective until the corporation has decided what kind of institution it is in todays' world, and what kinds of reforms are a necessary precondition to a vigorous defence–not of its every action but of its very survival as a quasi-public institution as distinct from a completely politicized institution. (Kristol, 1975)

3

Efficiency, Technology and Size

INTRODUCTION

As we pointed out in chapter 1 an important part of the case for big business rests on the claim that across a wide range of industries modern technology requires plants of a very large absolute size and this means that they can supply a relatively large fraction of the domestic market. Anything less would mean that unit production costs are higher than they need be and are therefore certainly above those of foreign competitors. A great deal of recent empirical work has advanced our knowledge on a number of questions concerning the relationship between scale of production and costs. The use of *production* and not overall size is deliberate: much more is known about the former than the latter and the importance of this point is discussed below. Used carefully, therefore, this kind of information can help answer the difficult question of whether technical efficiency in many industries requires firms of the massive size that we now have. The need for caution is great if we are to avoid the ham-fisted approach adopted by the British Government in the 1960s when enormity was seen as the hand-maiden of the new 'technological revolution'. The second part of this chapter, therefore, discusses the extent to which very large size is a necessary condition for technical efficiency.

But technical efficiency is only a part of the story. A sizeable part of microeconomic analysis is concerned with *allocative* efficiency. Subject to a number of important qualifications (some of which are discussed below) an efficient allocation of a given set of resources is one which yields both a maximum and 'correct' (in the sense of best meeting consumers demands) output. The central result from monopoly theory is that resource allocation will be distorted by the ability of monopolists to restrict output below a level that would best accord with consumer demand (that is price would be greater than marginal cost). Hence from a given bundle of resources economic welfare is likely to be lower in the presence of monopoly. To the extent, therefore, that large size is correlated with monopoly (itself a subject of some dispute[1]) allocative inefficiency will result. Section three of this chapter is thus mainly concerned with allocative efficiency. In particular it deals with two issues that have lately been much discussed in the literature. The first concerns the overall size of the 'welfare loss' that is likely to result from monopolistic output restriction. In other words, what does the empirical evidence tell us about the *extent* of the reductions in economic welfare that results from monopoly? Rather embarrassingly for those, including the author, who had filled blackboards with and spent much time expounding some of the central theorems of neo-classical price theory the answer seemed at first to be 'very little indeed'. As Stigler remarked in a review of one of the first attempts to measure these losses, 'If this estimate is correct, economists might serve a more useful purpose if they fought fires or termites instead of monopoly' (Stigler, 1956; p. 34). Stigler held the fort for a time by criticizing the statistical techniques and assumptions used. First-line reinforcements soon arrived in the shape of rather bigger estimates of the welfare losses from monopoly, obtained by changing assumptions (especially about the elasticity of demand). But the overall effects seemed meagre in comparison with the time and effort devoted to refining the theory of monopoly. The equivalent of the American cavalry only arrived rather later, in the form of Leibenstein's concept of X-inefficiency. As in the traditional Western, the arrival was in the nick of time, for who could enthuse for long about a misallocation of resources that led to a welfare loss equivalent to only a small fraction of 1 per cent of GNP? The second issue discussed, therefore, is X-inefficiency and its importance in the organization of industry.

Problems of technical, allocative and X-efficiency may still strike an uncommitted bystander as not getting to the heart of the matter. Increasingly high on the list of problems associated with very large firms is their alleged effect on the environment. What is the point of these firms ensuring, for example, that they are both technically and economically efficient in a *private* sense if, in their achievement, they are simultaneously generating very high social costs which do not enter their accounts but which nevertheless impose enormous burdens on the community? A large part of the 'radical' critique of 'big business' in the USA has centred on this issue rather than the more arcane questions of technical efficiency.[2] Our main concern in the fourth section of this chapter is, therefore, an analysis of how far these externalities are due to the presence of very large companies. Is it the case, for example, that industrial pollution would be significantly lower in the UK if the manufacturing sector was not so dominated by a relatively few giant firms?

Two general points should be noted about our subsequent discussion. First, there is frequently a large gulf between the theoretical concepts and the empirical measurement of those concepts. Secondly, on many of the most important questions our knowledge is still very often fragmentary. Neither of these points should surprise the reader who has any familiarity with the bewildering complexity of modern industry and who has heeded the warning given some time ago by a distinguished American economist in this field: 'No-one who is other than eclectic, methodologically speaking, has any business in the field of business organisation' (Mason, 1957). In the light of the difficulties he may be surprised only at the complete assurance with which leader-writers and politicians proffer solutions to our industrial problems.

TECHNICAL EFFICIENCY

There are now available for quite a wide cross section of UK manufacturing industries estimates of plants of minimum efficient size, that is the minimum size at which long-run average costs are lowest. The estimates generally employ the 'engineering approach' where the researcher obtains from production engineers in the industry the size of the plant which would minimize unit costs using the most up-to-date methods.[3] It is generally thought that this method may tend to bias estimates upwards to some extent, if only because the engineers may be basing their conclusions on sizes of plants which are theoretical rather than actual. Such estimates cannot, therefore, take account of all the economic pressures on plant size. Nevertheless so long as we are prepared to treat them as approximations rather than precise estimates the orders of magnitude will be roughly correct.

The research also gives two further pieces of information which are relevant to our discussion. First, estimates have been made of the extent to which unit costs rise for a plant only half the size of that where costs are minimized. This enables us to judge the feasibility of some (smaller) firms operating successfully plants of suboptimal scale. Secondly, estimates are given of the proportion of the UK market that would be served by one plant of minimum efficient size. Clearly if one such plant was sufficient to supply a very large fraction of the UK market in any time period there may be a conflict between efficiency and competition. Such cases are especially important in our context since they might imply further that only a firm of very large absolute size could operate an efficient plant. On the other hand, we need also to look carefully at whether the UK is the proper way of viewing 'the market'. Given membership of the Common Market, for example, the relevant market may be a large part of Western Europe. Alternatively, transport costs and product characteristics may make only part of the UK the effective market.

Before examining the estimates we should re-emphasize that they relate to economies of scale at the *plant* level. Although there may be cases where further *production* economies of scale can be realized by operating a number of plants simultaneously,[4] it is usually reckoned that the greater part of any technical economies arise at the plant level rather than at the firm level. The extent to which further economies can only be realized by the multi-plant firm is a very thorny issue and is discussed below.

Table 3.1 attempts to summarize some of the salient features of the detailed and painstaking study into the economies of scale carried out by C. F. Pratten and published in 1971. The expression 'attempts' is used advisedly because the complexities of the different industries and the problems involved in marrying the experience of actual cases with the theoretical concepts should not be underestimated. Readers interested in these issues should consult the excellent discussion in Part one of the book (Pratten, 1971). Subject to this general caveat, therefore, the table presents estimates for twenty-nine product groups of the size of a plant of minimum efficient size (MES) in relation to the UK market in the late 1960s (Table 3.1, column 1). It also gives estimates of the extent to which total costs are likely to rise for plants of only half the minimum efficient size, an indication of the possible scope for suboptimally size plants to persist in competition with larger, more efficient plants (column 2). The final column

Table 3.1 *Minimum efficient sized plants (MES) and the UK market (circa 1969), for a sample of manufacturing industries*

Industry	MES plant output as percentage of UK market 1969	Percentage increase in costs at 50 per cent MES compared with MES level	Five-firm concentration, 1968 (%)
Aircraft (one type only)	>100	>20	99
Electronic data processing equipment	100	10	87
Steel (wide strip rolling works)	80	8	>90
Electric motors	60	15	n.a.
Motor cars	50	6	98
Refrigerators or washing machines	50	8	84
Turbogenerators (range of designs)	50	n.a.	87
Synthetic fibres – polymer production	33	5	100
Steel (raw steel plant)	33	5–10	>90
Newspapers	30	20	n.a.
Sulphuric acid	30	1	78
Ethylene	25	9	90
Synthetic detergents	20	2.5	80
Synthetic fibres – yarn extrusion	16	7	100
Cement	10	9	89
Diesel engines	>10	>4	100
Petroleum refining	10	5	95
Bicycles	10	small	n.a.
Beer	3	9	64
Warp knitting	3	small	33
Book printing	2	small	32
Cotting spinning and weaving	2	small	50
Bread	1	15	77
Plastic products (range)	1	small	30
Iron foundries – large castings	1	10	42
Bricks	0.5	25	57
Machine tools	0.5	n.a.	41
Iron foundries – small castings	0.2	5	n.a.
Shoes	0.2	2	32

Sources: Pratten (1971), *Economies of Scale in Manufacturing Industry*, pp. 269–277, CUP; HMSO (1974), *Census of Production, 1968*, Part 158, Table 4; Business Monitor, PO 1006; HMSO (1979), *Statistics of Product Concentration of U.K. Manufacturers for 1963, 1968 and 1975*.

gives, as a further reference point the five-firm concentration ratio for a number of the industries shown.[5]

The estimates are arranged in descending order of the relative importance of the technical economies and thus highlight the considerable diversity of experience. In nine cases, for example, an MES plant needed upwards of one-third of the UK market. There are few surprises in this category. Most people would probably put motor cars, aircraft, computers, steel, and man-made fibres high on any list of industries where production scale economies are likely to be important. Generally speaking the cost disadvantage of operating sub-optimally sized plants in these industries was considerable (8 per cent or more in five of the cases). In view of the economies of scale implied by Table 3.1 for these industries the level of concentration is also hardly surprising. Indeed, in all of these cases there is barely scope for as many as five firms to produce efficiently, especially if they each operate more than one plant, as is usual.

On the other hand, in more than half of the industries shown an efficiently sized plant apparently required 10 per cent or less of the UK market. Again, amongst these fifteen industries there are a number of cases which are quite unremarkable: cotton spinning and weaving, book printing, iron foundries and plastic products are not usually associated with significant economies of scale. Other cases are much more surprising. The man on the Clapham omnibus might be surprised to learn that a general petroleum refinery or cement works only needed to supply a minimum of 10 per cent of the UK market to be efficient. In view of recent rapid changes in the structure of the industries and the nature and quality of the products he may be even more surprised to learn that an efficient brewery required only 3 per cent and an efficient bakery only 1 per cent of the UK market.

In general for this group of fifteen industries there is considerable scope, even within the confines of the UK market, for competition between separate plants ranging from ten in cement and petroleum refining, for example, to 500 in small castings and shoes. This is quite apart from the plants of sub-optimal size which can remain viable in the face of only small cost disadvantages in a number of industries indicated in Table 3.1, column 2. The actual structure of many of these industries is, however, rather different from that implied by a reading of the first two columns in the table. The level of concentration for most of the industries in this group bears little relation to what we might regard as the 'minimum level compatible with technical efficiency'. Even those at the top of the group have a concentration ratio about twice that of the 'hypothetical minimum level', while in cases like bread and beer, it is many times higher.

Part of the explanation for the divergence between the concentration level implied by technical economies at the plant level and observed levels is, of course, that all of the estimates given in Table 3.1 refer to *minimum* efficient size. If unit costs are roughly the same for plants considerably bigger than the minimum sizes indicated in the table, then clearly the concentration level may well be higher.[6] But the main part of the explanation is usually in terms of economies of size related to the *firm*, typically seen as operating a number of plants in different locations, although there is no reason why in some industries these factors should not operate in large single-plant firms. A suitable bridge between the discussion of the economies of large plants and those of the large multi-plant firm is provided by the striking series compiled by Prais and illustrated in Fig. 3.1.

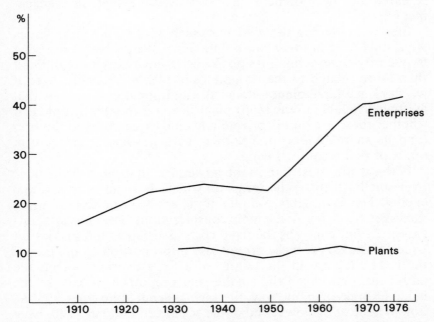

Figure 3.1 Share of the hundred largest enterprises and plants in manufacturing net output, UK

Source: Prais (1981), *The Evolution of Giant Firms in Britain*, p. 47, Cambridge University Press.

If we confine our remarks on the figure to the period approximately 1935–68 then it is clear that up to 1950 there was little change in the relationship between the hundred largest plants and the hundred largest firms. The former accounted for approximately 10 per cent of manufacturing net output and the latter rather more than double this at about 22–24 per cent of net output. If this approximate relationship had persisted, then we would have expected the hundred largest plants to account for something like 20 per cent of the sector's net output by 1968. Instead, while the share of the hundred largest *firms* practically doubled between 1950 and 1970 the share of the hundred largest plants remained remarkably stable at between 10 and 11 per cent.[7] Hence the explanation for the enormous growth in aggregate concentration must be found in factors other then economies of scale at the plant level.

A large number of factors can be introduced to help explain the growth and size of the largest companies. Amongst the most prominent are the economies of scale in finance, in marketing, in research and development and, to a lesser extent, in management.[8]

Before examining the evidence, such as it is, on these issues we should bear in mind two points. First, the problems of trying to quantify these economies of size are many times more difficult than those related to the economies of plants. Secondly, even if we think we have pinned down the additional cost savings that are only available to the multi-plant firm it is frequently not clear whether these are purely private advantages, accruing to the firm (and its shareholders) or whether there is some social gain in terms of real resource saving.

Perhaps the most important advantage that large firms have over smaller firms is the terms on which they can raise external capital. This is a highly complex topic and we can do little more than sketch in a few of the main considerations. The most straightforward point concerns the fixed costs associated with making an issue of shares. As these do not rise in proportion to the size of the issue they are in the nature of a fixed overhead. Thus the larger the sum raised the smaller the proportionate cost of the issue. Expressed in one way, the savings seem quite considerable. For an issue at the lower end of the scale, £250 000 in 1970, issue costs might amount to something like 10–15 per cent of the sum raised, whereas for an issue in excess of £1 million the costs may be as low as 3–5 per cent. But if these costs are capitalized and expressed as a higher required operating yield, the differences are much less important as Prais clearly illustrates: If a company, for example, requires a return of 10 per cent on its risk capital and on a very small issue costs amount to 15 per cent, then from the company's point of view this may be regarded as a requirement to earn not £10 on each £100 raised but £10 on each £85 which works out at a required yield of 11.8 per cent. For a company with a large issue and costs of 5 per cent similar reasoning points to a required return of 10.5 per cent, a difference in terms of 'annual running costs' of just over 1 per cent (see Prais, 1981; p. 108).

Another important point is the relationship between company size and risk. As size and diversification are directly related then it is generally argued that the risks of investing in a larger company are lower than in a smaller company and consequently the terms on which larger companies can raise capital will be more favourable than for smaller companies. The risks referred to in this context are not the particular risks that characterize any individual line of business. Clearly these are governed by the special features of the trade such as the natural and institutional factors affecting the demand and supply conditions. Natural factors will loom large in the supply of raw materials and agricultural produce; institutional factors, like the behaviour of trades unions may be a prominent influence on the smooth supply of some manufactured goods. None of these risks are changed simply by bringing a larger and larger number of possibly disparate activities under one corporate roof. This is quite an elementary point but it frequently seems forgotten in discussions of large companies which in some quarters appear to take on a kind of mystique more usually associated with religion than business.

The nature of 'risk reduction', of course, lies in the lower risk of complete loss where the company carries on a number of separate activities, when some are doing badly others will be doing well. In short, up to a point, the larger and more diverse the company the smaller is likely to be the profit *variability*. If it is possible to bring together product lines whose profit streams are substantially independent, then profit variation can be kept to a minimum.[9] Again, however, it is not commonly recognized how soon in practice the stabilizing effect of product variety peters out. On the basis of recent empirical work in the USA and Britain, for example, Prais suggests that most of the advantage of lowered risk can be obtained by firms with an employment of about 1000. Any further reduction in profit variability for firms of even much greater size are likely to be very small. Yet the average size of the hundred largest enterprises in 1972 was more than 31 000 and for the largest twenty-five was about 79 000 employees (Prais, 1981; p. 97).

In spite of unimportant risk reductions beyond quite modest sizes, a number of investigators in both the UK and the USA have found that shareholders still have a preference for large companies and this is reflected in the inverse relationship between earnings-yields and size. After a detailed examination of a number of British and American studies, Prais concludes:

> There is thus an exceptional consistency in the results . . . all pointing to a falling cost of equity capital as size of firm increases, with estimated elasticities all in a relatively narrow range of, say, −0.05 to −0.10 (p. 111).

He goes on to suggest that an important part of the explanation for this difference in costs may be the dominant role now played by the financial institutions (which we noted in chapter 2) and their preference for large issues. Whatever the preferences of the institutions may be, however, there is some doubt as to whether these financial advantages achieved by very large firms actually lead to savings in real resources which could be used elsewhere in the economy. It is at least arguable that they amount to no more than a private advantage with no beneficial social effects.

Similar doubts may be briefly mentioned concerning the advantages that large size may confer in terms of lower input prices. It is quite possible that genuine economies (of a resource saving type) arise when inputs are ordered on a large scale by multi-plant giants. The supplier may be able to achieve economies in production scheduling, long-runs, and inventory levels. But following the recent enquiries into the economics of multi-plant operations completed by Professor Scherer and his colleagues the occurrence of these kinds of economies of scale seems rare and insubstantial. Where advantages of large ordering did accrue to the large buyer they seemed to be mainly of the income-transfer type, without any accompanying social benefit. In other words the lower input prices resulted from superior bargaining strength and skill of the large firm rather than from any real saving achieved by input suppliers. As long as the buyer does not overplay his hand and demand prices that will yield a lower than normal long-run return for the input supplier, the effect of the bargain is to transfer part of what was previously the suppliers economic rent to the buyer (Scherer, 1974).

Perhaps the most controversial aspect of large-firm advantage over small is in the field of product promotion and marketing, especially where this involves advertising. The subject of advertising is so central to our main theme that it is discussed in detail in the next chapter. For the moment we may briefly note the following points. First, economies of scale in advertising arise in the same way as in any other area of printing. The initial set-up and first copy costs are high but thereafter running-off costs are very low. Newspaper advertising rates are, therefore, closely geared to circulation and readership figures: the higher the latter, the higher the cost of advertising but the lower the cost per person receiving the message. It is also sometimes assumed that beyond a certain absolute size (in newspapers) or coverage (on television) advertising messages become more effective (e.g. full-page advertisements are more than four times as effective as quarter page, three thirty-second peak-time spots have more than triple the pulling power of one such attempt, etc.)

Secondly, advertising expenditure is only of importance in some consumer goods industries, where customers are many and their product requirements not clearly specified. Even for consumer goods there is a wide range of experience, with very high advertising–net output ratios occurring in only a narrow range of products.[10] Furthermore where advertising is apparently heaviest and concentrated amongst a comparatively few firms the (private) advantages of size may be more apparent than real. An important conclusion from the Scherer study, mentioned above, was how often comparatively small firms, by catering for a special part of the market or by ingenious marketing methods, were able to overcome any apparent handicaps of size.

Thirdly, in the case of financial and input-price advantages enjoyed by large multi-plant firms we expressed some doubts about whether the acknowledged private savings could be translated into social gains. If possible an even larger question mark has been placed against the social benefits that might arise from the economies of large scale marketing. While recognizing that information costs are likely to be considerable in some consumer goods markets, the view is widely held, nevertheless, that much of the present level of advertising expenditure serves mainly to protect existing positions of market power by preventing the successful entry of fresh competitors. On this view advertising preserves and perhaps worsens the misallocation of resources rather than, for example, lowering costs and prices. This point is taken up in more detail below. For the moment we turn to the more promising area of research, development and innovation.

At last the corporate giants may come into their own. The uncertainties inherent in the process of innovation and the enormous capital requirements of some experimental equipment which may not show a 'return' for many years both point to the likelihood of considerable advantages in this area of very large size. Indeed some of the statistics accumulated over the years show the overwhelming importance of the largest firms. It is clear, for example, from evidence for the US and the UK that research and development (R and D) financed by the private sector of industry is largely (85 per cent) in the hands of the top 350 firms (Caves, 1968). Small firms (those with less than about 200 employees) for the most part undertake no research.[11] On the other hand, there is no clear evidence that beyond about 5000 employees (that is about the 200 largest firms in UK manufacturing industry) there are any *additional* advantages from R and D expenditures. Up to about the 5000 employees mark there is an approximately linear relationship between firm size and relative R and D expenditure. Thereafter the curve tends to bend downwards: the very largest firms spend relatively less than their somewhat smaller brethren (Scherer, 1980; pp. 418–422).

Research and development expenditures alone, however, give a very incomplete picture of the *innovation* process. It is after all the commercial introduction of new processes and products that should be our major concern not necessarily the size and sumptuousness of the research laboratory. The creative mind may be cramped and stultified by the bureaucracy that inevitably accompanies the highly structured system of responsibility and control in a large organization. Research scientists may find themselves spending much of their time supervising others and attempting to justify expansions in their next year's budget, rather than actually engaging in research. In short, the productivity of R and D effort in large organizations may be lower than in smaller ones. To test this view clearly involves fairly precise measurement of the output of R and D efforts in the form of 'innovations', a task inherently more difficult than simply gathering information on R and D expenditures.

To explain the difficulty we need to look a little more closely at the whole process of research and innovation. In the course of this discussion it should become evident why simple explanations of the relationship between size and innovation will not do. It is fruitful to think of the innovation process as having at least three stages. First an individual or group recognises the need or scope for an improvement or change in a product or process and have the tenacity, single-mindedness and good fortune to pursue it successfully. They may or may not be employed in the industry that eventually exploits the idea. Chester Carlson, for example, worked as a patent lawyer and recognized the need for a quick and easy means of duplicating documents. He worked for many hours in his spare time on the idea that eventually became photo-copying, although clearly his existing work was not directly related to the invention in any way. Peter Goldmark, on the other hand, was already a scientist in charge of Columbia Broadcasting System's research laboratory when he started work, partly at home and partly in the laboratory, on the techniques that later led to the introduction of long-playing records.[12] The initial insight and idea as to how a particular process might work or product be made and its demonstration, in perhaps a very primitive pilot plant, are now generally regarded as a vital but very often merely preliminary, first step on the long and difficult road to full, com-mercial exploitation. It may thus be at the second and third stages, involving *development* and full scale *production* that the industrial research laboratory, backed by the financial resources of the established firm, plays an essential role. To convert the new idea, demonstrated in a pilot plant into a product which can gain wide acceptance, is likely to require money and expertise beyond the compass of an individual or small group. In the first case quoted above, for example, it was twenty years before the process became commercially viable, assisted by an independent research institute and a moderately sized industrial company which eventually spent about $20 millions on development (Scherer, 1980; p. 412). At this stage, therefore, where the inventor has been working independently he may attempt to enlist the support of an existing company. The company may then quite correctly be credited with the innovation, even though the initial step may have been made by an individual or smaller com-pany.

This point should be considered when we refer to the data in Table 3.2 which show the number of innovations in the UK over the period 1945–70 by size of firm. The innovations, which were initially listed from independent sources, occurred in about 53 of

Table 3.2 Number and percentage share of innovations by size of firm in the UK

Period	Small firms (employment 1–199)		Medium firms (employment 200–999)		Large firms (employment 1000 plus)		All firms	
	Number	Percent of total	Number	Percent of total	Number	Percent of total	Number	Percent of total
1945–53	17	9	25	12	160	79	202	100
1954–61	38	10	43	11	313	80	394	100
1962–70	54	11	53	10	399	79	506	100
Total 1945–70	109	10	121	11	872	79	1102	100

Source: C. Freeman (1974), *The Economics of Industrial Innovation*, Penguin Books, Harmondsworth.

the 120 or so separate industries into which the manufacturing sector is commonly divided. The industries involved accounted for about half of manufacturing net output and in all, more than 700 firms gave information on their size at the time of the 1100 innovations listed. Every effort was made to ensure that the innovations in the sample were of roughly comparable importance but clearly with so many industries covered a certain amount of subjective judgement was involved. However, if the sample is treated as representative of innovations generally then the following points can be made. Firms in the largest size group (with 10 000 or more employees[13]) which unfortunately were not separately distinguished in the original table, had a disproportionate share of innovations: 54 per cent compared with a 28 per cent share in manufacturing net output (in 1958). But a sizeable share, about 37 per cent, came from firms in the middle size ranges (200 to under 10 000 employees).

What is more, while the medium-sized and small firms have experienced a decline in their share in net output[14] but have maintained their share in innovations, the reverse is true for the very largest firms. Their share in net output has risen from 28 per cent in 1958 to 38 per cent by 1970, yet their innovation share has remained unchanged. Just as the relative importance of R and D expenditures appears to decline for the largest firms, so their capacity to innovate may not match their capacity for growth.

Nevertheless, there is little doubt that the largest firms play a prominent role in innovation, especially at the development and production stages. There are clearly some industries (aerospace and atomic energy are probably the most outstanding examples) where the development costs are so great that only the largest firms, very often backed by government, can take them on. But there are also sufficient examples of pathbreaking discoveries by individuals and their subsequent development by firms of quite modest size to allow only the most dogmatic to accept the generalization that technical change is now the exclusive property of the industrial giants.[15] We would agree, therefore, with the recent conclusion of Professor Scherer:

> there are advantages of scale in research and innovation. They appear, however, to be fully realised (in the vast majority of cases) at firm sizes and concentration levels well below the upper size and concentration ranges of existing U.S. industrial structure. Exceptions to this generalisation can be found, but they must be recognised as such. (Scherer, 1974; p. 50)

Even if some allowance is made for the difference in size between the US and UK economies and largest firms, the broad conclusion is equally valid for the UK.

An interesting addendum to this brief discussion of innovation and size can be made by widening the definition along the lines suggested by Schumpeter when discussing the competitive process. The kind of competition that counted for him was 'the competition from the new commodity, the new technology, the new source of supply, the new *type of organisation* . . . competition which commands a decisive cost or quality advantage' (Schumpeter, 1965; p. 84: emphasis added). Discussion of innovation usually proceeds in terms of new procedures and products but for Schumpeter a new type of organization may have very similar effects and give a decisive competitive advantage. On this definition, for example, the new conglomerate enterprises that flourished, particularly in the US, in the late 1960s would be viewed as innovators. Another organizational change has been dubbed by an eminent economist as possibly 'American capitalism's most important single innovation of the twentieth century' (Williamson, 1971; p. 382). He was referring to the increasing use by the largest firms of a multi-divisional form of internal organization which allows a great deal of autonomy to the separate product or geographic divisions of the enterprise. Instead of having a central management board in charge of a number of functional departments (each with their own hierarchy of control) the multi-divisional enterprise will (in theory) consist of a number of semi-independent divisions responsible for their own profitability, although ultimately answerable to the chief executive's office.

Apparently not long before their untimely demise certain dinosaurs had started to develop a second brain in their tails. This was nature's response to the diseconomies of scale – in this case increasing difficulties with limb co-ordination – that the creatures had suffered. Co-ordination problems also seem to have prompted the managerial response in the case of giant companies that introduced the multi-divisional structure. In the case of the dinosaurs the development apparently came too late. It is Williamson's contention that in the corporate case the organizational change has been largely successful. If he is correct then the largest companies will have overcome an important threat to their continued growth and profitability. Earlier writers had relied on diseconomies of co-ordination to set an upper limit on the size of firms. Modern organizational methods (allied to the speed with which computers can handle large amounts of complex information) may effectively by-pass such limits. This innovation may thus have been the answer to the threat of stagnation and relative decline rather than initially to gain a competitive advantage. The result may be the continued growth of the giants and thus of aggregate concentration.

It is perhaps appropriate at this point to pull together some of the main conclusions of this section. The most telling advantage of large size may well be the sources of and terms on which finance can be raised. Recent research in the UK also suggests that existing advantages may have been accentuated by modern institutional changes in share ownership. There remains some doubt, however, about whether any social economy results from these scale advantages. Some sources of financial advantage (like profit stability) tend in any case to peter out at a firm size considerably below that of the corporate giants and the same is probably true of the second most important source of size advantage, research and innovation. The R and D input of the largest companies was not as high, relatively, as that of companies in the second rank and it may be the case (although here the evidence is more difficult to interpret) that their innovative performance may not have kept pace with their recent growth. On the question of economies of production and their importance for very large firm size, the picture from manufacturing industry is very mixed. For some industries production economies of scale, especially when viewed against a background of the UK market are of overriding importance and go a long way towards explaining the size of the largest firms. For many others, however, no such explanation emerged and there seemed to be a large gulf between economies in production and the scale and market share of the largest firms. On the whole the demands of technology seemed to play a comparatively minor role in their growth. Finally, the advantages of very large size in buying and marketing may be important in some industries (especially advertising in consumer goods) but the evidence here is still rather scanty. It is difficult to be convinced, however, either that scale advantages in these areas have played a predominent part in the growth of the giants or that they yield significant social benefits.

Part Two: Problems

ALLOCATIVE AND X-EFFICIENCY

In the neoclassical theory of resource allocation it was *assumed* that firms would be technically efficient in production and distribution. At any one time firms supplying a particular market may be of different sizes with different productive capacities. But all this meant was that the industry was not in long-run equilibrium. No firm was 'inefficient' in the sense of operating at unit costs higher than those indicated by its short-run average cost function. In competitive industries firms that failed to expand their capacity in the long run to ensure minimum unit costs would be eliminated while for the monopolist to tolerate costs higher than those indicated by his long-run cost function would imply that he was not maximizing profits which was assumed to be his basic motivation.

The central criticism of monopoly was thus not that it was technically inefficient but that it led to a less than optimal allocative performance. The profit maximizing monopolist, by charging a price greater than marginal cost, restricted output below the level that would prevail under competitive conditions and

Diagram 3.1

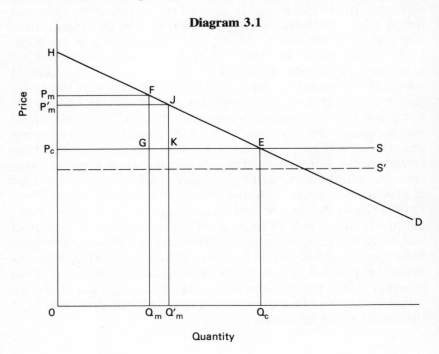

Quantity

reduced the level of consumer satisfaction. These points can be illustrated with the aid of Diagram 3.1.

HD is the demand curve for the industry and P_cS the supply curve of the competitive industry. Competitive output is OQ_c and competitive price OP_c. The long-run supply curve of the competitive industry (assumed perfectly elastic for simplicity) represents the aggregation of marginal costs of all firms in the industry and (in the absence of externalities) thus shows the marginal social costs of supplying any specified level of output. The social cost, therefore, of supplying the competitive output OQ_c is represented by OP_cEQ_c.

The area under the demand curve at any quantity represents the total money value placed by consumers on the utility of that quantity of the good. At a quantity OQ_c, therefore, the monetary value placed by consumers on this amount is $OHEQ_c$. This may also be regarded (under certain conditions) as the maximum amount they would be prepared to pay for the good rather than go without it altogether. With a uniform price, P_c, however, the total cost to consumers is OP_cEQ_c. The difference, P_cHE, is consumers surplus and represents the excess of utility, valued in money terms, over the resource costs.

The marginal valuation of the demand at E is equal to EQ_c. Thus under competitive conditions at the market clearing price P_c the marginal valuation placed on the last unit of output sold is just equal to the marginal social cost of producing that output. For any increment to the right of E marginal cost exceeds marginal valuation while a unit decrease in quantity sold (to the left of E) marginal valuation exceeds marginal costs. Consumers utility will therefore be maximized where resource cost and marginal valuation are equal, *ceteris paribus*. Thus the central conclusion of competitive theory is that under certain conditions (some of which we take up later) an optimum allocation of resources will result.

We now assume that the industry is monopolized but with no effect on supply conditions (the latter assumption is dropped shortly). The profit maximizing monopolist restricts output to OQ_m and can therefore charge a price OP_m. Resources necessary to produce output Q_m-Q_c are no longer required in the industry. Consumers surplus is diminished in two ways. An amount shown by P_cP_mFG represents an income transfer from consumers to producers and is usually assumed to take the form of a monopoly rent. In the customary analysis such a transfer is not regarded as a welfare loss or social cost of monopoly, even if it is thought generally desirable that government should take action through its fiscal policy to redistribute income. The amount GEF, however, is lost to consumers and gained by nobody. It was therefore dubbed by Marshall the 'dead weight' welfare loss of monopoly. By restricting output and charging a price in excess of marginal cost monopoly thus imposed a social loss on the community.

The question which a number of empirical studies have tried to answer is how great is this welfare loss in an economy like the US or the UK? In other words they have tried to measure the size of the triangle like GEF in Diagram 3.1 for the whole economy. Before discussing some of the estimates we should note the following two points. First, if the assumption of unchanged supply (cost) conditions is dropped, to accomodate the more plausible assumption that costs are reduced following reorganizations by the monopolist, the basic position is unchanged. If, for example, the monopolist's marginal costs becomes S', then his profit maximizing output will be OQ'_m and price OP'_m (the equality of marginal cost and marginal revenue, not shown in the diagram, is to the right of the previous position). The welfare loss of the monopoly pricing is then represented by the smaller triangle JKE. In effect the empirical estimates of welfare losses indirectly take account of any such cost reductions.

Secondly, the whole of this argument rests on the welfare loss of monopoly *in individual markets* and this may have very little to do with the overall size of the firms concerned. In the second part of this chapter we were particularly interested in the special advantages that the corporate giants – the 200 or so largest enterprises in an economy like the UK – may owe to their aggregate size, irrespective of their shares in particular markets. Now it is evident that in many cases the dominant firm in a market will also be a member of the corporate elite, even though sales in this market may only account for a small part of the firm's total sales. In other cases the monopolist may, by current standards, be of only moderate size. When speaking, therefore, of monopoly power it is important to keep this notion distinct from that of aggregate size: the share of, say, the largest 200 enterprises in any economy may rise considerably and yet the amount of *monopoly* power remain unchanged or even fall.

We indicated in the introduction that the initial estimates of the welfare losses were catastrophically low. Harberger (1971), the first to venture into the minefield, confessed that 'I was amazed at the result' (p. 24). His final estimate implied that if the resource misallocation due to monopoly were eliminated GNP (in the US) would have risen by about 0.1 per cent. An even lower estimate was obtained by Schwartzman (1960) using rather different methodology and completely different data.

Not surprisingly the size of the estimates caused some consternation amongst those who had regarded the distortions of monopoly as one of the major blemishes on the face of the market economy. Counsel for the defence of the importance of the social costs of monopoly made a large number of criticisms of the estimation procedures. In the calculations, for example, it was claimed that the elasticities of demand assumed were far too low and this led to downward bias in the estimates. Similarly, the industries used to estimate the extent of monopoly pricing were much too broadly defined to isolate monopoly power correctly. In effect high price cost differences (as reflected in profits) were averaged with low ones and this also meant underestimation. Some monopoly profits are capitalized at the time, for example, of a merger which results in monopoly, but the estimation procedures would fail altogether to measure these. Also taking the average profit in manufacturing industries as the benchmark against which to gauge the level of monopoly returns may lead to under-estimation when applied to the whole economy, since some sectors like agriculture and distribution may be much less concentrated than manufacturing. Consequently a lower benchmark should be used.

These and similar criticisms have been made of the original estimates or by subsequent writers explaining why their own efforts put welfare losses rather higher. In an important recent contribution, for example, Cowling and Mueller (1978) suggested that the welfare loss resulting from the operations of the 102 largest UK enterprises in 1968–9 amounted to about 4 per cent of gross corporate (not national) product. The estimate is based on the assumption that all firms working in non-competitive markets can charge the short-run monopoly price. In other words collusion in oligopoly is complete and there is no 'limit' pricing to prevent new entry. For an economy like that of the UK, which is open to considerable foreign competition this assumption seems especially strong and may have led to an over-estimation of the welfare loss. There is still probably a good deal in Scherer's original cautiously worded conclusion after a review of the earlier estimates for the USA that the dead-weight welfare loss due to monopoly lies somewhere between 0.5 and 2.0 per cent of GNP, with estimates nearer the lower bound inspiring more confidence than those on the high side (Scherer, 1980; p. 464).

Clearly this is not a subject where precision can be expected. Orders of magnitude, as most authors have stressed, is all that can be obtained. If, therefore, we accept that the order of magnitude of the estimates is correct we may still wonder at the fuss made by economists about monopoly especially if we accept, even partly, the view that some degree of monopoly may actually enhance the dynamic performance of the economy. That is to say, the static misallocation of the given bundle of resources may amount to about 1–2 per cent of GNP but part of that misallocation is the price paid to ensure that the growth of resources and output is maintained. If a higher rate of growth can be achieved in an economy with some degree of monopoly than in a comparably endowed economy without monopoly, then the compound effect of the differential growth rates will ensure that GNP in the former quickly outstrips that of the latter.

There are a number of replies to this view. A general point on which there may be agreement is that the dead weight welfare loss (represented diagrammatically by the Marshallian triangle) is only a part, probably an insignificant part, of a complex story of resource misallocation and waste. It is in the explanation of how these other important losses arise that considerable disagreement now seems to prevail. An explanation fully in accord with orthodox neoclassical analysis is given by Tullock and Posner. We deal with their view first. The alternative view which really lies outside conventional analysis was christened by Leibenstein 'X-inefficiency' although like most important ideas it had been lurking in corners of the literature for some time.

The Posner (1975) and Tullock (1967) view is that the dead-weight welfare loss considerably understates the full social costs of monopoly because it ignores entirely the resources devoted to achieving and maintaining monopoly power. Competition to achieve monopoly positions will mean that scarce resources are pulled into these activities instead of contributing to production elsewhere in the economy. They should therefore be included in the social costs of monopoly. Efforts to obtain preferential treatment from government or regulatory agencies in the form of patents, tariffs, exclusive licences as well as campaign contributions, lobbying and even bribery are examples of the kinds of expenses they have in mind. In cases where an exclusive position is won by firms who are then not allowed (by law) to compete on prices or agree to eschew price competition, non-price competition in the form of advertising and after sales services may dissipate what would otherwise have been monopoly rents. In other words to treat the area P_cGFP_m (Diagram 3.1) as a monopoly rent and therefore simply an income transfer (or neutral as far as social costs are concerned) is incorrect.

Posner in particular argues that the activities just described will convert monopoly rents into social costs. He therefore proposes that the full social costs of monopoly should include not only the triangle FGE but also the rectangle P_cGFP_m. Clearly, since the former only extends over the decrease in output that occurs if the industry changes from a competitive to a monopoly organization, while the latter extends over the whole monopoly output, the extent of the losses from monopoly will be significant. Not surprisingly the illustrative estimates that Posner included in his paper (although merely regarded as 'suggestive') imply much greater welfare losses than the earlier estimates mentioned above. When Cowling and Mueller (1978) attempted to take account of such expenditures their estimate of the social loss from monopoly rose to between 5 and 7 per cent of gross corporate product, although for reasons given below (see Chapter 4 p. 79) the estimate may be too high. If this analysis is accepted, then monopoly theorists can breathe again. They no longer need contemplate joining the fire brigade or becoming termite exterminators. They can continue to analyse the evils of monopoly in all its forms without fear that this activity is either trivial or esoteric. If necessary they can even call in reinforcements from Leibenstein and his secret weapon, X-inefficiency. The basic notion is very simple and probably as old as enterprise itself. In a recent restatement and defence of the concept Leibenstein explained it as follows: 'The degree to which inputs are *used* effectively represents the degree of X-efficiency, and the deviation between maximum effectiveness and actual effectiveness represents the degree of X-inefficiency' (Leibenstein, 1977: italics in the original). Thus although production engineers and economists may claim that with a certain technology and combining inputs in a particular way, a plant should yield an output of q units per time period, the performance of an actual plant may be considerably less than q. An alternative way of looking at the same thing is that costs per time period are higher than is apparently feasible with the available technology. In terms of Diagram 3.2 for example, attainable long-run average costs may be C but because of X-inefficiency costs actually achieved may be only C_m. In common with other writers Leibenstein[16] has argued in particular that where competition is effective, X-inefficiency will tend to be eliminated. Certainly some of the earlier cases of cartels in sectors of British industry investigated by the Monopolies Commission showed that large cost and profitability differences may be maintained under a monopoly price umbrella.[17] Once the shelter was removed the higher cost firms would have to become more efficient or leave the industry.

Now if such an analysis is correct (and as we shall see below features of it remain highly controversial) then the welfare losses from monopoly may again be considerable and certainly much greater than those represented by the dead-weight welfare losses alone. We can illustrate the argument with Diagram 3.2. In the diagram HK is the market-demand curve for a product which is monopolized. Under monopoly long-run costs are represented by C_mG and price by P_m.

If the industry became competitive, then through the elimina-

Diagram 3.2

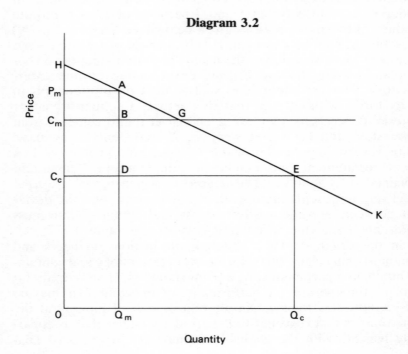

Quantity

tion of X-inefficiency costs would fall to C_c. While the monopoly is maintained, therefore, the dead-weight welfare loss is represented by the triangle ADE. But to this loss we should add an amount represented by the rectangle C_mC_cDB which is the extra cost of producing the monopoly output OQ_m.[18] Just as in the analysis of Tullock and Posner, the size of the welfare loss due to this cost increase is likely to be significant because it extends over the whole of the monopolist's output and not merely over the *change* in output that results from the organization of the monopoly rather than a competitive industry. Leibenstein explains further that X-inefficiency means that the dead weight loss itself will be greater. In Diagram 3.2 if costs were identical under monopoly and competition (the traditional starting point) then dead weight loss would be only ABG. But with X-inefficiency the dead weight loss is the greater area ADE.

By a different route, therefore, Leibenstein arrives at the same conclusion as Tullock and Posner: the welfare losses from monopoly are likely to be of great importance. The earlier estimates based on a simple comparison of monopoly and competition had therefore, grossly underestimated the position. Certainly this view is endorsed by Scherer in his general review of the wastes of monopoly. In his admittedly rough and ready estimates of the likely effects of X-inefficiency in the US economy he puts the figure as high as 2 per cent of GNP. We should emphasize that this was no more than a courageous guess rather than a detailed estimate.[19] It was based in part on a comparison of the existing estimates of the dead-weight loss which, for the reason given above, are likely to be considerably smaller.

But can we be sure that additional costs from X-inefficiency are a 'welfare loss'? A number of writers have taken a different view and before leaving this general subject we should mention their objections. Many years ago in a review of monopoly theory, Hicks (1953) wrote 'The best of all monopoly profits is a quiet life' (p. 369). Where a firm is apparently in an impregnable position the managers may well decide not to strain every nerve to maximize profits but simply ensure that profits are 'adequate' and take the residual in the form of leisure, perhaps cultivating their minds or indulging their bodies. In terms of Diagram 3.2 this means that the area C_mC_cDB should not be regarded as a welfare loss but as part of managerial welfare.

We may feel that it is quite reprehensible that managers do not ensure that costs are kept to a minimum, denoted C_c (in which

case the area C_mC_cDB would be part of the monopoly rent) but
this would be simply a value judgement favouring shareholders
vis à vis managers. As long as someone derives utility from the
move it is not possible, on this view, to count it as a welfare loss. It
is still the case, however, that if under monopoly costs are C_m
rather than C_c then the dead-weight loss, at ADE, is greater than
that of the simple analysis where costs are assumed to be
unchanged at, say, C_m, under both monopoly and competition. In
this case the loss would be only ABG. Furthermore, as Leibenstein (1977) has noted there is no reason to expect that the
increase in managerial utility exactly offsets the decrease in
efficiency.

The Leibenstein view involves the abandonment of cost minimization by firms and this is one of the basic assumptions of the
neo-classical analysis. It has therefore aroused considerable
opposition which has not been stilled by the alternative suggestion that firms now seek to maximize managerial utility. Stigler in
particular has warned of the dangers of espousing a non-
maximizing approach to economic theory (Stigler, 1976). The
analysis of Tullock and Posner retains the neo-classical
framework but also concluded like Leibenstein, that the extent of
monopoly welfare losses is considerably greater than either the
traditional analysis or most empirical estimates suggest. An
important part of Posner's case is that such losses are likely to be
far greater in the case of those industries which in the US are
regulated by government agencies and in the UK are nationalized, than in the private sector.

For the moment our conclusions about the 'pure' welfare losses
from monopoly have to be cautious. The initial estimates now
seem likely to have been too low for a number of statistical
reasons. But even when some allowance is made for underestimation the actual 'loss' may only be in the region of 1–2 per cent of
GNP. If the concept is broadened to include either the costs
involved in winning monopoly positions or in simply sub-
optimizing then the *scope* for loss seems much greater but so too
are the difficulties in even approximate measurement. The lower
bound of such estimates as we have are in the region of 2 per cent
of GNP. But some writers would put these losses three or four
times as high.[20]

The losses discussed in this section can be viewed as the opposite of the advantages outlined on pp. 44–52. Some of those
advantages were the result of large aggregate size, irrespective of

firms' shares in particular markets. To the extent that those advantages feed back into separate markets – by enabling, for example, the largest firms to expand their market shares at the expense of smaller rivals – then the growth of the corporate giants may go hand in hand with the growth of monopoly and monopoly costs. But we should not lose sight of the fact that allocative and *X*-efficiency depend mainly on relative rather than absolute size.

EXTERNALITIES AND SIZE

No-one who has lived through the last twenty-five years or even perhaps only the last ten, can doubt that externalities have not only grown enormously but now pose some of the most serious and intractable problems in all Western industrialized economies. The twin forces of rapid population and economic growth have immeasurably increased the tendency for individuals and groups to impose burdens or costs on others which escape direct calculation by the price mechanism and may therefore lead to a misallocation of resources. The chemical plant discarding untreated effluent into a river which is therefore unusable (or at only extra cost) to all downstream users is the traditional example of economics textbooks. But it has been joined in recent years by an almost unending series of polluters from which no individual is exempt. The executive whose trip on Concorde shatters the comparative calm of all counties to the west of Heathrow, no less than the motorist whose car exhaust poisons the atmosphere of a suburban street or the water-skier on Windermere whose power boat destroys the serenity of the lakes, all contribute in some measure to the deterioration of the environment.

An external diseconomy (or externality)[21] is said to arise when the activities of one party (producing chemicals, driving a car) impose costs on third parties (users of a river contaminated with chemical effluent, pedestrians in a congested street) for which they are not compensated and of which the polluter has taken no account in his own actions.

A moment's consideration of this definition and the illustrations mentioned above demonstrates first that externalities frequently arise from consumption activities by individuals, as well as from the production by large and small firms. Indeed a leading campaigner for severe or even draconian reductions in all kinds of externalities puts the consumption of automobiles at the head of his indictment:

> I once wrote that the invention of the automobile was one of the greatest disasters to have befallen mankind. I have had time since to reflect on this statement and to revise my judgement to the effect that the automobile is *the* greatest disaster to have befallen mankind. For sheer massive, irresistible, destructive power, nothing—except perhaps the airliner—can compete with it. Almost every principle of architectural harmony has been perverted in the vain struggle to keep the mounting volume of motorised traffic moving through our cities, towns, resorts, hamlets, and of course, through our rapidly expanding suburbs. Clamour, dust, fumes, congestion and visual distraction are the predominant features in all our built-up areas. (Mishan, 1971; p. 41)

One need not be quite so committed to accept, for example, that the externalities generated in the production of cars (by a small group of very large companies) are far outweighed by those generated in their consumption.

Secondly, externalities in production, while likely to be concentrated more heavily in some industries (like petrochemicals, chemicals and atomic energy) than others will nevertheless be generated across the whole field of industrial and governmental activities. Lake Baikal, for example, in the Soviet Union, was rapidly polluted by effluent from paper and pulp mills and the health of workers and the fabric of ancient buildings in Cracow in Poland have been ruined by an unfiltered aluminium plant. The Concorde, apart from being 'the least successful commercial venture in recorded history',[22] was developed under the auspices of the French and British Governments and is flown exclusively[23] by state-owned airlines. These last examples also give little ground for hope that collectivization or state ownership would provide any solution to these problems. On the contrary there are good grounds for believing that they may actually be made worse.

Where externalities are the result of production by private firms the irony is that the *level* may be higher under competitive than under the semi-monopolistic conditions customarily regarded as the natural home of the corporate giants.

We can illustrate this point within the partial equilibrium framework used in the previous section. In Diagram 3.3 DD', is the industry demand curve. Initially we assume that MC_p represents the aggregate marginal costs for all firms in a competitive industry. Under the pressures of competition firms would sell an amount OQ_c at price OP_c. The total private costs of this amount

Diagram 3.3

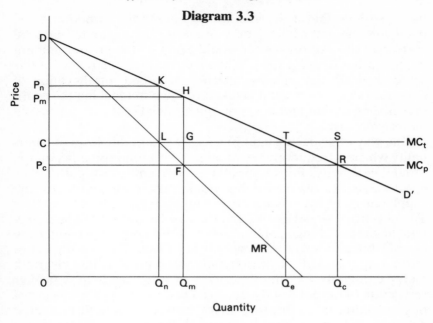

Quantity

are represented by OP_cRQ_c. In other words the costs taken into account by the firms in making their output decisions are OP_cRQ_c. However, if in the process of production external costs of CP_c per unit are generated by the firms in the industry,[24] the full *social* costs of output OQ_c are $OCSQ_c$. The external (or pollution) costs of this output are P_cCSR, and in particular, over the range Q_eQ_c costs (Q_eTSQ_c) actually exceed benefits (Q_eTRQ_c). Not only, therefore, is the industry generating costs of which no account is taken by the market but for part of its output the social costs are greater than the social gains. The invisible hand is clearly failing and resources are being misallocated.

Suppose instead the industry consists either of a single firm monopoly (or a small group of colluding oligopolists, successfully pursuing a joint profit maximizing policy). The marginal revenue curve of the monopoly is denoted *MR* and marginal costs by MC_p. The profit maximizing price and output are OP_m and OQ_m respectively. Under these conditions the monopoly earns a profit of P_cP_mHF but is creating total external costs P_cCGF. The restriction of output that occurs under monopoly thus has the incidental side effect of also restricting the total volume of externalities. (We may also note that if the monopoly is publically owned or regulated and charged with the duty of pricing according to marginal costs then the external effect would again be the greater amount P_cCSR rather than P_cCGF). While they may be 'restricted' in this sense they are nevertheless causing an added misallocation of resources since no account is taken of them in reaching the profit maximizing output and at Q_m marginal social cost exceeds marginal private cost.

One way of achieving a more socially acceptable level of externality which is frequently recommended is to impose a tax on the offending activity. For example a tax per unit of output of P_cC, exactly equal to the externality would raise costs and hence the supply curve of the competitive industry (Diagram 3.3) to MC_t. The new price would be OC and the new output OQ_e. The reduction in output brings a reduction in total costs represented by Q_eTSQ_c but a reduction in benefits of Q_eTRQ_c. There is thus a net welfare gain of TSR. Unfortunately the remedy is less clear cut under monopoly for the imposition of a tax leads to a further restriction of output to OQ_n sold at a price OP_n. The total cost of this reduction in output is Q_nLGQ_m while the benefit measured again by the area under the demand curve, is Q_nKHQ_m. Since the benefits exceed the costs, the tax has had the effect of reducing welfare (by the amount represented by LKHG). The result will clearly hold as long as the amount of the tax is less than the difference between price and marginal revenue at the initial monopoly output, (Buchanan, 1969). The difficulty can be seen as a conflict of interest between those who suffer from the externality and who wish it to be curtailed and those purchasers of the product of the industry who 'suffer' from the restriction of output by the monopolist and wish it to be increased (thus reducing the price). Some additional mechanism is required in this case to ensure that the optimal output (and externality) level of OQ_e is achieved.

The main point of this analysis in the present context is to show that externalities may well be higher under unregulated competition than under unregulated monopoly, but it also serves to highlight the problems facing the policy maker. Given that externalities are being generated in the course of production and consumption, and given that their abatement involves real costs what is the best means of achieving an optimal allocation of resources?

There is a strong tradition in welfare economics that the solution mentioned above, a system of 'externality taxes', will in many instances yield the best corrective behaviour. If liability for the tax is governed by the creation of external costs, firms and individuals will be encouraged to find ways of minimizing the burden by, for example, changing production techniques to use less pollution laden inputs, or consumption patterns by substituting 'cleaner' products (the water-skier takes up aqua-lung diving). By forming a close analogue of the price system, the taxes provide incentives for individuals and firms which are creating the externalities to make their own marginal adjustments, weighing costs against benefits, in a way that should ensure an improved resource allocation. That this result does not automatically follow was illustrated in the monopoly case above where taxes apparently caused further welfare loss. Moreover, in other situations marginal adjustments may not provide the desired outcome. The protection, for example, of a natural wilderness cannot be ensured by individuals making marginal adjustments to their behaviour. Like national defence and similar public goods the socially optimal level of provision may not be left to individual discretion. Collective provision and regulation by the government is the usual solution. Similarly some materials, like radioactivity, lead, mercury, and DDT which tend to become concentrated in the environment rather than dispersed and whose toxicity is severe, are most effectively controlled by direct government regulation and standards, rather than by a system of indirect incentives.[25]

Externalities are the unwanted side effects of attempts by households, firms, and Governments to optimize. They are generated by the efficient and the inefficient, the large and the small, the private as well as the public enterprise. Just as, therefore, the sources of externalities are manifold and their effects all-pervasive in the modern economy so also remedies will take a wide variety of forms depending on the circumstances. Direct government regulation and standard-setting, indirect incentives through taxation, and private abatement agreements are all likely to have a place in the system of control.

CONCLUSION

At the end of the second section of this chapter we suggested that the main advantages of the largest firms may lie in areas such as finance and marketing where gains remain private and where there may be little or no social pay-off in the sense of resource saving. There were certainly cases where technological imperatives went a long way in explaining giant size but these were probably much less frequent in manufacturing than might at first be thought.

The largest firms, as we saw in chapter 2 are likely to have considerable market power. Most operate in many markets and are frequently amongst the leaders. In the third section we therefore addressed the traditional question of how far economic welfare was reduced by the presence of market power and its attendant disincentives. On a question of such complexity only very tentative answers can be expected. When due allowance is made for data problems and possible downward bias the answer seems to be in the region of a 1-2 per cent reduction in GNP as a result of market power when narrowly interpreted. This last qualification stems from the criticisms levelled at the early estimates, to the effect either that they took no account of resources devoted to the creation and maintenance of market power or that they did not measure a potentially much more serious source of loss in the shape of X-inefficiency.

Clearly whichever path you choose will lead to a much greater welfare loss than the rather meagre amounts originally proferred. Some writers go much further and single out advertising as another important source of welfare loss usually exempted or ignored in calculating the effects of market power. We examine these issues in the next chapter.

We suggested in the third section that the common association between big business and pollution in all its forms was a caricature of the actual problem. It takes so many different forms and springs from so many different sources that a wide variety of policies, direct and indirect, are necessary if anything like the 'optimal' corrections are to be made.

4

Advertising and Consumer Choice

INTRODUCTION

When bishops are asked for their views on sin they apparently reply that they are against it. Many economists would give the same reply if asked about advertising. In the field of macro-economics, the monetarists do battle with the Keynesians over the main causes and mechanisms of inflation. But in an adjoining field a no less intense conflict continues between those who see advertising as one component of the basic right of free speech and information, a means of undermining existing monopolies, and those who believe that it destroys consumer sovereignty, buttresses market power and wastes resources.

By coincidence advertising in an economy like the UK amounts to roughly 2 per cent of GNP very similar to estimates of the direct welfare losses from monopoly. An initial reaction might be, therefore, why such a great fuss over a comparatively small amount? There are two answers to this query. First, as Johnson (1970) firmly points out, *any* microeconomic magnitude will almost by definition, be only a small fragment of a macro-economic quantity like GNP. The second and related point is that the direct costs of a particular activity may bear very little relation to its importance and influence. The costs of maintaining and running the Houses of Parliament are a much smaller fraction of GNP but few would doubt their power to affect profoundly the lives of all citizens.

In this area, where aesthetics may get the better of the economics, giant companies have not surprisingly taken the full force of the opponents' attack. For although heavy advertising (for a variety of well-known reasons) is confined to a narrow range of industries producing consumer goods, these are usually the industries where the largest companies dominate or have rapidly come to dominate. For example, the greater part of the outputs of manu-factured foods, drink, tobacco, household detergents, cars and petrol is produced by members of the hundred largest companies and is also heavily advertised.[1]

Within the framework of orthodox economics there is the defence that by advertising, the largest companies are providing information to consumers about existing and new products and this assists in the process of innovation and change. If the world is viewed as basically one of short-run monopolies, then advertising may be an important lever, making existing demand curves more elastic, as discerning consumers are tempted by rival products. On the other hand at least since Chamberlin (1962) wrote in the 1930s the more widely held orthodoxy has been that advertising differentiates one firm's products from those of close rivals and therefore has both the purpose and effect of making individual demand curves *less* elastic. In addition, in oligopolistic industries with differentiated products, advertising while making for intense rivalry amongst existing firms, actually hinders the entry of new competitors, deterred by the formidable costs of establishing a viable market share. The opposing views and contradictory evidence on these issues are discussed in section two of this chapter.

There is a much more heretical view which gives advertising a more dramatic role in modern society. This view, recently associ-ated with the name of Professor Galbraith, sees advertising as the main device by which the large companies control consumer demand so that it meshes in completely with their own production plans. The controllers of the companies can thus achieve their over-riding objective of stable growth. Underlying this vision of modern industry is the notion that the demands themselves are created by the combined efforts of the manufacturer and his advertising agent. Since most consumers expenditure in wealthy economies does not go to meet some primal need such as for food and shelter then, it is argued, the vast majority is spent on fulfil-ling artificial, frivolous and unnecessary wants. The implications of this view are far reaching and needless to say have not gone unchallenged. We examine the claims and counter claims in sec-tion three.

ADVERTISING AND COMPETITION

We can consider two main issues in the controversy over advertising and competition. First does advertising in oligopoly generate barriers to new entry sufficient to allow a joint monopoly return to existing firms applying a minimum of respect for their mutual interests? Secondly, does competition through advertising lead in oligopoly to a wasteful use of resources? We examine these issues in turn looking first at the *a priori* arguments and then the empirical evidence.

Some of the main conclusions of Chamberlin's *Theory of Monopolistic Competition* (1962) have not retained that position of central importance with which they were initially greeted. The famous 'excess capacity' theorem is now treated either as a rather special (and not particularly important) case or shown merely as an intermediate stage on the road to a more stable equilibrium (see for example Dewey, 1969). But an important effect of the book has been to focus attention on selling costs in general and advertising in particular as a crucial aspect of competition and one which may have important implications for public policy. Perhaps ironically, in view of the interest originally provoked by Chamberlin's 'large group' case (where a large number of producers selling differentiated but close substitute products were in competition) the main controversy today essentially concerns the 'small group' case of a few large firms competing mainly through advertising. A landmark in this phase of the discussion was the publication in 1956 of Bain's work on barriers to new competition. His empirical findings still form the basis for one side of the conventional wisdom on advertising and competition, and both in the US and UK have been quoted at one time or another by official agencies to back up their reports on individual industries.

Bain defined the condition of entry as 'the advantages of established sellers in an industry over potential entrant sellers, these advantages being reflected in the extent to which established sellers can persistently raise their prices above a competitive level without attracting new firms to enter the industry' (Bain, 1956; p. 3). He thus viewed entry conditions as a structural characteristic and in theory they could vary over a whole range of values. At one extreme entry conditions may be so easy that existing firms would have no scope for maintaining prices above competitive levels. At the other extreme their advantages may be so great that, so long as they can (tacitly) agree on a joint profit-

maximizing strategy,[2] then prices can be maintained at the equivalent of the monopoly level. The entry barriers would effectively
prevent the emergence of new competition. Between these two
extremes there might be a great number of different levels of
impediment to potential entrants. Bain identified product differentiation advantages that existing firms might have, as one of
the main factors governing the condition of entry. In his initial
conception these were viewed quite widely and included superior
product designs protected by patents, favourable distributive outlets as well as 'accumulative preferences of buyers for established
brand names and company reputations' (Bain, 1956; p. 16).
Although he concludes from his empirical work that in
consumer-goods industries advertising was the most important
source of product differentiation advantages, he was careful to
maintain in his final assessment that 'product differentiation' was
a complex concept and indeed that it may be that

> advertising *per se* is not necessarily the main or most important key to
> the product differentiation problem as it affects intra- industry com-
> petition and the condition of entry. Although instances are found in
> which it is, we may need in general to look past advertising to other
> things to get to the heart of the problem. (Bain, 1956; p. 143)

Later writers have been much less cautious in their approach and
in their anxiety to pin down the effects of *advertising* have
allowed these other characteristics of product differentiation to
be elided altogether from their analysis. In this way Bain's finding
(1956; p. 216) that product differentiation is the most important
barrier to entry, has almost casually been converted into the
much narrower view that advertising may be the most important
barrier. This view has recently been justified by Mann (1974) on
grounds of manageability and econometric convenience. A sceptical bystander may feel that the last reason is rather similar to
that given by the drunken man searching for his door key under a
street lamp. He explains with the impeccable logic of the intoxi-
cated that he dropped the key over the other side of the road in
the dark but was looking over this side where there was more
light.

Since Bain wrote, suggesting rather tentatively that there may
be a direct correlation between entry conditions, other structural
characteristics (such as the level of concentration) and the performance of industry as reflected in the persistent mark-up of
price over long-run average costs (measured by the rate of return

on capital or sales) a fairly continuous stream of articles have filled the academic journals attempting to measure the relationship. It would be satisfying to record at this point that empirical studies have reached a number of reasonably firm conclusions that command general support. Unfortunately on this subject perhaps more than others, the positive methodology so enthusiastically embraced by many applied economists since the mid 1950s has served merely to accentuate differences rather than settle them, as we shall see below.[3]

Part of the explanation for differing hypotheses and empirical results may be a certain lack of clarity over what constitutes a barrier to entry, especially in the case of advertising. In an important monograph on advertising and competition Comanor and Wilson (1974) quote the Bain definition which we have already given above and then add that this is consistent with a rather different definition given by Stigler: 'a barrier to entry may be defined as a cost of producing . . . which must be borne by a firm which seeks to enter an industry but is not borne by firms already in the industry' (Stigler, 1968). This emphasis on the *differential* advantages of existing firms over new entrants and not merely on the costs of entry which may have been required of established firms in the past, is emphasized by Comanor and Wilson. They argue, for example, that as existing firms were 'first in the field' they have advantages that cannot be neutralized by entrants investing an amount comparable to the present value of existing firms' past advertising outlays. Entrants will have to spend more. When existing firms were creating the market for their product they will have met little resistance and may have been able to proceed at a more leisurely pace than new entrants can now allow themselves for the latter are confronted by the established brand preferences of consumers. To capture a viable market share the entrant has, on this view, to spend proportionately more than existing firms to win customers away from established brands. By coming late to the field the entrant must 'shout louder' to make his voice heard above the insistent clamour of the existing brands. But the Comanor and Wilson view probably overstates the case of advertising and entry barriers. They allow existing firms a comparatively easy passage into their position of dominance on the ground that they were 'creating the market' and were the first in the field, while entrant firms run into the opposition of existing brands. This complete antithesis between existing firms and entrants is underlined: 'When existing firms entered the market,

their entry was probably associated with an innovation of some
sort or with a period of rapid growth of demand. . . . Prospective
entrants in the present, unaccompanied by innovation, faced different contingencies' (Comanor and Wilson, 1974; p. 51). This
seems to be a much too simplified view of the competitive process
especially in that comparatively narrow range of consumer-goods
industries on which Comanor and Wilson concentrate. In these
industries product innovation (supported by heavy promotional
outlays), although not of the world-shaking kind, is the very
essence of competition and is a frequent occurrence. New products are just as likely to run into consumer resistance whether
they come from an entrant or not. The cycle of new products
partially superceding existing products and so on is a more or less
continuous process and not one which has been laid down for all
time a decade or so beforehand.

The Comanor and Wilson suggestion that existing firms also
tend to have an advantage since they were the first to make a new
product acceptable to consumers can also be stood on its head.
Once a certain type of new product, say soapless detergent or
wrapped bread is accepted it seems just as convincing to argue
that entrants would have *less* difficulty overcoming consumer
scepticism and ignorance that greeted the initial promotional
efforts of the innovators. Once the produce is familiar, therefore,
entrant firms may actually reap part of the benefit that, 'by
rights', belong to the innovator. *A priori*, therefore, there seems
little ground for the view that advertising creates a *differential*
advantage for existing firms.

Comanor and Wilson (as well, incidentally, as most other
researchers outside of Chicago) add a further strand to their
argument. Economies of scale in advertising, in the form of both
reduced prices charged by the media for larger volumes of repeat
messages and also of the greater effectiveness of messages
beyond a certain volume per unit of time, may further increase
entry barriers. But this extension of the idea beyond that of differ-
entially higher costs of new firms clearly does not square with
Stigler's definition. In fact he explicitly rules out scale economies
as forming a useful part of the definition of entry barriers. Certainly the substantive issues raised by them, especially policy
issues, seem more clearly defined if scale economies are treated
simply as a possible determinant of firm size rather than an
impediment to new competition. Indeed this argument has often
been used to support the view that advertising and concentration

will be positively correlated. If economies of scale in advertising (and related selling costs) are substantial then this would lead, over time, to the survival of only a few giants. Without denying, therefore, that the past advertising expenditures of existing firms may continue to have an important effect after they were incurred and that there may be important economies of scale in advertising we can remain sceptical of the hypothesis that treats advertising *per se* as an important barrier to the entry of new competition. Our scepticism is based on two points, (a) advertising is only one part (and possibly an insignificant part) of the much wider concept of product differentiation, as discussed by Bain, and (b) there is little ground for believing that advertising by a firm 'first in the field' with a particular product gains a *differential* cost advantage over potential rivals (see also Schmalensee, 1974).

Unfortunately for many of those researchers who have worked with great diligence and ingenuity to test the relationship between advertising and concentration the results have so far been singularly anaemic. At best, the observed relationship has been weak and at worst non-existent, with the issue clouded inevitably by the interaction of many other factors. Telser's scepticism of the validity of the hypothesis was apparently matched by his results (Telser, 1964). But others have complained that his measurement of the variables may have been too gross (industries too widely defined, for example) and caused the negative results. Their own more refined measurement, they claimed, produced a definite and positive relationship (Mann *et al.*, 1967). Subsequent empirical work (surveyed by Comanor and Wilson, 1979) has unfortunately done little to settle the controversy.

Instead the emphasis has tended to shift back to the more fundamental problem first tackled by Bain: the relationship between profitability and advertising. If intensive advertising makes an important contribution to high entry barriers then this will be reflected in persistently high profits with possibly important implications for resource allocation. As we have raised doubts about the likelihood of advertising giving existing firms a *differential* cost advantage we are sceptical about this interpretation of any links between advertising intensity and profits. Comanor and Wilson, amongst others, argue extensively for a positive relationship and their empirical analysis supports this view. They summarize their main finding as follows: 'Industries characterised by heavy advertising earn profit rates that are typically between 3 and 4 percentage points higher than those in other industries.

This differential represents up to a 50 per cent increase in rates of return' (p. 245). They argue further that as long-run average costs in the manufacturing sector are probably constant over the relevant range of output for the market leaders, then their results imply that prices in industries selling heavily advertised products, exceed marginal costs. Furthermore their later results[4] were robust enough to stand up to an energetic critique mounted by Brozen that in their original article profit rates were over-estimated since no account was taken of the *capital* value of past advertising outlays. Most students of advertising are agreed that it has similar characteristics to capital investment. In effect it earns a return for a number of years after the expense is incurred. Hence it should be treated like any other capital asset and depreciated over a number of years not simply treated as a current expense as it is for accounting purposes. Rates of return on capital, therefore, that do not include the capital value of advertising assets in the denominator will, on this argument, be biased upwards. Profitability comparisons between industries where advertising is heavy and those where it is not, will favour the former. But this is simply a result of the bias and not of barriers to entry.

In the event, when Comanor and Wilson adjusted the measurement of profits to take account of this point their results were little changed: profitability was positively related to advertising intensity. Similar results were obtained by Weiss, although he was somewhat more circumspect in his interpretation: 'It is possible that the net relationship between advertising and profit rates would fall to non-significance if ads could be depreciated over more reliable lives' (Weiss, 1969; p. 428). The issue is therefore left unsettled because if there are grounds for disagreement about how fixed assets should be depreciated, *a fortiori* there will be disagreement about the true rate of decay of advertising assets.

Recently a more subtle point on the interpretation of any positive relationship between advertising and profitability has been made. One response to the result that profits are correlated with heavy advertising might be to ask whether the firms concerned could increase their profits simply by increasing their advertising? If that were true we may wonder why advertising formed such a small part of GNP. Comanor and Wilson attempt to dispel any such idea with the following explanation:

> Advertising in this analysis acts as a proxy for product differentiation, or, more specifically, for the product and market characteristics that

permit heavy advertising expenditures to differentiate effectively the products of a firm from those of its rivals. Although these product and market characteristics are not easily measured, they are typically characterised by heavy advertising expenditures. (Comanor and Wilson, 1974; p. 130–1)

Those who feel that this comes uncomfortably close to circular reasoning are in good company: Comanor and Wilson (1979) have themselves conceded the point.[5] All that we really know, therefore, from such research is that certain product and market characteristics determine both advertising and profitability but we do not know what they are.

The alternative hypothesis on the basic issue is that advertising is a means of entry into imperfect markets for new competitors and that in its absence prices would be even higher. Far from being a barrier to entry, therefore, advertising is seen as a key to entry. An interesting study which supports this view is one by Benham (1972). He compared the price of spectacles in states in America that allowed advertising of the product with those that had banned it. He found that prices in the states without advertising were about twice as high as in the others, where advertising was permitted. The wider market developed by advertising allowed larger sales volumes, smaller margins, and lower prices. Compared with the cross section analysis of forty-one industries by Comanor and Wilson this study refers to only one industry and perhaps for that reason may be considered of rather limited applicability. More studies of this kind would clearly be highly desirable, but there must be very few products which allow such clear-cut (almost laboratory-like) divisions between advertised and non-advertised regions.

Some writers have suggested that there may be significant differences between manufacturer and retailer advertising. The information content in the latter (as in the case study of spectacles[6]) may be much higher than in the former (the Comanor and Wilson sample) and, therefore, genuinely reflect pro-competitive forces. Others have suggested that within consumer goods there may be different categories which are affected in distinct ways by advertising. The demand for 'convenience' goods of low unit price and purchased at the most accessible outlets without much thought for price and quality comparisons may be much more amenable to advertising than 'shopping' goods which are highly priced and where the gains from price and quality comparisons easily outweigh the costs of searching.

In view of these complexities a certain degree of agnosticism is indicated. As a recent reviewer of the literature put it:

> the differences between the two schools of thought are not as irreconcilable as they might at first appear. There is no contradiction in believing both that advertising is crucial in facilitating firms' entry into new markets and that these entry costs might be steep enough to discourage entry. It is not inconsistent to hold that indivisibilities associated with advertising on nationwide television create market power in certain industries, but that a government policy to severely curtail advertising in these industries would cause prices to become even higher. (Butters, 1976; p. 395)

Agnosticism, however, has not found favour amongst most observers of this emotive subject. Advertising is heaviest in oligopolistic, consumer goods industries because it can be used as a major competitive instrument in place of price changes. As is well known from the theory of oligopoly, overt price competition can be extremely damaging for the firms concerned and therefore may only be used in exceptional circumstances. It is therefore argued that advertising, with its less clear-cut and predictable results can be used extensively by rival firms in their struggle for an increased market share without undermining the price structure. In these industries indirect methods of price co-ordination may be relatively easy to maintain[7] because firms know the dangers if they are upset. It may be much more difficult to reach agreement on limiting and restraining advertising expenditures, for the same kind of reason that makes it almost impossible for the super powers to agree on nuclear-arms control. A price cut can be matched quickly, precisely and with certainty. An increase in advertising may have a much less determinate outcome. Some campaigns, for no apparent reason capture much more public attention than others, equally expensive. Monitoring the outcome of a particular advertising campaign is also much less precise than that of an (unmatched) price change. On this view there is an ever present temptation, therefore, to spend just that much more to ensure a major rival does not gain an advantage.

For these reasons it is often claimed that advertising in consumer goods industries is 'excessive' and leads to waste. Thus Scherer is led from the hypothesis that the competing advertising claims by firms in oligopoly may cancel each other out and lead to a waste of resources to the unwarranted conclusion that the prime offenders include 'soap, proprietary drug, cosmetic and toilet goods, cigarette, cereal, beverage and automobile industries',

(Scherer, 1980; p. 404). The clear inference that we are invited to make is that most of the resources used in these industries' advertising campaigns are wasted. Presumably the reason for listing these industries is that their advertising sales ratios are high. The list would be similar for the UK or any other 'advanced' economy. There is still a good deal of controversy over whether, even in principle, the volume of advertising may be excessive (see, for example the exchanges provoked by Dixit and Norman (1978)). It is extremely hazardous, therefore, to attempt to measure the extent to which resources devoted to advertising lead to a social loss.

Nevertheless, Comanor and Wilson carry the Scherer view several stages further by estimating the social costs (welfare loss) of 'excessive' advertising. They suggest that advertising is excessive in some industries first because of the extreme skewness of its inter-industry incidence and secondly because of the correlation between profit rates and advertising-sales ratios. As we have already observed, all that these points suggest is that there are some product and market characteristics, as yet not fully understood, that determine both advertising and profits. It is not a justification for concluding that advertising leads to social waste. Comanor and Wilson's estimates of the social costs of 'excess' advertising amounted to about 1.5 per cent of the value added in consumer-goods manufacturing which puts them roughly at 0.6 per cent of GNP. To this they add an estimate of a similar size attributable to the maintenance of suboptimal capacity that advertising allows.[8] They conclude that advertising accounts directly and indirectly for a large proportion of the total costs of market power in consumer goods industries and that these costs are especially concentrated in a small group of industries.

We have indicated above that we are less than happy with the logical foundations on which these conclusions rest. That unease is compounded when we read in a more recent study which attempts to measure the social costs of monopoly power that 'all of advertising is added to the welfare loss. This takes the extreme view of advertising as merely an instrument for securing market power' (Cowling and Mueller, 1978; p. 733). Comanor and Wilson at least restricted their estimates to those industries which had, in their judgement, high advertising–sales ratios. Not surprisingly the estimates of the social costs of monopoly in this later study are much larger than in most previous efforts (cf. chapter 3 above; p. 59).

Before turning to the subject of advertising and consumer choice it is perhaps appropriate to mention briefly policy towards advertising, although policy matters are dealt with more fully in Part three of the book. Recent experience in the UK of restrictions on the use of cigarette advertising illustrates the general point that unless policies are well thought out they may have the opposite effect from that intended. The decision to end cigarette advertising on the commercial television channel was made on health grounds. But the restriction was the signal for the tobacco companies to redouble their efforts elsewhere. Resources formerly used in television advertisements were channelled into sponsorship of a wide range of regular sporting events. The first irony was, therefore, the unholy alliance of an apparently lethal product with activities designed to promote bodily health. The second irony had a special British flavour. The BBC which of course carries no direct advertisements prides itself on the breadth and excellence of its sports coverage. No sooner, therefore, do tobacco companies sponsor a new event, in show-jumping, snooker, cricket, tennis or rugby league (with the accompanying brand name, image, and advertising hoarding in the arena itself) than the BBC arrives to give it comprehensive coverage. Not only is the association between sport and smoking maintained but it is promulgated on a television channel which has to deny, because of its Charter, direct access to other advertisers. Truly a masterstroke for the advertising agent and a perfect example of a policy misfiring.

It might be argued that in a private enterprise economy if there is widespread dissatisfaction with the information provided by advertisements and frequent complaints that consumers are led into purchases that they subsequently regret, an industry would spring up providing, for a fee, unprejudiced information based on scientific tests of advertised products. If the extent of the dissatisfaction was genuinely great then, on this argument, firms in this 'information' industry would make handsome returns, producers of inferior brands would have to mend their ways or see their market share dwindle and consumers would no longer be deceived. It is true that organizations of this kind do exist both in the UK and the USA but they are usually non-profit-making bodies and hitherto have had rather limited appeal. Certainly subscribers to *Which?* the magazine of the Consumers Association in the UK are miniscule compared with the number of regular customers for advertised products.[9]

Unfortunately we cannot conclude from this that the lack of response on the part of information-providing firms or information-seeking consumers necessarily signifies general satisfaction with the current state of advertising. The reason lies in the 'public good' attributes of the kind of information that such agencies or firms can provide. If the Consumers Association offers the results of its tests to one subscriber that, for example, on a number of relevant criteria Brand X is the 'best buy' then the use of this information by the subscriber in no way diminishes its value to the subscriber's friends, neighbours, casual acquaintances and so on. Indeed if the subscriber regards himself as in the vanguard of protecting consumers interests, he may well feel it is his duty to give the information to as many people as possible. In contrast there is a flourishing trade in market research carried out by specialist agencies and commissioned by producers. To know what consumers expect from a breakfast cereal, deodorant, or toilet soap will be useful to the manufacturer when planning his packaging and marketing strategy. Clearly he has a strong incentive to keep this information to himself otherwise any competitive advantage may be lost.

Thus the non-exclusive nature of unbiased information on consumer products means that there will be too little investment in its provision. For this reason policy discussions of advertising usually include proposals for government funded agencies to undertake the necessary testing and publicity to make up for the shortfall in private investment (e.g. Mann *et al.*, 1967; p. 345: Scherer, 1980; p. 404). They are often accompanied by other suggestions for direct or indirect measures that will curb the volume of advertising (see chapter 7).

ADVERTISING AND CONSUMER CHOICE

The disagreements that we have so far reviewed in this chapter have, by and large, been within the mainstream of neoclassical theory. Central to the dispute has been the role of product differentiation and especially advertising in the competitive process. The power that advertising may confer was seen either as a means of barring the entry of new competition or alternatively as a key to effective entry. We have so far heard little about the consumers themselves, except that they may desire access to more unbiased information.

The consumer plays a much more important role in what is claimed to be a more profound attack on advertising mounted over a number of years and through successive volumes by Galbraith. The main thrust of his attack is on the notion of consumer sovereignty in modern, wealthy societies.[10] According to the conventional view, in market economies resources are allocated to their most important uses in order to meet the most urgent needs in response to consumer demand. Changes in tastes will be reflected in upward pressure on prices, lower stocks and lengthening waiting lists for those products favoured by an increase in demand while the reverse will occur for those products now relatively unpopular. As a result more resources will be devoted to the production of the first group of goods and less to the second group. As the whole of economic activity is devoted to the satisfaction of consumers' wants, the greater the bundle of goods and services consumers can buy the higher will be their utility or welfare, *ceteris paribus*.

According to Galbraith the logic of this argument fails once it is recognized that the wants themselves are being created by the same process by which they are satisfied. For many products in wealthy economies demand no longer arises spontaneously in the breast of the consumer but is implanted there by the wiles of the advertising industry. Like Iago sowing the seeds of discord in the noble soul of Othello, so the road-side hoarding, the television commercial and the full-colour newspaper spread creates dissatisfaction with his current possessions in the pliable mind of the consumer. In this way he becomes the servant of the producer instead of the other way round, as the conventional wisdom has it. Now, argues Galbraith, if consumer demand is really the creation of the producer in order that his production, growth and profit plans may be fulfilled, it is a short step to recognize that we can no longer assume that the more of these kinds of goods the consumer has, the higher his level of satisfaction. The goods in question are those heavily advertised which we have discussed on pp. 78–79 above.

This apparent reversal of the roles of production and consumption by which 'wants depend on the process by which they are satisfied' Galbraith called, in his early work, the 'Dependence Effect'. It is integrated into the main argument in his last book in this area which contains the important statement:

Production is great not necessarily where there is great need; it may be where there is great capacity for managing the behaviour of the individual consumer or for sharing symbiotically in the control of the procurement of public goods and services, all in the interest of bureaucratic growth. This is in sharp contrast with the neo-classical view of power which holds that power restricts output in the manner of the classical monopoly. But a moment's thought directed to the areas of abundance in the economy—automobiles, weapons, soaps, deodorants and detergents—will suggest that the present analysis is not in conflict with common observation and common sense. (Galbraith, 1975; p. 161)

This passage has been quoted because it helps us to see the implications of Galbraith's argument. Prices are no longer any guide to what needs to be produced and hence in the allocation of resources. As prices can no longer be relied upon even as rough benchmarks against which 'needs' are to be gauged some other mechanism will have to be substituted. Since we cannot rely on benign Providence we shall, presumably, have to depend on committees of wise men who will be able to decide for everyone what 'need' in an 'exclusive or dominant sense' is. What a heavy responsibility for the wise men but what a comfort for the consumer to be relieved of the onerous task of choosing between different brands in their multi-coloured packets. For the wise men will surely eliminate much waste and make certain that everyone has access to the uniform and standard products.

If Galbraith's view is taken seriously the logical outcome would seem very close to this caricature. But very few producers would recognize themselves amongst those supermen portrayed by Galbraith. Similarly very few consumers whether they frequent senior common rooms or the local discotheque (or perhaps both) would recognize the demeaning portrait painted of them. Although many producers may at times wish they had such powers to control demand for their products, few if any come within hailing distance of such mastery. To take one of the very few industries that Galbraith mentions to illustrate his argument, motor cars, both in the United States and Europe (and particularly Britain) the well-established and firmly entrenched enterprises which over the years have spent millions of pounds advertising their brand names and made them household words have recently been groaning under the burden of intense competition from Japanese models. In the space of very few years names which were formerly unknown have captured more than a tenth of the British market. To argue that this merely demonstrates the

powers of advertising, since the Japanese campaign was launched
with heavy promotional expenditures, misses the point at issue. It
is not logical to argue simultaneously that firms are in control of
the demand for their products which they themselves have created yet at the same time to hold that they are at the mercy of any
determined competitor using methods similar to their own. Nor is
it sufficient to suggest that it is not the position of the individual
firms which is in question but that of *all* firms in the industry, for
in many cases what constitutes an 'industry' is very difficult to
define. Over time changes in demand, technology, or income
levels decimates the size of some industries and multiplies that of
others. At one period products that are regarded as close substitutes and hence (conceptually) belonging to the same industry
may at a later period be regarded as more distant substitutes.

> The joint but unco-ordinated efforts of the producers merely creates
> one element of the environment by which wants of the consumer are
> shaped. It is because each individual producer thinks that the con-
> sumers can be persuaded to like his products that he endeavours to
> influence them. But though this effort is part of the influence which
> shapes consumers' tastes, no producer can in any real sense 'deter-
> mine' them. (Hayek, 1979; p. 9)

There is, however, a much more fundamental criticism of the
Galbraith position. The essence of the argument, after all, rested
on the notion that most consumers' expenditures in wealthy
economies are spent on satisfying wants that are far from 'basic'.
Soapless detergent, perfume, electric toothbrushes and so on
would do little to help Robinson Crusoe keep body and soul
together. Since most expenditures are on products that do not
have this life and death urgency then psychologically grounded
desires take over. Hence, says Galbraith, the vulnerability of the
consumer to the allurements of the advertising man.

If psychologically grounded desires take over as soon as basic
needs for food and shelter are met the scope for the advertising
industry is great indeed. If further, the goods and services that go
to meet these 'desires' may *all* be regarded as illegitimate or at
least as not improving man's utility, then the greater proportion
of GNP of many societies for many decades if not for several
centuries must fall into this category.

A moment's reflection, however, suggests that the Dependence
Effect rests on a very shaky foundation.

> The innate wants are probably confined to food, shelter and sex. All

the rest we learn to desire because we see others enjoying various things. *To say a desire is not important because it is not innate is to say that the whole cultural achievement of man is not important'* (Hayek, 1979: italics added).

All of the great works of art in architecture, literature, music and painting fail the Galbraithian test of meeting a real or genuine 'need' and therefore man is no better off with them than without them. His welfare would be improved if the resources devoted to the creation of works of art were made to serve some more 'useful' purpose.

The argument has only to be stated to demonstrate its absurdity and yet it is logically the same as that which Galbraith invites us to accept in the case of other, humbler artefacts. In most societies most of the time the demand for the great majority of products is culturally determined rather than derived from an innate need. We leave the last word to Hayek:

> Professor Galbraith's attempt to give an apparent scientific proof for the contention that the need for the production of more commodities has greatly decreased seems to me to have broken down completely. With it goes the claim to have produced a valid argument which justifies the use of coercion to make people employ their income for those purposes of which he approves. (Hayek, 1977; p. 10)

We ended the previous section by noting that there may be a case for non-profit making agencies to increase the supply of unbiased information because of its 'public good' characteristics. Similarly we conclude this section with a brief comment on the view that some forms of private consumption should be encouraged by public subsidy. In view of the general tenor of the last few pages which has favoured the notion that the consumer still knows his own mind best despite the efforts of advertisers it may come as a surprise to read general support for public expenditure of this kind.

Perhaps the most eloquent advocate has been Tibor Scitovsky who has for some time warned of the dangers of taking a too uncritical view of the sanctity of consumers choice as expressed in the market.[11] He recognizes the enormous benefits that have been brought by economies of scale but he also points to an important drawback. The widespread application of mass production techniques while lowering unit costs also raise wages and this makes it costly and possibly uneconomic to produce on a small scale and cater for specialized, minority tastes. As a consequence, they may

have become comparatively neglected and unless given special
treatment may die out altogether. Scitovsky argues that this may
have undesirable consequences for the development of the preferences of the majority. As we have already said most tastes in
advanced economies are learnt rather than innate. If the market
economy is catering to a wide variety of tastes, consumers have
the opportunity of learning from those with highly developed or
informed tastes. Consumers who *now* have such tastes were once
not in that happy position and thus have the considerable advantage of experiencing both states:

> I cannot claim that an informed person's tastes are better by any test,
> than an uninformed person's, or that they are more conducive to
> happiness or more appropriate to the atomic age; but I can claim that
> they are based on knowledge of a wider range of alternatives, which
> includes the alternatives available to the uninformed person. (Sci-
> tovsky, 1964; p. 246)

But in the wake of important economies of scale in mass production, the market alone may fail to cater for specialist, minority
tastes with the eventual consequence that majority tastes may be
based on a progressively narrower range of alternatives simply
because the example and knowledge of other preferences – poetry
over pushpin, mountaineering over sunbathing, baroque over
rock music, or whatever – are almost totally lacking. In order,
therefore, that 'specialist' tastes may compete on an almost equal
footing with 'general' tastes and perform this important educational function some public support for these artistic and sporting
activities can be justified. Scitovsky underlines this point by
observing that such activities only yield up their full 'pleasures'
after perhaps a long period of relative 'pain'. Most artistic and
sporting pursuits involve this reversal of the usual sensations in
consumption (immediate pleasure or satisfaction) and therefore
many potential consumers, for the lack of information, practice,
or expert example, may 'under-consume' on a whole range of
activities. The case for subsidy may thus be further strengthened.[12] Other commentators who have ventured to write on
'Economics and the Arts' have frankly admitted that the question
of subsidy is not one which can be answered by reference to
scientific economics, but is one of basic political philosophy.
Peacock tries to fit the arguments in favour of subsidy into a
'public goods' or 'externalities' framework but is not very happy
with the results (Peacock, 1976). The case for subsidy is recog-

nized in varying degrees by the governments of most wealthy economies (although as Scitovsky points out there is little correlation between wealth and public expenditure on the arts) and ironically by many of the largest companies who are increasingly using their shareholders money to underwrite Shakespeare, art exhibitions, and concerts.[13] To some extent, therefore, they are helping to offset the adverse effects that scale economies in mass production may have on the formation of public taste.

CONCLUSION

Advertising has always had an uneasy place in neo-classical economics which much of the time assumes perfect knowledge of the opportunities available to consumers. On the other hand, the main rationale of advertising is usually claimed to be precisely to fill gaps in consumer knowledge by bringing to their attention the goods and services on offer. As a result there is bound to be some ambiguity and conflict about the proper role of advertising, especially if it is conceded that consumers may derive genuine utility from product variety which will entail branding and other product differentiation activities.

In recent years the older controversies about the possibility of separating the persuasive from the informative content of advertising and precisely where production costs cease and selling costs begin, have largely given way to a discussion of the nature and importance of product differentiation (particularly by advertising) in creating barriers to the entry of new competition. Given that effective entry barriers allow existing firms to maintain prices in excess of long-run average costs, then to the extent that product differentiation contributes to such barriers, it impairs the competitive process and requires some policy response. In part II of this chapter we noted that for this argument to hold, advertising and related activities had to give some *differential* advantage to the established firms over potential entrants, otherwise the latter could simply match the (past and present) expenditures of the former and win a viable market share. On *a priori* grounds a *differential* advantage from advertising seems difficult to sustain and the empirical evidence is mixed. If we unravel the statistical problems that have frequently led to claims and counter-claims about the efficiency or iniquity of advertising, there is some evidence that certain product and market characteristics lead to both high advertising and high profits but as yet we do not really know what they are or in what direction the causation flows. On the other side there is some case-study material that suggests that advertising may tend to keep prices lower than they might otherwise be. More investigations of this kind are really needed before we can be confident about their general applicability.

We are inclined to reject entirely the Galbraithian thesis that in affluent societies wants are created by the process by which they are satisfied and that therefore 'it can no longer be assumed that welfare is greater at an all round higher level of production than at a lower one'. Most wants in all societies except those in the most piteous poverty are learned rather than innate but this makes them no less urgent or desirable. On the contrary, some of those acts of consumption which by common consent involve participation in the greatest achievements of man—the arts—depend so much on learning, practice, and example that they require direct intervention in the market with subsidies.

5

Competition and Conglomeration

INTRODUCTION

We have seen in chapter 2 that the enormous size of the largest companies means that they are usually not only amongst the leaders in some markets but also lesser participants in a number of others, owing to their diversification. In each case their role in the competitive process has given rise to a great deal of controversy. Although much more is now known than 30 years ago about the nature and implications of competition in oligopolistic markets the very nature of the problem makes it more prone to violent disagreement than the straightforward cases of competition and monopoly.

While for some, therefore, large firm competition in oligopolistic markets is thought likely to lead to an allocation of resources that is efficient in both a technical and allocative sense, for others, there is little to choose between a single-firm monopoly on the one hand and a few large firms which by (tacit) co-ordination can achieve a monopoly result, on the other. In both views it is recognized that the interaction of modern technology and the size of the market may allow only a few firms to flourish but on the first view competitive forces are considered strong enough to keep prices generally in line with long-run average costs. In the second case, competitive forces are viewed as either fully neutralized by firms' agreement on a joint profit maximizing strategy or simply channelled into 'wasteful' product differentiation and advertising which we discussed in the previous chapter. We discuss this aspect of large firm competition in the second section of this chapter.

More recently, as the breadth of large firms' activities has increased, another feature of competition has received considerable attention. Where firms are of a very large absolute size and operate in a great number of different markets with varying

89

amounts of market power they may be able to compete in ways which are not normally covered by the traditional analysis. In particular, it is argued, a large firm's power over prices in an individual market may no longer depend on its relative size in that market but on its overall size and financial strength. Above-normal profits in some of its markets, where it may be amongst the leaders, can be used to subsidize losses in other markets where it is cutting prices in order to win a larger share at the expense of more specialized rivals. By this and similar means the large, diversified firm may change adversely the structure and performance of industry.

We do not have to look far to find writers who have no time for these views. For them diversification is seen as a means of gingering up existing competition, rather than undermining it. In a manufacturing sector where many industries are quite heavily concentrated, entry in the form of diversification by a prosperous large firm is thought likely to improve rather than worsen performance. These issues are discussed in the third section.

COMPETITION IN OLIGOPOLY

In the field of industrial economics one of the most influential works since the war has undoubtedly been Bain's *Barriers to New Competition* (1956) and his subsequent textbook which drew very largely on his previous researches (Bain, 1959). The paradigm for the economic analysis of industry (in terms of structure–conduct–performance) which, following E. S. Mason, he pioneered, has served both teachers and researchers well for a very long time and has greatly improved the way in which the mass of detail about individual industries can be organized and assessed.

In a sense the critical stance that we assume for the remainder of this section is largely a result of the almost total success which Bain's work had on much subsequent empirical research. The focus of his work was on the effect that the threat of entry by new competitors could have on the price and output behaviour of existing firms. He was justly critical of previous discussions of oligopoly which had concentrated almost exclusively on the competitive behaviour among *existing* rivals. But as a result of his work the pendulum seems to have swung completely in the opposite direction: conditions of entry and their effects are emphasized, while competition amongst existing rivals are relegated to a back seat. Much of the empirical work that has been done in the Bain tradition has relied largely on a simple theory of oligopoly which was recognized by Cournot (but largely ignored as uninteresting) and developed by Chamberlin.

The main point of this theory is that firms in oligopoly will recognize that it is in their mutual interest to co-ordinate their policies on price and output, for once this is achieved they may well share a monopoly profit. Under certain circumstances, therefore, independent firms in oligopoly will arrive at a joint profit maximizing strategy where price and output are at the monopoly levels. The most straightforward case would be a perfect cartel where firms agree to restrict output in order to maintain a monopoly price in return for a share in the resulting profits. Even where the law allows such a degree of collusion, however, it is doubtful whether conditions will be such that firms would be prepared to give up their independent sovereignty so completely. Where overt collusion is illegal the approximation to such a strategy which may emerge will depend largely on the extent to which the desire to share in a joint maximum profit outweighs the desire to retain complete independence in price setting and the feeling by individual firms that they can improve on their own profit by operating independently, even though this may reduce the total profit earned by the industry as a whole. The joint profit maximizing hypothesis does not deal with how the spoils are actually divided up amongst the rival firms but it is usually emphasized that such a policy will be more successful where firms are of roughly equal size and costs. Clearly the stronger the influences leading firms to pursue an independent policy, the more price and output levels will depart from the monopoly level. In the limit, where (tacit) co-ordination breaks down altogether, price will settle at the competitive level.

The key question is then to identify leading features of industrial structure that will produce a co-ordinated policy. For Bain these were the number and size distribution of firms, the degree of product differentiation and the conditions of entry to the industry.[1] Thus he hypothesized, for example, that where the number of firms was small, each with a large share of the market, tacit co-ordination would be probable, especially if existing firms were shielded by onerous entry conditions that gave them a differential cost advantage over potential entrants. Alternatively where there were a large number of firms, none with a dominant market share and where entry to the industry was comparatively easy, then tacit co-operation to achieve joint profit maximization would be difficult or impossible. In this case prices would be kept roughly in line with long-run average cost by the forces of competition. Using his detailed analysis of entry conditions in twenty US manufacturing industries Bain then attempted to test the hypothesis empirically. Broadly speaking his results supported his theory: in particular industries where the level of seller concentration was very high[2] and where entry barriers were also substantial, then profit rates (measuring the average difference between price and average cost)[3] were higher, on average, than where one or other of these structural variables had a lower value.[4] Much subsequent empirical work, although often based on a much less detailed analysis of precise entry conditions, has until recently tended to support Bain's central contention. Some recent work has, however, challenged both the validity and interpretation of the earlier results and we shall discuss these further below.

For the moment there are one or two direct effects of Bain's work that should be emphasized. There was a tendency almost to take for granted that where one or other index of industrial structure was 'high' this necessarily meant that firms were successfully co-ordinating their price policies to ensure a joint monopoly profit. Thus if the level of seller concentration was say, above 70–75 per cent and/or if the ratio of advertising to sales was 'high', then it was assumed that there was a strong probability that excessive prices and profits prevailed. In this way the main problem in the analysis of oligopolistic industries, namely how to handle competitive move-response and counter-move was sidestepped by the over-simple assumption that recognition of a mutual interest in tacit co-ordination to secure a joint monopoly profit would inevitably lead in many cases to its actual long-run achievement. In practice control of the market may be much more complex and difficult.

The point is well illustrated by the recent discussion in the UK of price leadership. In 1973 the Monopolies Commission reported on parallel pricing, 'the practice by which two or more sellers in an oligopolistic market, when changing their prices, do so together, by similar amounts or proportions and having regard to the interests of the group of sellers as a whole', Monopolies Commission (1973b), para. 10. The Commission first makes the distinction between price determination in 'highly competitive' industries where prices and price changes are determined by the impersonal forces of supply and demand, and in oligopolistic markets where individual sellers will be aware of their mutual interdependence and seek to co-ordinate their policies 'with the aim of balancing the interests of all' (para. 9). Where explicit collusion is ruled out by law, sellers in the second kind of market may adopt a system of price leadership as the method of co-ordination. The burden of the report is then a discussion of various forms of price leadership and their likely consequences for the 'public interest', as well as a review of some rather sketchy evidence from five industries. For our discussion the most interesting point is the distinction in the report between 'collusive' and 'barometric' price leadership. As a subsequent critical article suggested (Polanyi, 1974) the central issue which will govern the whole attitude to policy is whether *most* price leadership is of the collusive or barometric type. Under collusive price leadership, co-ordination of price changes may, according to the Commission, be so tight and complete that even though there is no formal agreement, prices will be above the competitive level and 'may indeed approach the monopoly level depending upon the conditions of entry to the industry' (para. 29). The Commission admits that this behaviour and result would be indistinguishable from the case of an industry dominated by one very large seller with an additional fringe of much smaller sellers. (They excluded this latter category from further consideration since in effect the dominant seller, like a monopolist, can act independently.) For the collusive leadership result to hold, however, it is also clear from the report that a large number of structural conditions have to be met. Apart from a high level of seller concentration, the Commission mentions, for example, standardization of products making price differences easily identifiable; industry demand that is price inelastic so that a single seller has little to gain from an independent price cut; high ratios of fixed to variable costs, making the industry prone to periodic excess capacity; similar cost levels between firms, so that mutual interests are clearly defined; infrequent innovations so that technology is stable and known, and finally high entry barriers allowing above normal profits to be earned without attracting new entry.

Now amongst the great variety of industries in the modern economy it is quite likely that there are some where all of these are more or less met. It seems equally likely that if any antitrust agencies exist, these industries would be amongst the first to

engage their interest and energies. The list of conditions, however, seems long and detailed enough to make it more probable
than in most oligopolisitc industries, the absence of one or other
of them will ensure a different form of pricing behaviour and
consequently a different industry performance. To characterize
this much looser form of price leadership where the results are
unlikely to be very different from what would occur if firms set
their prices independently in response to the underlying conditions of supply and demand, Stigler (1947) suggested the term
'barometric'.

The 'barometric' price leader only retains his position as
initiator of price changes so long as he accurately gauges the
feelings of the other leading sellers as to the 'correct' response to
a change in costs or demand that affects the whole industry.
Unless he is unusually perceptive the 'barometric' firm is unlikely
to get important changes 'just right' for any length of time. He
may over-estimate the effect of a cost change, for example, and
find that another large firm or firms have not followed his price
increase so he may have to rescind it. Thus in these conditions the
identity of the 'barometric' leader is likely to change fairly frequently, compared to the collusive case where the leader may be
expected to retain his position for some considerable time.
Despite its looseness, given the structure of the industry leading
firms may find this informal recognition of a leader a useful
short-run device for co-ordinating their response to an important
change in the underlying market conditions. For in oligopoly
there is the ever present danger that an individual firm may have
his price change misunderstood by competitors: too large a price
cut may be treated as the opening shot in what turns out to be a
very costly price war for all firms; a too hasty price increase may
not be followed, with the consequent loss of sales for the firm
concerned.

As we have mentioned, this second form of price leadership is
likely to yield price levels that would prevail if firms acted independently in response to market conditions and since all of the
conditions necessary for collusive price leadership are unlikely to
be met frequently, the most common form of leadership is likely
to be of the less damaging 'barometric' type. Rather surprisingly
the Monopolies Commission did not agree. They accepted that
'prices may be less successfully co-ordinated by "barometric"
than by other forms of price leadership and it follows that levels
of prices and profits are likely to diverge less from the competi-

tive norm than with the stronger forms of parallel pricing'. But they did not accept that the result is likely to be the same as the competitive norm. 'However oligopolists choose to co-ordinate their behaviour, the result is likely to be a level of prices and profits higher than would prevail with a larger number of sellers, and a price structure more rigid in the face of changing cost and demand conditions' (para. 35). By the 'competitive norm' the Commission seems to have in mind something very like perfect competition, judging from the discussion in para. 7. Given that firms in an oligopolistic industry may have quite different production functions to what a greater number of smaller firms in that industry would have, the comparison lacks plausibility. But from a policy point of view the implications of this dubious comparison are serious as we may observe from the last part of the quotation. It is made clear that whatever form price determination in an oligopoly may take is likely, to some extent, to be viewed unfavourably by the Commission. In view of the admittedly sketchy evidence that they themselves present, this position, as Polanyi has persuasively argued, is difficult to support. Chapter 2 of the report contains a brief review of five industries in which price leadership prevailed: bread, electric lamps, gramophone records, petrol and tyres. In each case there was direct and indirect evidence that the form of price leadership was barometric rather than collusive due to the absence of one or more of the necessary conditions and that therefore the likely outcome was similar to what would have emerged from a large number of firms operating independently. For example in the bread industry there were thought to be no substantial entry barriers (para. 45); in electric lamps no direct evidence on entry barriers was given but there was evidence (from an earlier Monopolies Commission report) of successful growth by a previously small, independent company and of active competition (in discounts) by other leading companies (subsidiaries of international concerns) as well as countervailing power by large retailers; in gramophone records growth of demand in the 1960s and lack of sufficiently high entry barriers led to the erosion of the market share of the previous leaders and the emergence of barometric price leadership; in petrol, despite being 'highly oligopolistic', the leading sellers had suffered a steady decline in market share at the hands of fringe sellers (which were usually part of much larger international concerns); in tyres there had been a number of significant innovations—contrary to one of the conditions necessary for successful collusive price leadership–as well as active retail-price competition, imports accounting for nearly one-fifth of the market and considerable countervailing power by motor manufacturers in the initial equipment market.

In all cases, therefore, the forces of competition of one kind or another were far from inactive even though a superficial glance at the structure of the industry may give the impression that complete collusion was probable. The difficulties of maintaining the kind of price leadership that the Monopolies Commission was justly concerned about can be fully appreciated by considering the list of conditions necessary for its success. We would suggest that only if all of these conditions can persistently be met are there likely to be serious adverse consequences such as monopoly profits or inefficiency. The probability of this happening in a *large* number of apparently oligopolistic industries in an economy like the UK, open to the uncomfortable disciplines of foreign competition, seems very remote.

The evidence in the report on parallel pricing was from a hand picked sample of only five industries and was qualitative rather than quantitative. Other students have tried to determine the issue – essentially whether oligopolies can persistently earn abnormal profits – by taking a wider cross section of industries and using statistical methods. A pioneer in this approach was Bain (1956) to whose work we have already referred (p. 92 above). A key contribution, published in 1951, reported on the effect of concentration on the profit rates of leading sellers in a sample of forty-two US manufacturing industries in the period 1936–1940. Where concentration was high[5] profit rates were apparently above those of other industries. Bain's work formed the starting point for a mass of subsequent investigation, much of which used the more sophisticated methods of multiple regression analysis. In a useful survey published in 1974, Weiss summarized more than forty-six separate studies dealing mainly with the US but also including the UK, Canada, and Japan. Since that date the flow may have abated slightly but the diligent inquirer would not be hard-pressed to find at least another dozen studies that dealt essentially with the same hypothesis.

The result of all this energy has not been, unfortunately, an unambiguous harvest of hard facts. The division of opinion on this issue is aptly caught in the title of the paper by Demsetz that precedes that of Weiss: 'Two systems of belief about monopoly.' Upwards of two-thirds of the studies yielded a moderate to weak positive relation between concentration and profits (with a variety of other structural features held constant). Thus they seem to give some support for what Demsetz terms the 'self sufficiency' view of monopoly and oligopoly. On this view firms in concentrated industries can, by a variety of methods, maintain their prices and profits above the 'normal' level without the assistance of government. This conforms with the collusive view of price leadership, for example, that we have just discussed. The minority of studies which either find no relationship at all between concentration and profits or that any relationship is short-lived, support what Demsetz terms the 'interventionist' view of monopoly power. On this view most monopoly power can be traced directly to some government agency or regulation which either confers a long-term privilege on some existing firms or deters the entry of new firms. Without such government action any market power is short-lived: undermined either by an internal conflict of interest amongst existing firms or successful new entry. This is very much in line with the type of industrial performance that would result from 'barometric' price leadership. An influential empirical study which supports the second view reworked and extended Bain's material but obtained very different results. Having enlarged the sample of industries and the number of firms observed within some industries Brozen (1971) could find no positive correlation between profits and concentration (a result similar to that of Ornstein for a later period (Ornstein, 1972)). These studies refer to the US but a similar conflict of results can be quoted for the UK (compare, for example, Hart and Morgan (1977) with Cowling and Waterson (1976). Much seems to hinge on the precise sample included, the way variables are measured and the time period considered. Under these circumstances it is again advisable to record a verdict of not proven. Even many of those convinced that the direct concentration–profit rate relationship is well established and indicative of monopoly power are uneasy at the prospect of major reconstructions in industrial organization. They favour instead merely a more active and tougher application of existing antitrust laws (Weiss, 1974; cf. chapter 7).

In the face of the many different studies that do find some, albeit modest, relationship those holding a basically 'interventionist' view of monopoly power have offered several explanations. The one to which Demsetz gives most weight is that leading firms in concentrated industries are likely to be the most efficient and

forward looking and for these reasons will earn high profits. If it is
to the concentration level (and by inference monopoly power)
that firms in certain industries owe their high profitability then,
argues Demsetz, the relationship would still hold even when firm
size is taken into account. Thus smaller firms in concentrated
industries may be expected to be more profitable than firms of
similar size in less concentrated industries. In a test of this
hypothesis, however, the results were negative: 'after the size of
firm is taken into account, *no* significant correlation between profit rate and market concentration is apparent even though the
correlations which ignore firm size are positive' (Demsetz, 1974;
pp. 177–78). Any positive association between concentration
and profit rates is, therefore, on this view, simply recording the
fact that the largest firms tend to be more efficient and hence
more profitable.

We may summarize this section of the discussion as follows.
Oligopoly can be used to cover a whole host of different industrial
structures. Some will have only a handful of firms of similar size
while others may have many firms of different sizes. Some will
sell differentiated products, others homogeneous products, but
these are not two discrete and easily identifiable categories since
both the form and degree of differentiation or homogeneity can
vary enormously. Barriers to entry may be very high for some
industries and very low for others but, as with the growth of
demand, these may vary at different periods. The list could be
extended but the point is probably clear enough. To the extent
that structural conditions affect industrial behaviour then we can
expect considerable variety in the pricing behaviour of different
industries. Very often some form of price leadership will be used
to co-ordinate price changes but we have argued that only where
a rather long list of structural conditions are met is this likely to
be of the more damaging 'collusive' kind which can produce
results similar to monopoly. In view of the great variety of structural features that are encountered in practice a much more likely
outcome is price leadership of the 'barometric' kind where prices
are adjusted to the underlying conditions of the market. For those
who consider that collusion is fairly readily attainable where a
market is reasonably concentrated (for example a US market
where the largest eight firms have 70 per cent or more of the
sales) this should show up in higher profit rates. For those who
consider collusion much more difficult, if not impossible, to maintain (unless aided in some way by the government) any relation-

ship between concentration and profits would be at worst short-lived and at best negligible. Results in this research field (which now resembles that used by elementary textbook writers to explain what happens to the marginal product of labour when too much per time period is applied to a fixed resource) are profuse but ambiguous. By a margin of something like two to one the empirical studies have suggested a weak, positive association between concentration and profits. The robustness of some of these results has been challenged and even where they appear to hold up, an interpretation with quite different policy implications has been offered, namely that larger firms in concentrated industries owe their high profits to the efficiency of large scale production not collusion.

FREQUENT ENCOUNTERS OF A CONGLOMERATE KIND

The orthodox view of market power depends on firms' size *relative* to the market. If two firms share a particular market their market power will depend on that fact alone regardless of their overall size.[6] Thus even if one firm is part of a much larger diversified group its power in the particular market is unaffected. This view was energetically challenged in the early 1950s by Edwards (1955) and the continued rapid growth and diversification of the corporate giants plus the sudden appearance (and equally rapid demise in some cases) of a new breed of 'conglomerate' organizations in the middle 1960s have given it greater prominence in more recent discussions.

The economic strength of the largest diversified firms (or conglomerates[7]) is said to rest on two factors. First, the breadth of their activities will inevitably ensure that in some of them they will enjoy a good deal of market power. Thus if the economy as a whole contains some markets where monopoly is present, others amenable to joint long-run profit maximization by oligopolists, as well as some that are more persistently competitive, then the conglomerate firm's interests are likely to reflect these different market situations. As a result some industries will yield above normal or even monopoly returns and these may be used for a variety of purposes. Secondly, the largest firms are likely to be able to raise new capital on more favourable terms than smaller rivals, not least as we have seen (chapter 3 pp. 44–47) because of the preference by large financial institutions who now hold a substantial fraction of manufacturing industry shares, for holdings in the largest companies.[8]

This strength of diversified companies may, it is argued, have a profound effect on competition and economic performance. High returns in some lines of the firm's business may be channelled into other lines where there may initially be strong competition from smaller, more specialized firms. These funds may be used either to charge uneconomic prices or mount lavish promotional campaigns (or both), in order to gain a larger market share for the conglomerate at the expense of smaller rivals. While the expenses incurred in the short-run are greater than the short-run returns, in the long run when competitors have been eliminated or demoralized, prices can be raised so as to recoup previous losses. Smaller, specialised firms may thus be undermined, not because of any inefficiency on their part but because of the financial strength of the conglomerates derived from their aggregate rather than relative size.

There are additional refinements to this line of reasoning to which we return shortly, but for the moment we need to consider in more detail this pessimistic view of modern competition, where the 'long purse' of the conglomerate can by cross subsidization apparently be used to such devastating effect. Two central questions are immediately raised by the preceeding argument. First, what was the form of competition and structure of those industries subjected to the invasion of large conglomerate firms? Secondly, what is the condition of entry to those industries once the conglomerates have made their appearance? Consider an industry in which a large number of firms compete on price; entry is easy and long-run returns 'normal'. If a large diversified firm enters such an industry, either by acquiring existing firms or by new building, the long-run performance of the industry is unlikely to be seriously affected unless the firm can both acquire a substantial market share and then prevent the entry of other new rivals. Undercutting on price may have the short-run effect of temporarily closing down some competitors but as soon as prices are raised to make up for previous losses, new competition will appear eager to take advantage of the improved profit prospects. Thus although such industries are vulnerable to entry by large diversified firms (as well as any other kind of firm) they are likely to be unattractive.

Consider, alternatively, industries where a few firms share a large part of the market and can, through some form of tacit, joint co-ordination earn (at least intermittently) abnormally high returns. Successful entry to such industries is likely to be more difficult. If it is achieved by acquisition, the purchase price will reflect the future prospects for exploiting any market power, so that unless the acquirer is to be content with a normal return he must expect to be able to increase the market share and profitability of his purchase. In this case, however, he will encounter the competition of the other market leaders which (by assumption) have enjoyed high returns in the past and may be expected not to give them up lightly. Although their overall size may not be as large as a conglomerate entrant their resources and perhaps more important their expertise in their special market, may make life very difficult for the newcomer. While the profit prospects in such industries may thus seem attractive to a diversifying company their actual attainment may prove difficult. Cross subsidization by an entrant may indeed be used not to eliminate rivals but to compete successfully against them. We examine below such evidence as there is on this aspect of conglomerate competition.

Apart from cross subsidization it is also argued that large diversified firms can subvert normal competitive processes by negotiating dense networks of reciprocal agreements with component, raw material, and even final product firms. In this context a reciprocal agreement is one where firm X agrees to buy from firm Y if Y similarly agrees to buy from X. Clearly if X is a large conglomerate with many subsidiaries in all parts of manufacturing and services while Y is a specialist component producer the scope for X to conclude such agreements is much greater than for Y. Now as long as Y is satisfied that the terms he receives from X (both in buying and selling) are competitive, there can be no objection to the trading. Indeed it might be argued that transactions costs are lowered and resources saved by the two firms engaging in two transactions rather than one.

Opponents of large diversified firms have, however, argued differently. They have claimed that even where a firm Y could obtain better purchasing terms in the market, it will hesitate to do so for fear of losing the custom of X for its own products. By such means specialist producers[9] may, on this view, progressively lose their independence even though ostensibly they retain it. It is no longer open to such firms to seek out the most competitive supplier (of components, or raw materials or whatever) with a resulting misallocation of resources, as more transactions are *de facto* removed from the market. The argument has been carried one stage further by the Federal Trade Commission (1969) which saw in the increased diversification of large companies and the accompanying scope for reciprocal agreements a new source of entry barriers. It envisaged a greater and greater portion of market transactions 'foreclosed' to potential entrants because they would be tied to reciprocal agreements. The only successful entrants would themselves be diversified companies with the ability to overturn established relationships by offering new reciprocal agreements from their own varied activities. The Commission, vying with the Old Testament both in tenor and cadence reaches the awful conclusion: 'As the victims of reciprocity . . . are squeezed they too seek shelter in diversification and reciprocity. Conglomerate mergers thus beget more conglomerate mergers, and the ultimate prospect is a highly rigidified industrial structure' (Federal Trade Commission, 1969; p. 330).

We are not alone in questioning this whole line of reasoning. Stigler (1970) for example, says bluntly that if a specialist firm obtains no advantage from a reciprocal agreement or can get better (buying) terms elsewhere it will do so. Certainly the opportunities open to smaller, more specialized firms envisaged in accounts like that above are extremely limited and static. Where any semblance of competition remains, a specialist firm will have a number of different outlets for its product both at home and abroad. If it disagrees with the attempts of a conglomerate customer which tries to enforce reciprocal purchases even when better terms are available elsewhere it can sell to other customers. Only where specialists are confronted by monopoly or near monopoly will they have no choice but to accept unfavourable terms. But this is hardly new. The power of monopolists has long been known and most countries have laws to prevent its abuse. But it is not *monopoly* power that the opponents of large diversified firms are attacking but rather the power they allegedly derive from their *overall* size. The key characteristic of these firms is the multiplicity of their interests, in markets of varying structures. In those where they have comparatively small market shares they will be unable to maintain reciprocal agreements which the other party regards as unfavourable. Where they have a monopoly they will be able to earn a maximum return without recourse to such complicated refinements. When the Federal Trade Commission and others cite cases where a firm has maintained a reciprocal agreement even though better terms are apparently available elsewhere, they are perhaps underestimating the value to a firm of its existing trading relationships and the costs that it would have to incur in seeking out and evaluating new customers or suppliers. Any firm seeking new custom must offer terms and conditions which more than compensate for such costs.

If we follow Professor Edwards and others of similar views a little further down the road of competition among the conglomerates we come to a sign marked 'Mutual Forbearance'. This condition is found in economies that have reached a certain level of aggregate concentration (the UK where more than two-fifths of manufacturing output is made by the largest hundred firms may qualify). The subsidiaries of the giants are then found in most if not all markets and their frequent encounters lead to mutual recognition that active competition may not serve their best interests. 'Like national states, the great conglomerates may come to have recognised spheres of influence and may hesitate to fight local wars vigorously because the prospects of local gain are not worth the risk of general warfare, (Edwards, 1964; p. 45). The result is a general dampening of competitive forces. Entry to a new industry by one giant may not, therefore, produce a competitive effect because of the likely consequences in other industries where relative shares may be reversed.

It is not usually made clear in these discussions whether the firms are simultaneously pursuing a policy of cross subsidization in some markets and mutual forbearance in others. Perhaps the latter only comes into operation once the conglomerates have secured pre-eminence by use of the former. In any event some evidence would help to determine how far this analysis has already proved accurate

We have already suggested in chapter 2 (pp. 24–25) that although the largest firms have been diversifying their activities quite rapidly in recent years, for many two or three primary industries form a sizeable core of their activities although they are also likely to have a large number of peripheral interests in other industries. What then is the direct evidence that such firms are able to manipulate the structure of these industries to their own advantage, using the methods just discussed? It is certainly true that the antitrust authorities of both the UK and USA uncover cases of cross subsidization by firms seeking to undermine or weaken a rival. For this purpose short-run prices may be quoted without regard to costs. In the UK the reports of the Monopolies

Commission on matches, industrial gases, electrical equipment
for motor vehicles, cellulosic fibres, librium and valium all contain instances where a dominant firm used this tactic.[10] The Fed-
deral Trade Commission (1969) has cited similar cases in the
USA. But without exception these examples deal with firms in an
almost unassailable position in their respective industries. In all of
those cited from the UK the leading firm had 90 per cent or more
of the British market. What we are observing in such cases, therefore, is not the action of a large diversifying firm attempting to
gain control of a market but that of a monopolist using predatory
pricing or cross subsidization to protect its dominance. From this
pre-eminence the outcome of such a policy is almost assured (so
long as it can be kept from inquisitive antitrust agencies). In
contrast, as we have suggested above, for a diversified firm to
take on the established market leaders in a price war may be
extremely costly and the outcome uncertain. Unfortunately since
the Monopolies Commission has to deal mainly with established
positions of dominance rather than those possibly in the process
of creation we have, as yet, no test cases on which to draw.[11] We
must, therefore, fall back on various pieces of indirect evidence.
If, for example, large diversifying firms are able to reshape industries that they enter to their own advantage and at the expense of
smaller rivals we might expect a positive relationship between
entry and concentration increase in such industries. But two painstaking studies in the US into the effect of diversifying mergers on
concentration were unable to discern any association (Goldberg,
1973; Markham, 1973).[12]

We may also note at this point one other feature of large firms
which probably deters them from a deliberate policy of cross-
subsidation. It is estimated that a very large proportion of these
firms have adopted a multidivisional framework in their internal
organization (Channon, 1973). Broadly speaking this means that
the management in each division is responsible for its own performance to a central executive committee and if it falls short of
its targets it will have to give an explanation. It is thus a useful
means of monitoring and controlling the performance of different
parts of the enterprise. Each division is likely to be very jealous of
its position, particularly since in most cases it is dependent on the
central executive committee for capital investment funds. In these
circumstances it seems very unlikely that a system of inter-
divisional cross-subsidization would be either practical or desirable. The firms themselves may use this structure for assessing

divisional performance but unfortunately it is not published in a form or in sufficient detail to allow an outsider (even a shareholder) to make a similar judgement. However a detailed examination of nine conglomerate organizations in the USA, although critical of the amount of 'information loss' to all outsiders, nevertheless failed to find any significant evidence of cross-subsidization (Federal Trade Commission, 1972).

On the other hand there is some evidence that the effect of increasing diversification by large firms may be pro-competitive rather than the reverse. Berry, for example, found that entry by large firms into other industries tended to be at the expense of the previous market leaders rather than more vulnerable competitors: 'the projected impact of entry to concentrated industries by large firms is not small . . . 70 per cent of the market share of entering large firms is acquired at the expense of the leading four firms' (Berry, 1975; p. 140). In other cross section studies which have attempted to measure the relationship between profitability and large firm diversification, the effect appears to be negative, that is the greater the participation in an industry by large firms primarily engaged in other industries, the lower (on average) are industry profits (Rhoades, 1973; Utton, 1979). For a number of technical reasons these results should be treated with caution,[13] but they do point in the opposite direction to the mutual forbearance hypothesis. If anything they support the view that under current conditions of relatively high average industry concentration effective entry may come mainly from firms already established elsewhere. At least in the short-run, therefore, the impact may be pro-competitive and lead to an improvement in the allocative performance of industry.

CONCLUSION

We have tried to emphasize in this chapter the complexity of competition in oligopoly. The form that it takes will depend on many factors in addition to the relatively few structural characteristics on which large-scale cross section studies have inevitably to rely. In particular, the conditions sufficient to ensure successful 'collusive' price leadership are probably met with much less frequently than is often assumed. The looser, less damaging 'barometric' form is, therefore, likely to be much more common and when considered in conjunction with an active antitrust

policy may result in most cases in an efficient industrial performance.

More recent criticisms of large size have focussed on diversification and the multiplicity of interests and encounters amongst the
giants that this involves. As yet this line of argument has been
longer on hypotheses than positive evidence. In fact such evidence as there is tends to indicate that diversification by large
firms may be pro-competitive rather than the reverse. But it is
probably still too early to draw any firm conclusions. Quite apart
from data problems mentioned above there is a more substantial
problem of interpretation. The simultaneous occurrence of considerable diversification and a high level of aggregate concentration that we now have in the UK is, as we indicated in chapter 2, a
recent phenomenon. Comparatively little is known about industrial performance in such circumstances. The long-run effects
may, therefore, be much more serious for the vitality of manufacturing industries than the present, essentially short-run evidence,
suggests.

6

A Preliminary Assessment

If the government wished to draw up a set of accounts for the whole big-business sector similar to those for an individual public company but with a wider, social perspective, the task, judging from our foregoing discussion, is likely to prove very daunting. Parts of the account may be filled in without too much difficulty or controversy. Thus the basic facts about the relative size, character and growth of the corporate giants are now established. For example in the manufacturing sector in the near future the hundred largest firms are likely to be responsible for half of the total sector output; their operations will reach into every manufacturing industry and in many of these most of the sales will be made by four or five firms.

As soon as we move into the more complex area of the accounts, however, there is likely to be great difficulty not only with the definition and measurement of the variables themselves but also with their interpretation and significance. Thus the measurement of economic efficiency, a concept on every commentator's lips and one which the layman may therefore expect to be readily measurable, in practice proves extremely difficult to pin down in any comprehensive way. Even if we accept the estimates of efficient *plant* sizes as being reasonably precise this says very little about those further economies that may be available to the multi-plant *firm*. On this central issue we have very little quantitative information. It is thus not yet possible, except in a few well-known instances, to determine the extent to which the size of the largest firms is governed by the demands of efficiency. Similarly despite the large amount of empirical research that has attempted to isolate the rewards of market power, we would be hard pressed to know whether the results should be entered as a 'profit' or 'loss' in the social account, especially if we remembered the writings of Schumpeter on the needs of innovation.

107

An initial impulse to enter the advertising and promotion efforts of the corporate giants as an unequivocal 'loss' on the grounds that they deceive and dishearten the consumer while acting as a buttress of market power would have to be resisted. The final verdict has to be more measured. To identify precisely those resources devoted to advertising and promotion that have harmful effects from those that are beneficial is, as we have seen, much more difficult than some commentators would have us believe. Where high advertising and high profitability go together the direction of causation is by no means clear. While it may *a priori* be plausible to argue that much advertising in mature oligopolies is self cancelling and therefore socially wasteful in practice it may be impossible to disentangle this kind of advertising from that designed to launch a new product or defend an established one from the attention of a fresh rival.

As far as the commentary on the figures in the account are concerned we would need some assessment of whether the dramatic rise in the share of the corporate giants, especially in manufacturing in the UK, has had a profound effect on the nature of competition in many industries. The tendency of theorists to concentrate on the static equilibrium properties of fairly simple market models has helped to deflect attention from competition as a dynamic process – it is more akin to a movie than a snapshot. Consequently when confronted by giant firms which have grown to prominence in one particular industry where they may have a very large market share, but whose recent growth has pushed them into many different industries, the conventional response has been simply to extend the notion of monopoly. Thus the concept of monopoly power, even though it does not readily fit the experience of industries dominated by three or four large firms, is nevertheless frequently carried over into the realm of diversified or conglomerate firms via the 'deep pocket hypothesis'. On this view high returns in one industry can be converted eventually into high returns in other industries by means of cross subsidization and predatory pricing. This interpretation is widely held even though systematic evidence is lacking. The closer one moves to actual cases, however, the more convincing becomes the alternative suggestion that competitive processes are at work. The fact that a number of the competitors are members of larger groupings should not obscure what is actually taking place in the market. Rather than indicating less competition this recent trend in the development of large firms seems on the contrary, to indicate greater competitive intensity.

Part of the difficulty that economics has had in handling the development of very large diversified firms can be traced to the highly ambiguous notion of 'power'. As we indicated in the opening chapter many people have a general feeling of unease about the obtrusiveness and dominance of the corporate giants. The feeling which may not be properly articulated most of the time may quickly turn to open hostility when the unsavoury activities of some appear to confirm their worst fears. Although there have been some attempts by economists to define the 'power' of large companies, notably Edwards (1955) as we have seen, these have generally not been well received or adopted into the main stream of economic analysis. Edwards' main thesis was that the total power of the large companies is greater than the sum of the market power that they may have in individual markets. He had in mind both the opportunities for switching resources between market which can be handled by the traditional analysis but also and perhaps more important a host of extra-market activities which the companies could finance to gain a more secure environment for their operations. They would, for example, make political contributions, hire lobbyists and political advisers, undertake prestige advertising and sponsor charities all of which may appear to make little sense if interpreted in narrow profit maximization terms, but according to these writers are easily understood as the exercise of political and social power.

At this point, however, an analytical difficulty arises. The 'extra' market power on which all of the rhetorical skill of these writers is brought to bear is not defined, even approximately. Rothschild (1971) not only admits this but seems to regard it as a virtue. In his introduction to a book of readings entitled Power in Economics where we might reasonably expect to find some specification of the concept, he writes

> The problem [of making the selection for the volume] is further complicated because 'power' is such a vague concept. In relation to economic affairs it can take on very different forms. Even if we do not bother about niceties of definition and details of form we can easily see that very different things fall under the power-economics complex (Rothschild, 1971; p. 15).

He excuses this vagueness further by retelling an old anecdote about a professor of medicine who finds no definition of 'illness' satisfactory and so tells his students: ' "Now look, if a patient comes to me and tells me he is ill, *he* knows what he means and I know what he means, and that after all, is important." Power is probably a concept not so very different from illness' (Rothschild, 1971). Neither the patient nor the policy maker can take much comfort from these remarks. It is difficult to see how the diagnosis of power and its effects is helped by allowing it to mean practically all things to all men.

We have seen in chapter 3 that *market* power can be precisely defined and if carefully handled can be used in the analysis of many different market structures. It can also be extended in the ways suggested by Tullock and Posner to include something akin to the kinds of political activities that Rothschild had in mind in an earlier paper (Rothschild, 1953) even though in his later comments he not only chastises economists for not paying sufficient attention to such matters but denies that the usual analytical approach can be extended in this way (Rothschild, 1971). Yet the 'investment' that large oligopolistic companies make in such things as lobbying, public relations, prestige advertising and even bribery can be treated as being financed out of monopoly profits. In this case, as we have seen, they should not be treated simply as an income transfer – from consumers to producers – but as a social cost. Interpreted in this way it may even be possible to make approximate measurements of the amount of resources used up in these socially inefficient ways, as the recent studies by Posner and Cowling and Mueller indicate. This approach seems much more fruitful both for analysis and policy (cf. chapter 7) than amorphous generalizations about 'power' that are likely to lead to mystification and muddle.

None of this, however, should deflect us from recognizing the subtle dangers to economies dominated by a relatively few giant companies. Their importance should not be underestimated simply because their influence may be unspectacular or difficult to quantify. The first point, which we owe to Schumpeter, concerns the gradual slowdown and perhaps the elimination of change and adjustment once aggregate concentration in an economy reaches a certain level. This very important conclusion in Schumpeter's classic work (Schumpeter, 1965) seems to have been obscured or even forgotten by those whose main interest has centred on the narrower point of what structural characteristics are most favourable to technical change. But a major part of his thesis was the gradual 'institutionalization' of change in the hierarchies of very large organizations which would lead inevitably to the stifling or at least dilution of most important innovations. Since for Schumpeter flexibility in adapting to change was the dynamo of capitalism he therefore envisaged its eventual transformation into some form of socialism. The point is reinforced if powerful trade unions with a large stake in present methods and techniques have grown up alongside the giant companies. They too are likely to slow down the process of change. Economies where this process has proceeded furthest, therefore, are likely to have a poorer growth record than others and both the UK and USA are sometimes cited as examples (Brittan, 1978).

Secondly the situation may be made worse where a number of factors conspire to 'crowd out' or dry up the possibilities for the foundation and growth of small firms. Prais (1981) has traced the sorry record of the UK where, since the Second World War, small firms have been caught in a kind of pincer movement. On the one hand very heavy rates of personal taxation and death duties dried up what in other countries forms an important source of risk capital (that is family fortunes) while on the other, as we saw in chapter 2, the enormous growth of large financial institutions with a natural preference for equity holdings in the largest industrial companies has made it more difficult for small companies to raise capital on the Stock Exchange. The result has been a dramatic decline in the number of small firms which now play a much smaller role in manufacturing industry in the UK than in comparable European economies or the USA. To the extent, therefore, that small firms add to an economy's flexibility and adaptability to change and also provide the seedbed for the future business leaders that Marshall envisaged, then the UK economy has been weakened, although the effects may be very difficult to quantify and only make themselves felt over a long period.

Thirdly, the emergence of the giant enterprises alongside powerful trades unions with governments committed to 'manage' the economy so as to achieve the major economic objectives brings all of the dangers of 'Corporatism'. In broad terms this is the feeling amongst politicians and civil servants as well as some business and trade union leaders, that the main economic problems faced by the country can be solved by meetings at various levels of the representatives of government, industry and labour. Common objectives can be agreed upon, difficulties pinpointed, conflicts resolved and policies settled 'in the public interest'. Economic problems will thus be diminished if not altogether resolved. Successive British Governments since the Second World War have until recently, accepted some variant of this view. In the numerous bodies associated with the National Economic Development Office (NEDO) – the National Economic Development Council, the industrial sector working parties, and the development councils for individual industries – the UK has the organizational fruits of this philosophy. Yet the political and economic dangers of this approach are well known. The political danger is that these non-elected bodies may gain considerable political power to push through their objectives at the expense of other groups which are neither represented nor featured in the plans for the future. The economic danger is equally acute. Even if the diagnosis of the problem is correct the accompanying view of participants to the debate, that the solution lies in their hands is, in a democratic state, doomed to failure. The failure is made worse by the belief, nevertheless, that 'something is being done' and that in time the problem will as a result be solved. By this means not only may policy take entirely the wrong direction but many people are lulled into a false sense of optimism. Furthermore the corporatist approach is likely to lead to a conflict of economic policies. At this point it is appropriate merely to mention one or two examples from recent experience. A fuller discussion is reserved for chapter 8. In order to supervise and control positions of market power a number of countries have some policy towards mergers, especially where large market shares will be strengthened or created. The UK has since 1965 had a fairly innocuous policy in this respect (cf. chap. 7) whereby certain proposed mergers can be referred to the Monopolies and Mergers Commission which then reports on whether the proposal is likely or not 'to operate against the public interest'. Between 1966 and 1971, however, the government, through the Industrial Reorganisation Corporation (IRC) also sought to promote mergers to ensure that British firms were large enough to compete successfully in international markets. For this purpose it was able to call on public funds if necessary although in many cases its role was merely one of persuasion. While it confined itself to small- or medium-sized concerns little conflict of policy was likely to arise, although in those cases where financial support was involved other British competitors not favoured with IRC patronage might justly complain that others were being given an unfair advantage through access to funds below market rates. Its sights, however, were on a number of occasions raised far above the ranks of the modest or the obscure. Both British Leyland (BL) and the present General Electric Company were sponsored by the IRC. Had these merger proposals arisen spontaneously in the market it is quite possible that one or both would have been referred to the Monopolies and Mergers Commission. Under the sponsorship of the IRC, however, the mergers were guaranteed a clear run. The implications for market power were thus sidestepped in the interest of promoting the alleged benefits of very large size.

The second example also relates to antitrust or competition policy. Possibly one of the most successful aspects of UK competition policy since the war has been the abolition of several thousand restrictive agreements mainly as a result of the Restrictive Practices Act of 1956. There is general agreement amongst economists that broad classes of such cartels serve mainly to protect a sectional interest at the expense of the public and should therefore be made as difficult as possible to sustain. But more recently there have been pressures to modify this position. The first of these was embodied in a later Restrictive Practices Act which simultaneously extended the scope of existing legislation in an important respect but also included a clause allowing the minister to exempt firms from the provisions against restrictive practices where this was 'in the public interest'. The second appears in a volume on Competition Policy published by NEDO (1978) calling for the general exemption of certain categories of restrictions. In fact the general tenor of the document is that the task of individual firms, not to mention that of NEDO officials would be made very much easier if co-operation could be substituted for competition. As we shall see later (chapter 9) a case can be made for allowing all forms of cartels to exist on the grounds that in a general atmosphere of competitive markets and against a background of innovation and change they will be short-lived and collapse due to internal conflicts of interest. But the proponents of this view would certainly oppose the notion of officially sponsored agreements backed by the authority of a governmental body like the NEDO, able to bring a number of sanctions against those firms which chose to remain outside the fold.

The presence in the private sector of most Western economies of giant companies clearly poses a very serious challenge to the policy maker. The challenge is especially pressing in the UK where the relative growth of the largest companies has been very rapid. Under these circumstances is it still possible to adopt

policies of a basically antitrust kind that many critics claim belong
to an earlier era but which are now impotent in the face of the
'power' of the giants? One view is that antitrust weapons can be
resharpened to cope with any new forms that the old problems
may take (chapter 7). An alternative view which periodically has
found favour since the war, as we have just seen, is for policy to
embrace large companies together with large unions in the hope
that co-operation can replace that competition which their joint
growth has undermined (chapter 8). Although these two
approaches are quite different both in their diagnosis of the problem and their remedies, both broadly speaking can be fitted into
the mainstream of policy thinking. There are two other schools of
thought whose diagnosis and prescription involve more fundamental changes. On one side are those who believe that despite
recent developments, efficiently operating markets can achieve
most economic objectives. The role of policy should, therefore,
essentially be to frame laws which ensure that markets can operate smoothly with the minimum of disruption and rigidity (chapter 9). At the opposite pole are those who view the most recent
trends in the growth of giant companies as merely part of the
inevitable development of late capitalism as predicted by Marx
and look forward to the further evolution of society towards
socialism and ultimately communism (chapter 10).

Part Three: Policies

7

Antitrust and Related Policies

INTRODUCTION

The main policy response in a number of Western economies to the problems raised in Part two has been in the form of antitrust or competition policy.[1] These vary considerably in scope and form, from the comprehensive legal approach used in the USA to the mixed legal and administrative system in the UK. But all, by and large, are seeking to correct and control the market power of enterprises in the private sector. The policies are applied to three main areas namely monopolies and oligopolies, mergers and cartels. It is thus the first two that are most likely to involve the corporate giants although the breadth of their operations is also likely to draw them into cartels, especially where these have an international flavour.

With the exception of the control of conglomerate mergers these policies are aimed quite clearly at power in a particular market, whether this derives from the monopoly of a firm which may, for example, control an essential raw material, or from a group of firms acting in concert to fix prices and market shares. The overall size of the firms is not the issue. We review the strengths and weaknesses of these policies especially those of the UK and USA on pp. 118–138.

In recent years a number of writers have argued that a useful supplement to these policies is for the state to finance new enterprise in industries where the antitrust problem seems especially acute and where existing firms are judged to be performing badly. The role of the new enterprises is seen by their supporters as gingering up the performance of their privately owned competitors but clearly the proposal raises a number of very important issues. On what terms, for example, should the state enterprise be funded and what criteria should govern their pricing and

117

dividend policies? If they wish to diversify out of their original industry by merger or even by new investment, should they be free to do so? State enterprises as supplements to antitrust policies are discussed in the third section.

If, however, an important part of the problem posed by the giant enterprises is their absolute rather than their relative size it is legitimate to ask what other policies are available to restrain their apparently insatiable growth. Antitrust policy and (possibly) state enterprises may help to curb their powers in individual markets, but with the one exception noted above these policies leave untouched the question of absolute size and growth. In the fourth section, therefore, we examine a number of proposals which aim to restore the balance between large and small firms, a balance which has been upset, at least in the UK, by a number of recent financial developments.[2] Essentially the proposals consist of changes in the way the largest and smallest companies are taxed and in the sources available for small companies to finance growth.

ANTITRUST POLICIES

It is convenient to discuss these policies under three headings: monopoly and concentrated oligopoly, mergers and cartels. From what we know of the difficulty of defining monopoly and market power, of the wide range of possible outcomes in oligopoly, and of the ambiguity of much of the empirical research in these fields we can anticipate a number of problems that antitrust policy is likely to encounter.

Monopoly and concentrated oligopoly

The British approach can perhaps be described as pragmatic and tentative: pragmatic because the underlying view is that monopoly or oligopoly may perform badly or well depending on a large number of circumstances, and tentative in that the agency investigating these industries has no direct power to order changes. The body chosen to undertake the enquiries is the equivalent of a permanent royal commission. The Monopolies and Mergers Commission, as it is now known[3] has part time members drawn from industry, trades unions, academic and public life as well as a permanent chairman and deputy chairman and a small permanent research staff. It has no power to initiate enquiries itself but has to await references either from the Minister or from the Director General of Fair Trading. A reference will relate to a single product or to a narrow range of products[4] (for example wheat flour and bread, insulated electric wires and cables, frozen foodstuffs) or services (for example mens' hairdressing, estate agents, fire insurance) and the Commission has then to perform three tasks. First, it has to determine whether or not a 'monopoly' as laid down in the Fair Trading Act of 1973 actually prevails, that is that one firm controls one-quarter or more of the production, process or sales of the product or products in question. Since it is now most unlikely that any reference of this kind would be made where the research staff of the Office of Fair Trading had not already determined a clear case of 'statutory monopoly' this stage is usually a formality. Secondly, the Commission has to explain what types of market conduct the firms concerned use to preserve or enhance their 'monopoly' and thirdly, to decide whether or not they operate or may be expected to operate against the public interest and to make recommendations. The reports are often very lengthy, amounting in effect to a monograph on the firm or industry concerned. They usually contain a great deal of statistical information on sales, prices and profits at a level of detail which is not generally available. For example many of the firms involved in the enquiries are large and diversified. The information that such firms have to publish in their annual accounts refers to their consolidated activities whereas that in the Commission reports will usually be concerned with only a narrow range of products. An analysis of a number of their reports (especially the sections covering the market conduct by monopolists) gives a fascinating insight into the process of competition in a great variety of oligopolistic and semi-monopolistic industries, for the statutory criterion of 25 per cent of a market allows a much wider range of industries to be covered than the term monopoly in its theoretical sense implies. Furthermore since references of this kind are to a particular product or products the Commission does not have to spend a great deal of time deciding whether or not they constitute a separate market, although in the course of their discussion of the price and other policies of the leading firms they assess the extent to which close substitute products act as a constraint on market power.[5]

It is important to remember when reading the subsequent discussion not only that the legislation contains no condemnation of monopoly or 'monopolising' but also that the Monopolies and Mergers Commission has no remedial powers. The most it can do is to make recommendations. Whether or not these recommendations are carried out depends entirely on the Minister. This approach stands in stark contrast to that adopted in the United States whose antitrust policy has a much longer history than that of the UK. For example according to Section 2 of the 1890 Sherman Act persons who monopolize or attempt to monopolize any part of trade amongst the separate States will be deemed guilty of a misdemeanour. Antitrust in the USA has always been a branch of the law and cases are thus heard in a court and subject to the normal rules of evidence and procedure and can on appeal travel all the way to the Supreme Court. Such a journey is usually very long and very expensive both for the state and the defendant companies and in some cases the penalties can, at least by European standards, be extremely severe.

It is not our purpose to give a detailed review of the work of the Monopolies and Mergers Commission, still less of the Sherman Act, both of which would deserve separate volumes to themselves.[6] What we can do is to gain some impression of the effectiveness of antitrust policies in dealing with near monopolies or industries so concentrated that some form of concerted action by the existing firms is inevitable. We are thus concerned with how market power shows itself in the behaviour and performance of companies in these industries, what remedies have been applied and what results have been produced.

In the course of its enquiries into concentrated market structures the Commission has had to assess the impact of a wide range of competitive practices. These have varied, for example, from the use of fighting brands or companies, and predatory pricing (matches, industrial gases, librium and valium) discrimination against non-integrated firms (man-made fibres) discounts based on exclusive dealing (metal cans, frozen foods) excessive prices (man-made fibres, colour film, librium and valium) secret, illegal market sharing (telecommunications cable) and excessive advertising (detergents). Perhaps we should add that the descriptions used in the previous sentence are intended to reflect the judgement of the Commission. In some cases there may be considerable disputes as to whether their interpretation is strictly correct. But the more important point that these and many other cases help to illustrate is that while market conduct in oligopoly or semi-monopoly can be extremely complex, the main policy issue is whether its effect is to exclude new entrants (which may, of course, include ICI as well as Joe Bloggs). Exclusionary tactics can be direct (by for example using a fighting company to undercut rivals without any regard to costs) or indirect (by giving preferential discounts to dealers signing exclusive contracts). The Commission has usually condemned exclusionary behaviour on the ground that it tends to rigidify market structures and slow down or prevent the entry of new competitors: in short that it impairs the workings of the market.[7] They usually recommend therefore, that such practices should be ended and in most cases the firms have complied, after discussions with the Office of Fair Trading or relevant government department. Note, even if the Commission has found what it regards as blatant abuses of market power in a whole array of exclusionary practices, the companies concerned are not liable for fines or damages. Nor are there any provisions for the executives to be given prison sentences, because in British law they have not been guilty of any legal misdemeanour. There have been cases where the companies concerned did not accept the judgement of the Commission. Two cases where this occurred were detergents (Monopolies Commission, 1966) and librium and valium (Monopolies Commission, 1973a). The Commission recommended that the two leading synthetic detergent manufacturers who shared more than 90 per cent of the market should substantially reduce their advertising and sales promotion so that price reductions could be made. Not only would the consumer benefit from lower prices but it was thought that the reduced advertising would eventually lower entry barriers. A long wrangle between the Minister and the companies followed. The companies regarded any restriction on their advertising policies as unworkable and likely to hamper their efficient operation. After considerable delay each of the companies rather grudgingly agreed to market one of their established brands at a lower price and with much reduced 'promotion'. Their other brands continued at the former 'high' price with no restriction on their promotional expenditures. Not surprisingly within a comparatively short time the chairman of one company was able to report that the low-advertised, cheaper brands had lost a large part of their market share.

The other case was much more acrimonious and in its later stages took on something of the character of an American antitrust suit as it ended in the final court of appeal, the House of Lords. Apart from the abandonment of a number of discriminatory practices between different classes of customers the Commission also recommended that Roche Products, the pharmaceutical firm, should make large reductions in the prices of librium and valium. Furthermore, it suggested that in view of the 'excessive profits on a very large scale' earned by the company in its contracts with the Department of Health and Social Security (DHSS) repayment of 'large sums' to the DHSS should be negotiated. The company decided to challenge the recommendations of the Commission. It did not accept the interpretation put by the Commission on its prices and profits. Instead of the usual procedure following a Commission report, therefore, of negotiations between the Minister and the companies concerned, in this case a lengthy series of court hearings ensued which involved the House of Lords. Ultimately a compromise agreement was reached between the Company and the Minister whereby the price reductions remained but the repayment of past profits by Roche was lower than originally demanded (see *Economist*, 15 November 1975, pp. 90 and 94).

The two cases just mentioned, however, are rather exceptional. Generally within a short time of a report being completed the objectionable aspects of the firm's market conduct are dropped or altered. Many observers would probably agree that in the 'monopoly' enquiries this has been the most successful aspect of the Commission's work: a large number of dubious competitive practices in heavily concentrated industries have been removed. On the other hand, critics claim that the companies would not in the majority of cases have been so acquiescent and accommodating if the conduct complained of had really affected their interests in an important way. The companies may realize that agreement and minimum publicity will leave the way clear again for them to introduce slightly modified tactics that can achieve the same results. Although it is possible to re-open a case if, say, the Office of Fair Trading receives fresh complaints from customers or competitors, in practice the companies know from past experience that this is unlikely. Although the Office attempts to monitor the market conduct of companies recently the subject of an adverse Commission report it is unlikely to be able to do this in anything but a very superficial way. After all, market conduct which the Commission has found objectionable is based on a lengthy and detailed investigation including access to data which will no longer be available to the Office of Fair Trading after the report has been completed. In other words the critics believe that there are many ways of exploiting market power and if some of the cruder ways are stopped they will soon be replaced by subtler and perhaps more insidious methods.

Furthermore, the critics can, with some justice, argue that the complex details of the market conduct of oligopolists tend to obscure the fundamental issue of market dominance. Tinkering with market conduct may have a marginal short-run effect but the performance of the companies is not affected to any important extent. In making their case the critics can point to the failure of antitrust policies to cope with parallel pricing behaviour in concentrated oligopoly and, in the UK at least, of the almost complete lack of any attempt to change the structure of industry as a result of antitrust findings. These issues are clearly related because if parallel pricing is a successful way for oligopolists to maintain a joint-profit maximizing policy, then a structural remedy appears to be the only solution. Since parallel pricing is almost inherent in the structure of the industry it can be effectively attacked only by changing that structure not simply by getting the firms to change some features of their conduct. In its general report on parallel pricing (Monopolies Commission, 1973b) the Commission was fully aware of the intractability of the problem and therefore somewhat lamely emphasized the need for an active policy (especially against mergers) to prevent the growth of structural conditions which would allow the practice to flourish. The American position also demonstrates the difficulties faced once concentrated oligopoly has emerged. Parallel pricing *per se* is insufficient to sustain an antitrust suit. But parallel behaviour that could not possibly have been arrived at by each firm simply seeking its own interests, especially where the resulting performance (as reflected, for example, in profit levels) is considered far from competitive, would probably be judged as a violation of the anti-trust laws. The penalties in such cases would be fines and possibly heavy damages. In neither country, therefore, has the remedy been to change the structure of the industry.

The closest the Monopolies Commission in Britain has been to recommending structural remedies was probably in 1956, in the case of British Oxygen, when a minority of the Commission proposed nationalization; Imperial Tobacco, in 1961, when the Commission recommended that Imperial's hitherto undisclosed and substantial shareholding in their main competitor should be sold; and (more indirectly) in the Kodak, and Courtaulds cases, when they proposed tariff reductions as a means of increasing competition. All of these suggestions were a long way from the break-up of monopoly but even these were judged inappropriate by the government.

In the USA also it is fair to say that since the opening years of this century when antitrust fervour was probably at its height, structural remedies have generally not been employed to cope with the monopoly problem. Leaving aside merger cases which we discuss below, there has been nothing to compare recently with the legally enforced dismemberment of the original Standard Oil or American Tobacco Companies in 1911. The recent revival of political interest in 'deconcentration measures' which produced the presidential 'task force' to review antitrust policies, although stimulating a great deal of interest in academic circles[8] and leading to concrete proposals in the form of the proposed Concentrated Industries Act (1968) and the proposed Industrial Reorganization Act 1973, did not lead to changes in the law.

Have the critics, therefore, established their case that in the face of apparently formidable market power from monopolists or oligopolists, antitrust policy is impotent and has only a minimal effect because in practice it cannot or (in the British case) the government will not rely on structural remedies?

While conceding that spectacular changes have not occurred as a direct result of antitrust policy, a reasonable defence of the approach adopted might proceed along the following lines. First, a dramatic structural remedy may make matters worse rather than better. A change involving the break-up of large firms may be highly inefficient, not only because of the impact effect of rupturing the operations of a possibly long-established and going concern but also because scale economies may be sacrificed for the sake of creating several 'new' firms out of the old. Secondly, an acceptable performance by dominant firms may in most cases be achieved without such drastic remedies. If companies are made to drop exclusionary tactics, the forces of competition will, over time, reassert themselves. For example, the four cases quoted above were, as we have indicated, amongst the most extreme encountered in the more than thirty-year history of the Monopolies Commission. Yet in three of them the market share of the dominant firm has subsequently been eroded. In industrial gases Air Products now has about one-quarter of the market gained from British Oxygen (Price Commission, 1979; p. 11). Since 1968 imports of man-made fibres have increased considerably and now account for more than one-third of UK sales. In the cigarette market the final abandonment of the global market-sharing agreement between American Tobacco and Imperial Tobacco in 1972 meant the almost immediate entry of American Tobacco into the UK market. Other cases examined by the Commission were thought to require less substantial remedies in any case and by having to abandon or modify objectionable aspects of their market behaviour a 'workable' performance was expected.

One advantage of the British approach to this problem is that it allows the Commission to make a fairly detailed assessment of the technical, allocative and innovation performance of the leading firm or firms. It is very unusual for the Commission to give an adverse judgement on all aspects and in fact in many cases it has found the leading firms to be technically efficient and progressive.[9] Although it has probably been more ready to criticize profit levels, it also recognizes that high profits may result from efficiency and growth. For example, both Metal Box and Pedigree Pet Foods were earning profits much higher than the average for manufacturing industry but these were judged acceptable, given the high degree of efficiency of the companies.

The variety of experience in heavily concentrated industries which is reflected in the Commission reports merely underlines the conclusion reached in chapter 5 about the relationship between concentration and profits. Part of the weak positive correlation may be due to an abuse of market power but part is also probably due to the efficiency of large companies. The defenders of antitrust in approximately its present form would thus summarize their position as one which prevents the worst effects of market power by eliminating objectionable conduct while maintaining the benefits of size and avoiding the social costs that more fundamental structural remedies would bring.

Mergers

This conclusion appears to place a great responsibility on merger policy. If positions of dominance are not readily removed by antitrust action but only by the re-emergence of competition, then as the Monopolies and Mergers Commission itself remarked (Monopolies Commission, 1973b) it is important to prevent the creation of market power by merger. Mergers between sizeable companies in the same market may give sudden access to market power not won as a result of superior performance. For this

reason growth by merger may generally be viewed more sceptically by outside observers than that achieved by 'internal' investment. There is also the point that internal growth means a net
addition to society's assets whereas merger in itself amounts
merely to a change in ownership of a given bundle of assets.

Certainly American antitrust decisions, at least since 1950,[10]
have reflected a strong aversion to mergers. Even where quite
modest market shares have been involved the Courts have been
prepared to find a substantial lessening of competition. For
example, Bethlehem Steel with 16.3 per cent of US ingot capacity
was not allowed to acquire the Youngstown Steel and Tube Co.
with 4.6 per cent of US capacity; the merger between the Brown
Shoe Co. and the G. R. Kinney Co. was struck down largely on
the grounds that Brown Shoe's supply of 8 per cent of Kinney's
retail requirements 'foreclosed' a substantial portion of the retail
market to other shoe manufacturers, even though their combined
sales in the relevant markets never exceeded 20 per cent. A
merger between two grocery supermarket chains creating a market share of 7.5 per cent in the Los Angeles area was similarly
disallowed (Scherer, 1980; pp. 549–50). Success in these and
other cases encouraged the Justice Department to issue formal
guidelines in 1968 showing which mergers they would challenge
in the courts. To many British observers these seemed extraordinarily severe: for example, where concentration was high (four
largest firms controlled 75 per cent or more of the market) and
where an acquirer had 15 per cent or more of the market, any
acquisition involving 1 per cent or more of the market would be
challenged. Even where concentration was below this, acquisition
of a market share of 3 per cent or more would be challenged.
Moreover, it was clear from a number of cases that a substantial
lessening of competition was sufficient condition for mergers to
be struck down. Even where important economies were expected
to grow out of the merger these 'cannot be used as a defence to
illegality' (quoted by Scherer, 1980; p. 556). As the policy
evolved, therefore, in the 1950s and 1960s at least in horizontal
and vertical cases (that is between firms operating in the same
market or previously in a seller-customer relationship) mergers of
any importance at all were in effect illegal.[11]

It was essentially in response to this development that Williamson (1972) suggested a more rational trade-off approach in
merger cases. The first step in his argument was that if a merger
simultaneously increased market power and produced economies

it was more logical for policy to admit those economies as a possible defence than simply to ignore them or treat them as 'immaterial'. The main points can be illustrated with Diagram 7.1. The average costs of the firms wishing to merge are shown by AC_c, price by P_c and demand by AD. In the event of the merger, costs would be lowered to AC_m but price would rise from P_c to P_m as a result of the increase in market power. (Clearly if there was no change in market power then only benefits would flow from the merger and no antitrust problem occurs.) Also a monopoly profit of GP_mBE would be earned after the merger was completed but only the amount P_cP_mBF represents a transfer of consumers surplus to producers. In this, the simplest of the cases mentioned by Williamson, he argued that the antitrust authorities should weigh the loss in consumers surplus-labelled L in the diagram – against the gain due to cost reductions – labelled S.[12] If the savings outweigh the added burden then, *ceteris paribus*, the merger should be allowed. He then shows that on plausible assumptions about the elasticity of demand and pre- and post-merger levels of market power, quite modest reductions in cost resulting from merger would be sufficient to offset considerable price increases. For example, if elasticity of demand were 2, a 20 per cent increase in price (and consequent loss of consumers

Diagram 7.1

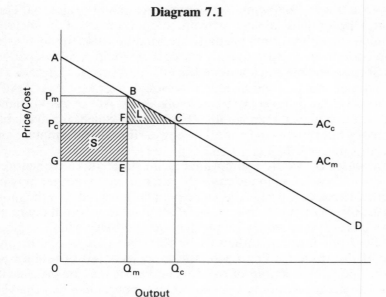

Output

surplus) would be offset by a cost reduction of 4.4 per cent, assuming that pre-merger market power was absent. If pre-merger market power already allowed firms to raise prices 5 per cent above minimum cost levels then the cost reduction required to offset a 20 per cent post merger price increase rises to just under 7 per cent, still one might think a fairly modest requirement.

In view of what we have said about the likely fate of monopoly profits or levels of X-inefficiency in chapter 3, the simple trade-off approach clearly needs to be modified, quite apart from other dynamic considerations mentioned below. As in our previous discussion we can proceed along two fronts. Following Posner and Tullock we can question whether the post merger monopoly profit should be considered on the benefit side of the equation. If it will be consumed subsequently in the hectic quest to maintain the position of market power, then we may wish to remove at least some of it to the other side of the equation: in particular that part that was previously consumers surplus, $P_cP_m\text{BF}$.[13] Naturally this has the effect of converting many mergers that would have yielded net benefits into ones yielding net costs, since monopoly profit applies to the whole output (OQ_m in the diagram) while the original consumers surplus loss applies only over the change in output ($OQ_c - OQ_m$) resulting from the merger.

Alternatively, following Leibenstein, we might argue that cost savings potentially available from merger may not in fact be attained, or at least only partially attained because the increased protection from competitive pressures that would result will allow the firm to become slack and inefficient. In terms of Diagram 7.1 this implies that following merger, although average costs of AC_m are possible, realized costs are actually above AC_m.[14] As Williamson rather obviously concludes: 'Economies which are available in theory but by reason of market power are not sustainable, are inadmissable' (Williamson, 1972; p. 131).

The cases considered so far have been static and have ignored the possibility that in many cases the alternative to merger may be internal expansion. In fact it can be plausibly argued that the most worthwhile economies from a social point of view are likely to be those closely concerned with production and these will flow more readily from internal rather than 'external' expansion. In any case, if the trade-off approach is to be considered in relation to merger policy the *timing* of benefits and costs may be crucial. If, for example, all economies promised by a merger can be achieved after a time lag by internal expansion but without any adverse market power effects the correct trade-off is then the present value of *net* benefits of the merger compared with the present value of benefits from the internal expansion. Clearly if there is no difference in the timing of the economies that can be achieved by internal expansion compared with merger, then on this approach the merger should be disallowed. On the other hand, the greater the time lag necessary before the economies can be achieved by internal expansion compared with that of merger, the more likely the merger is to be accepted. Thus, in this trade-off the information required concerns not only the size of any economies that might flow from the merger but also the timing.

We have dwelt on the Williamson approach because it provides a useful framework for assessing UK policy. Mergers involving a market share of one-quarter or more or the transfer of £5 millions or more of assets may be referred by the Minister to the Monopolies and Mergers Commission which has to decide whether or not they are likely to operate against the public interest. Although not specifically charged with carrying out the cost-benefit type analysis that this approach implies, the Monopolies and Mergers Commission weighs the potential advantages against the possible detriments. Unlike the American antitrust authorities, it can, for example, take expected economies into account in its assessment. British experience also illustrates, however, the formidable difficulties that stand in the way of a more formal adoption of the Williamson approach. Its analytical and 'rational' appeal may, therefore, fail on very practical grounds. Consider, for example, the information that would be required in a specific merger case. First, it is necessary to define the relevant market, a problem which the precise lines in diagrams like 7.1 tend to obscure. In practice it may be very difficult to decide just where one 'market' ends and another starts both geographically (is the market for cod in Britain the whole country, East coast ports, or only some East coast ports?) and technologically (are wrapping materials of all substances close substitutes or only some of them? Do cheap suits compete closely with expensive suits, or do they compete only with separate jackets and trousers?). The examples from the USA and UK could be multiplied many times over but the definition finally accepted in any particular case may be of crucial importance because the more narrowly the market is defined the greater will be the apparent impact of horizontal mergers on market power. Secondly, even if a satisfactory definition of what constitutes the market can be agreed, estimating economies that might arise from the merger is likely to be very complicated. As we have seen in chapter 3 estimating the economies of multi-plant firms is particularly difficult. While production economies of scale at the plant level have now been estimated for quite a wide range of manufacturing industries, those additional advantages that accrue to enterprises operating a number of plants are only available for a small number of products. If measuring realised multi-plant economies is problematical, an attempt in a comparatively short time[15] to forecast *potential* economies must be even more hazardous. The problems are compounded where there is the possibility that the merger may be disallowed or where the company to be acquired objects to the merger. In such cases neither party involved will be anxious to disclose too much to the other about its cost levels and the means envisaged for improving them for fear of being at a severe competitive disadvantage should the merger not be completed.

Despite these considerable problems, in a number of its enquiries the Monopolies and Mergers Commission has asked the companies concerned to provide them with estimates of the expected cost reductions. The replies received have ranged from bland assertions that the company 'was not able to make any present estimate of the cost savings that might be achieved, but was convinced that they would be "real and substantial" '. (Monopolies Commission, 1967a) to quite detailed attempts to show how cost savings might arise in both production and distribution (Monopolies Commission, 1967b, 1968).[16] Where the projected savings were put in percentage terms they were generally of the order of 5 per cent or less which moved one critic to conclude that 'the economies, where they are quantified at all, are strikingly small, even as promises' (Sutherland, 1969; p. 123). It is, of course, in the nature of the problem that the economies are potential rather than realized yet while the increase in market power may occur more or less simultaneously with the completion of the merger, achievement of cost savings may take some considerable time during which any number of unforeseen changes in demand or input prices or technology may intervene to prevent their fruition. For quite genuine reasons, therefore, actual cost savings may be smaller than the forecasts.

Even in cases where cost savings could be made the fact that they only occur some time after the completion of the merger implies that the antitrust authorities should have the means to monitor subsequent performance. In other words, if the increase in market power has only been allowed on the understanding that reduced costs would follow, then it is logical that they should be demonstrated to the authority. At present there is no mechanism for such detailed post-merger assessment and it seems highly unlikely that any feasible method of appraisal could be worked out without a considerable extension to the powers of the Commission or the Office of Fair Trading. In any case this solution may raise more problems than it solves because it could easily lead to what with some justice might be considered 'interference' in the internal affairs of the companies concerned. Furthermore, what sanction should be used against a company which anticipated important economies within, say, five years of merger and then failed to achieve them? Should the merger be dissolved even though it has operated as one unit for such a time?

Here we come to an important difference between the experience of the UK and the USA. In the UK there is no precedent for a merger already completed being forcibly unscrambled, even though the Minister does have sufficient powers under the Fair Trading Act. The aversion to breaking asunder what the market has blessed was perhaps most clearly shown in two early mergers considered by the Monopolies Commission. The cases involving GKN's acquisition of Birfield and BICC's acquisition of Pyrotenax were exceptional in that both mergers had been completed by the time the Commission made its report. Both also involved very substantial increases in market share (to something over 90 per cent),[17] and the Commission was clearly uneasy about the consequences for competition. In the GKN case it relied, perhaps rather lamely, on the countervailing influence of large customers.[18] In the BICC case the anxiety was especially acute for the Commission considered that 'the most satisfactory safeguard for the public interest would undoubtedly be the continuance of competition between two producers of comparable stature' (Monopolies Commission, 1967b). But then concluded just five pages later that the merger would *not* operate against the public interest. Especially in this last case it seems very probable that if the merger had not already taken place the result would have been different. It also seems possible that if there had been anything like the American precedents for annulling well-established corporate marriages, the Commission would have recommended a dissolution. For example, in two of the American cases mentioned on p. 126 above, the time lag between merger and dissolution was seven years (Brown Shoe Co. and the G. R. Kinney Co.) and eight years (Von's Grocery Co. and Shopping Bag Food Stores).[19]

Although the problems of unscrambling a merger may not be as great as those involved in breaking up a monopolistic enterprise considered in the previous section, there are clearly difficulties in re-establishing competition between companies that have been jointly owned for some time. Significantly, since the early cases involving GKN and BICC, merger proposals which might lead to reference to the Commission have been quickly screened by an internal mergers panel[20] before any action is taken. Any references can then be made before the companies have merged so that an adverse recommendation simply involves dropping the proposal rather than divestiture.

As in monopoly cases the Commission has to decide whether a merger is likely to operate against the public interest and according to a recent official review 'present policy operates on the basis of a favourable view towards mergers' (HMSO 1978; para. 4.17). We have already noted that only a tiny fraction of all mergers are actually referred to the Commission and then only about one-third of these receives an adverse report.[21] (But we should also note that about another third of all mergers referred are actually abandoned without a report being made. This seems to indicate either the light-heartedness with which company boards make bids or the blatantly monopolistic intent of the proposals which would not pass the close scrutiny that the Commission could give.) After examining the evidence on the recent effect of mergers on industrial structure and firms' performance in the UK, the policy review recommended a change in emphasis for merger policy. At least those closely concerned with these matters regard it as a change and Holmes could probably discern a perceptible difference after close scrutiny through a magnifying glass. Others may be more uncertain. The review recommended a shift

> from the present policy which tends to operate in favour of mergers to an essentially neutral approach that would have due regard to the dangers of abuse of market power resulting from reduced competition and to the possible dangers of further increases in aggregate concentration but would also recognize the economic benefits that may accrue from improved industrial structure. (HMSO, 1978; para. 5.18)

The response to this passage by members of the Commission who are veterans of a number of merger enquiries has unfortunately not been published. Monsieur Jourdain in Moliere's comedy was astounded to find he had been speaking prose for many years without knowing it. Commission members must have been equally astonished to find that apparently they had *not* been considering the possible adverse competitive consequences or the possible benefits that might flow from mergers.

The review rejected the possibility of adopting a negative stance on mergers, that is that companies wishing to merge where an increase in market power was involved should be required to demonstrate that post merger benefits would outweigh detriments. Such a change was considered 'too drastic' and the 'neutral' position was recommended. If adopted the proposal might have the effect of increasing to a certain extent the number of references made to the Commission but would be unlikely to make much substantive difference to the actual content and conclusions of the reports. Even this suggested change, which was hardly visible to the naked eye, provoked quite a sharp reaction from the NEDO.[22]

It is unfortunate that the review felt it necessary to tread so cautiously on this important issue. There are a number of grounds for believing that a tougher approach is required. First, as we indicated above, although Williamson's trade-off analysis is attractive on theoretical grounds in practice it poses very formidable estimating problems, especially as it is desirable to have the matter settled speedily. Secondly, analysis of the effect of mergers on industrial structure suggests that they have played an important, possibly predominant role, in increasing concentration and furthermore that the effect on subsequent performance may be adverse (although this result is perhaps less firmly grounded).[23] Thirdly, the scope for social as opposed to private gains from merger may be much less widespread than is commonly supposed. In terms of Diagram 7.1 for example, this would simply mean that average costs post-merger may remain at AC_c so that the only effect is the loss of consumers surplus, L, and the transfer of the value represented by P_cP_mBF from consumers to producers. This point is strengthened if we recall the discussion of the economies of the multi-plant firm (as opposed to economies within the plant) in chapter 3. Apart from some aspects of research and development and possibly some in distribution, the scope for economies of a resource saving type seemed limited. Yet mergers are between going concerns, each with its own plants which presumably already enjoy all possible production

economies.[24] The bulk of any economies from merger are therefore likely to be of the more questionable kind. Fourthly, even if
policy was strengthened the number of mergers involved would
still be a very small fraction of the total, where the likely adverse
effects on competition are clear-cut and substantial.

For these reasons it now seems timely to consider a limited
application of a *per se* rule in some merger cases. For example,
mergers which created or extended a market share above a certain level would be illegal and there would be no provision for
arguing that the eventual economies would outweigh the market
power detriments. A branch of the High Court, constituted similarly to the existing Restrictive Practices Court, would have the
responsibility of determining whether the proposed merger would
produce a market share above the specified level. There is clearly
some ground for disagreement about what market share should
be illegal (if acquired by merger). As we envisaged the court
would have discretion as to how the 'market' should be correctly
defined both as to close substitutes (including imports) and geo-
graphical area (which might mean in some cases the whole of the
EEC, rather than simply the UK) the crucial share could be
50 per cent or less. If the social economies that flow from merger
are as improbable and scanty as present evidence seems to suggest,
the damage from such a policy is unlikely to be great and yet the
cumulative effect over a number of years on the upper end of the
size distribution of firms might be quite profound.[25]

As this proposal involves such a large departure from any previous British experience it is important to emphasize that the
number of such cases is likely to be very small. Indeed the knowledge that such special 'last resort' powers are available may be a
sufficient deterrent. Similarly, the number of predominantly vertical mergers (that is between companies in a seller-customer
relationship) which involve the substantial increase in market
power rather than its transmission from one stage of production
to another, is also likely to be very small and the same market
share criterion could be used.[26] In these cases the existence or
creation of a market share of 50 per cent or more at any stage in
the production–distribution process would be sufficient for the
merger to be challenged in the court.

The third broad category of mergers, those of a diversifying or
conglomerate kind, are especially interesting in the present context. Recently they have aroused some of the strongest opposition

in both the USA and Britain since they frequently seemed to have no product or industrial logic and yet increased rapidly and dramatically the size of the acquiring company. Through a series of such mergers in the late 1960s and early 1970s a number of obscure names were catapulted into the ranks of the largest American companies.[27] By definition conglomerate mergers increase the overall size of the acquirer rather than its relative size in a particular market and for this reason no increase in market power may be involved. In chapter 5 we examined the view that conglomerate size may nevertheless bring special dangers to the competitive process, but both on *a priori* and empirical grounds we were inclined to reject the hypothesis. In the case of conglomerate mergers there may be another reason for allowing companies a relatively free hand. If companies with market power become X-inefficient, although the net benefits to an individual shareholder of trying to unseat the unsatisfactory management may be negative, for shareholders taken as a group the net benefits could well be positive. The threat of a take-over bid by an uncouth conglomerate may therefore help to concentrate the minds of managements on internal efficiency rather than on the allures of a quiet life. Nothing is likely to upset the security of tenure of existing managements more than a change of ownership. It thus seems important to keep the 'market in corporate control'[28] as open as possible. Furthermore, if companies see that the path to horizontal growth through merger is partially blocked because of a more stringent policy like that mentioned above, they may be more inclined to seek out others of a more diversified kind.

The main focus of merger policy should, therefore, remain market power and this means horizontal (and perhaps in a few cases vertical) mergers. Despite the attractions of Williamson's trade-off analysis, its practical feasibility remains very doubtful and we would therefore favour a *per se* rule where the probability of a substantial post-merger increase in market power was high. If genuine unexploited economies are possible then these should be realizable by internal expansion. The number of cases likely to be affected by this changed emphasis is very small so the vast majority of mergers would remain untouched. In general the active threat of a possible takeover bid may be a potent means of ensuring managerial efficiency.

Cartels

Formal agreements between companies in the same industry to control the conditions and terms on which they trade are illegal in the USA and very likely to be found 'against the public interest' in the UK. Although neither absolute nor relative size of company is the issue in cartels policy, the corporate giants are likely to feature quite frequently in any antitrust cases. First, as we have noted above, in the UK the spread of their activities is now so wide that their subsidiaries are found in every branch of manufacturing, and secondly in perhaps half of these industries, they will be among the market leaders.

There is probably more unanimity amongst economists on the effects of cartels than on other antitrust issues.[29] The conventional view is that they tend, on the whole, to inhibit the dynamic and efficient while protecting the slothful and inefficient. But the former group are prepared to tolerate restrictions as the price of stability in the market. If the conflict of interest between members becomes too great or the temptations to cheat irresistible then the formal price structure will crumble, at least for a time, until a new agreement can be reached. As long as cartels remain intact, however, both prices and costs are likely to be higher than otherwise and, perhaps more important, the structure of the industry may remain more or less frozen like a pre-historic monster entombed in glacial ice. The shift of resources from the inefficient to the efficient in response to variations in profitability may be neutralized especially if entrants can be kept out by the cartel's use of discriminatory techniques.[30]

The corollary of this is that if a strict anti-cartel policy is introduced into an economy (like the UK), large areas of which have been quite legally cartelized for a considerable time, the after effects are likely to be dramatic and profound. Following the Restrictive Trade Practices Act of 1956 more than 2500 agreements between firms were abandoned in the course of the next sixteen years.[31] In some cases, as Swann and his colleagues reported (Swann *et al.*, 1974) the end of a formal price agreement led to quite severe short-run price competition and elimination of excess capacity. More important from our point of view was the quite frequent resort to mergers by companies seeking a substitute for their abandoned cartels. If cartels are viewed as simply one means of keeping prices consistently above marginal costs for existing producers, then it is to be expected that their abolition will be the signal to find some other method to achieve the same end. It is difficult to be precise on this issue, especially as the general level of merger activity was considerably higher throughout the 1960s than either before or since, but one conclusion of the Swann study was that mergers 'were in fact an important phenomenon in many cases studied' (Swann *et al.*, 1974; p. 172). In such cases the net social benefit of an anti-cartel policy might not be clearcut. Merger is a much more final step than a cartel which is subject to a number of internal pressures and, as we have indicated, even complete breakdown from time to time. On the other hand, mergers may only have been artificially restrained by the presence of a formal agreement. Most commentators are agreed that the shake-up following the 1956 Act was desirable, even if it meant in some cases that concentration increased. The general unfreezing of industrial structure that is likely to follow the abandonment of cartels may not only improve the efficiency of those firms that remain but also make entry more feasible and attractive.

Thus part of the upsurge of merger activity that took place in the 1960s in the UK and hence some of the increase in domestic concentration was probably due directly to the adoption of a tougher anti-trust policy towards cartels. It is true that in some industries looser forms of collusion (especially information agreements, until they too were caught in the legislative net) followed hard on the heels of formal agreements. It is also true that in a few industries the sanctions of disregarding the law were thought trivial enough when set beside the advantages to be gained from deliberately ignoring it, to persuade firms to form unregistered and therefore illegal cartels – telecommunications cable and ready-mixed cement are two cases that have recently come to light. But after the once-for-all change has taken place, the continued application of an active anti-cartel policy is likely to make for a more flexible and dynamic industrial structure. We suggested in chapter 5 that an important form of price determination in oligopoly was probably price leadership of the 'barometric' kind. By making formal contacts between firms relatively difficult[32] cartel policy can help to ensure that this kind of price leadership is not replaced by the potentially more damaging 'collusive' type. For this and other reasons Adam Smith's advice is equally applicable today as when it first appeared more than 200 years ago: 'though the law cannot hinder people of the same trade from sometimes assembling together, it ought to do nothing to

facilitate such assemblies, much less to render them necessary'
(Smith, 1977; p. 117).

STATE-OWNED ENTERPRISES IN THE
PRIVATE SECTOR

A number of writers have argued that state-owned enterprises
operating in the heart of the 'private' sector can act as a powerful
supplement to antitrust policies by improving the performance of
the other firms and restraining the power of the giants. The
Italian organization known as IRI (the Institute for Industrial
Reconstruction), despite its unfortunate birth at the height of the
Fascist era, is frequently taken as a model which others would do
well to emulate. The scope of the IRI is now very wide indeed and
extends into nearly every sector of the Italian economy. According to the editor of a recent panegyric it has served as the inspiration for the state intervention agencies in Britain, France,
Canada, Australia, Sweden and possibly Germany (Holland,
1972). Although to its supporters the objectives of such a body
are manifold and all-embracing we confine ourselves here to its
possible role as a reinforcement to antitrust policy.

At first glance the presence of a publicly owned firm in the
heart of a highly concentrated oligopoly of private enterprises
might be considered a much more potent antidote to the abuse of
market power than the more traditional antitrust policies. Thus
another optimistic commentator anticipated that such a firm with
a mixture of private-public motivation could 'cause improved
pricing and efficiency in tight oligopoly markets. Its takeover
threat to firms in other tight-knit oligopoly markets could indirectly induce increased efficiency in them too' (Shepherd, 1975;
p. 161). Clearly the optimism rests on some very large assumptions about the comparative efficiency levels of private and public
enterprises. The incentives to become X-inefficient which may
affect managements in large private enterprises may, in the case
of public enterprises, be re-inforced rather than diminished.
There are two main reasons for this pessimism. First, despite the
ostensible limitations imposed by the legislation creating such
enterprises, there is almost bound to be, at the back of management's mind, the feeling that if all else fails the government will
step in with financial assistance. In some measure, therefore, the
pursuit of efficiency is likely to be modified. (In Britain this

argument unfortunately may have more force than in other countries, because support for public enterprises of whatever form has become almost purely a political issue. As a result a Labour Government could not allow any experiment with such a public enterprise to fail, whereas a Conservative Government is unlikely to try.) Secondly, the pursuit of 'mixed' public and private objectives may force the firm into less efficient operations than its private competitors would choose. For example, it may feel obliged to maintain plants in operation in areas of high unemployment even though on private efficiency criteria the resources should be withdrawn. The overall efficiency of the firm would suffer as a result and extra finance would have to be made available from the Treasury.[33] In either case, if the government stands ready to act as a financial long-stop, what starts as a short-run emergency aid may, before anyone is really aware of what is happening, turn into a long-run subsidy with no coherent criteria governing the performance of the enterprise or the magnitude of the assistance.[34]

It may be argued that the above remarks are unfavourably coloured by recent ill-starred cases of support for ailing British firms, and that this experience is irrelevant to the case of public enterprises deliberately thrust into highly profitable industries with the prime task of correcting market performance. The problem is that once the public enterprise is there it is likely to become a permanent part of the industry which will not always be growing and profitable. If the public firm is not to run into the problems mentioned above it has to be completely free to act entirely on its own commercial judgement and be prepared to raise funds at market rates. This implies that it has no special social responsibilities, that it can diversify out of slow growing lines and close unprofitable plants. But in this case the rationale for the enterprise to be public rather than private has vanished.

In the quotation given above, Shepherd suggests that public enterprises would be able to 'improve pricing' in heavily concentrated industries. As far as antitrust policy is concerned this could be interpreted in two ways. The most obvious is that if existing private firms had been able to achieve abnormal profits by tacit agreement on a joint maximizing strategy, the public enterprise, with its wider brief, would be able to force price reductions below the monopoly level, presumably to bring them more into line with long-run average costs. In other words, the public enterprise would, on this view, become the price leader, driving prices down and in inflationary conditions keeping price increases to a minimum. If we examine this idea more closely we get a clearer impression of the magnitude of the task set for the public enterprise.

Entry to the offending industry could either take the form of new investment or of the acquisition of an existing firm. In the case of new investment even if we set aside the reservations made above about the likely cost levels achieved by a public enterprise, initially it is going to be very vulnerable. Like any new entrant to an industry, whatever its overall size, it will be at a disadvantage *vis-à-vis* existing firms simply because it lacks experience and expertise.[35] While making 'shake-down losses', therefore, it is unlikely to be able to cut prices without special financial provision from the Treasury. In addition, as we explain further below, the position of the public enterprise entrant will clearly depend very much on what form the entry barriers to the industry take.[36] In the case of what Bain christened 'absolute cost advantages' of existing firms which include special privileges like patents and licences, in the absence of giving the public enterprise privileged access to such assets it is difficult to see how it would be able to compete with existing firms without further subsidy. On the other hand, if established firms enjoy product differentiation advantages (including accepted brand-names, prime site distribution outlets, and the cumulative effect of past heavy advertising) the new public enterprise entrant, like any other firm, would have to make very heavy initial outlays to overcome its disadvantages. In this case there would be the added problem of a public enterprise participating in and thereby escalating competitive advertising which many would argue already leads to resource misallocation in some consumer goods industries.[37]

For these and other reasons the public enterprise may view 'entry' by acquisition as a better alternative and this is the method that Shepherd explicitly mentions. The price that the public enterprise pays for its acquisition, however, will be of central importance. if we rule out the case of simple expropriation, the purchase price will either be at market value or some 'adjusted' value. The market price would be approximately equal to the present value of the future profitability of the company under its present management. By assumption that profitability reflects the degree of monopoly power exercised by the company. If the public enterprise purchases at this price future profits have thus been capitalized. But the whole purpose of the exercise is to ensure that the new owners do *not* in future act like a monopolist: their role is to reduce prices, not to maintain them. In this case they are likely to be squeezed between the costs of servicing the outlay incurred in making the acquisition and the requirement to reduce prices. The fact that no private firm has made a bid for the target company also suggests that at the market price no outside management is confident that it could so improve on the performance of the company as to make more than a 'normal' return.

The alternative is for the public enterprise to be allowed to make the acquisition[38] at a price 'adjusted' to take account of monopoly. Formally this would require an assessment of that fraction of the market price that is attributable to the prospects of the future *monopoly* profits under the firm's existing management and the subtraction of this amount (or some part of it) from the market value. The public enterprise would then clearly be in a strong position to reduce prices. But merely to state the possible procedure seems to raise far more problems than it is likely to solve. Apart from the difficulty of estimating the 'monopoly' element in the current market valuation of the company deliberate acquisition by the public enterprise of assets below the current market price would involve such a large departure from previous practices as to make it wholly unacceptable as an antitrust remedy.

In sum, it is difficult to see how a public enterprise, charged with the task of reducing prices and then keeping them in line with long-run average costs, would be able to fulfill this objective without a subsidy or the promise of a subsidy. Far from finding this prospect daunting, however, Holland sees it as an important element in the strategy of the public enterprise. He suggests, for example, that a central function of a public enterprise would be to counter what he terms 'the "no entry" and "elimination" pricing tactics emphasized by Bain and Sylos-Labini' (Holland, 1972; p. 37). According to Holland the 'no entry' price tactic is where 'firms already established within a sector and in a position to influence price will *temporarily* set price at a lower level than that which they had previously established in order to deter a would-be entrant' (p. 35; italics added). This interpretation, to put it politely, gives a somewhat optimistic gloss to Professor Bain's classic work. It allows Holland to argue that if the potential entrant was a public enterprise backed by the national treasury, the 'no entry' price tactic would soon fail, and having entered the industry the public enterprise could then perform its role of maintaining prices at the competitive level. This analysis overlooks completely the central thesis of Bain's work. As is well known he emphasized that where existing firms had some cost advantage over potential entrants, they would be able *persistently* to charge a price in excess of long-run average cost without entry occurring. The extent of their ability to maintain prices in this way was a measure of the entry barriers behind which they could shelter. In some cases by co-ordinating their policies existing firms would 'limit' their prices below the short-run profit maximizing price to ensure that entry did not occur. Where the entry barriers were high enough there would be no need for prices to be limited in this way. In the present context the most important point is that if firms had been able to earn abnormal returns because they enjoy some cost advantage over potential entrants, the public enterprise is bound to make losses until the cost difference is eroded. The need for subsidy to cover these losses, far from being temporary, as Holland implies, may continue for a very long time. The cost advantage may, after all, derive from a patent, brand or dealer network not easily reproduced.

The second case that he mentions, 'elimination' pricing seems at first glance a more promising area for the public enterprise. The more usual term in this case is 'predatory pricing' by a firm already dominant in an industry where 'it can temporarily reduce its price below that of variable costs . . . of a competing firm, and very quickly eliminate it from the market concerned' (Holland, 1972; p. 35). Again the emphasis is on price *reductions* as an abuse of market power and the temporary nature of the expedient. As we saw in chapter 5 the Monopolies Commission has uncovered a number of instances where firms in an apparently unassailable position have nevertheless resorted to pricing below cost to restrain or even eliminate a rival.[39] An important feature of these cases was that the firms involved were much closer to monopoly than oligopoly. The public enterprise is, therefore, likely to be faced with the unenviable task of either entering the market on a very small scale or taking over the monopolist, and incidentally, then having to *raise* prices. Many would probably argue that the public enterprise solution would simply exchange one set of problems for a new, more intractable set. Whereas the private monopolist caused problems by protecting his excess profit by dubious competitive tactics, the public monopolist may cause concern by being unable to maintain its internal efficiency. In addition recent British experience suggests that government, whatever its political complexion is very likely to treat existing public enterprises as an additional instrument for use in their general economic policy, for example, as a spearhead in restraining prices and thence wages (Labour) or as a means of reducing the public sector borrowing requirement (Conservative). What may begin, therefore, as an antitrust remedy may rapidly deteriorate into another industrial problem. There may be less direct but more efficient remedies available and these are reviewed briefly in the next section.

OTHER POLICIES

At its simplest an abuse of market power involves the restriction of output below the competitive level in order to earn a monopoly profit. In theory it is possible to correct the resource misallocation that arises from the output restriction by the government paying a subsidy per unit equal to the difference between marginal revenue and price at that output that would be produced under competition. The subsidy would then just be sufficient to ensure an expansion of output to the competitive level. The monopoly return that would result from this process could in theory be recovered by levying a lump-sum tax on the firm. Unfortunately the theoretical simplicity of this sleight of hand is not matched by its practicability. It is likely to be very difficult to adjust the lump-sum tax precisely to recoup the monopoly profit without affecting the level of output, even assuming that the subsidy level can be accurately assessed from the available information. For this reason the subsidy-tax solution is likely to remain a textbook curiosity rather than an active remedy for the market power problem.

After observing the apparent correlation between surplus profit and market share (rather than the combined share of the leading four or five firms, which we discussed in chapter 5) Shepherd made the singular proposal of a progressive tax levied according to market share. Below a threshold level of, say, 10 per cent market share, the proposed tax would be at a standard rate. Thereafter it would rise progressively in line with market share up to a limit of perhaps 45–60 per cent (Shepherd, 1975; p. 197). According to Shepherd because the tax would be levied on market share it would not lead to the X-inefficiency and waste that are frequently mentioned as consequences of a progressive tax on profits. Apart from the formidable difficulties that are bound to arise over market definition (which Shepherd recognises without perhaps appreciating their complexity in dynamic conditions) there is the serious point that such a tax may fall with greatest weight on the most efficient companies. As we have seen, there is some evidence to suggest that in concentrated industries the largest companies earn high returns because they are more efficient, not simply because they are taking advantage of market power.[40] Profitability and growth are generally correlated, but under this proposal firms would have little incentive to pursue those opportunities that might appear to offer the greatest scope for growth in case this pitched them into a higher tax category. Despite Shepherd's reassurances it is difficult to escape the conclusion that such a tax would have an adverse effect on incentives.

As it is aimed at market power, the market share tax would have no effect on the overall size of companies. Indeed one side effect would be an increase in diversification, probably by acquisition, in order to minimize the tax burden. In view of the enormous growth of the largest companies in the UK other writers have proposed the introduction of a progressive tax geared to a company's overall size. Meade (1975), for example, has proposed the abolition of the present Corporation Tax which is levied on the profits of all companies,[41] and its replacement by a progressive tax on the numbers employed by a single enterprise. Beyond a threshold level of employment, the tax would then be levied in accordance with the company's total number of employees. It is thus clearly aimed at the overall size of the company rather than its relative size in a particular market but for firms paying this tax relative factor prices would be distorted and the incentive to economise on labour would be reinforced. A similar proposal but based on the net assets of the company, has recently been made by Prais (1981; p. 169). Both writers couple this general suggestion with a number of other tax proposals which they hope might slow the overall growth of the largest companies and lead to a greater dispersal of ownership amongst a greater number of medium-sized and especially small concerns, thus invigorating the private sector and increasing competition.

In view of the disincentive effect of the progressive tax on size it may be important to make it much more attractive for a parent company to sell off a subsidiary or division which is considered either viable on its own or as part of another enterprise. At present in the UK a large firm still has much greater incentive to continue to grow by merger than to dismantle those sections of itself that may have outgrown their usefulness. Until recently, for example, large firms have been able to finance the purchase of the equity of another company by issuing debentures at negative real rates of interest while on the other hand, the sale of part of their assets would probably attract capital gains tax or (if the proceeds were distributed to shareholders) be subject to a high marginal income-tax rate. Prais, therefore, suggests that the privileged position that interest (on debentures) presently enjoys for tax purposes should be re-assessed with a view to bringing the UK position more into line with the US since 1969.[42]

Both Meade and Prais ally their proposals aimed at restraining the growth of the largest firms with other measures which would help the development of small firms. Meade tends to favour special government-assisted bodies which could seek out and finance promising firms with less than a specified number of employees (Meade, 1975; p. 47). He does not rule out some element of subsidy but in any case envisages the government underwriting their borrowing requirements. The difficulty with such a scheme is that it may place too much discretion in the hands of the management of the government-aided bodies. It is not clear why they should make more efficient judgements in distinguishing between the viability of various small firms projects than those of the capital markets. For this reason, if the need for some kind of assistance is accepted, then a more indirect method of encouragement might be preferred. Prais, for example, suggests that interest on bank loans which at present can be deducted by all firms before computing profits liable to Corporation Tax could be disallowed for companies above a certain size, so that small firms would gain an additional tax advantage. The Corporation Tax envisaged by Prais, therefore, would have two elements. The first, progressive element would be assessed on company size (assets) while the second, assessed on profits, would discriminate in favour of small firms.

Although the effect of the various measures would not be seen overnight their cumulative impact over a number of years could be significant. Thus if the largest firms were encouraged to look very closely at their overall size because of the progressive tax and could with comparative ease divest themselves of unwanted divisions, part at least of their relentless growth may be slowed. Coupled with a toughened approach to horizontal mergers, as part of a revised antitrust policy and dearer finance for acquisitions, the policies may help to restore the balance between different sized firms which in the UK at least appears to have been seriously upset since the 1950s.

The literature contains a number of other proposals usually designed to curb or correct the activities of the corporate giants. Meade, for example, is especially hard on 'advertisement'. While recognizing that 'much advertisement of an informative nature is necessary and desirable' he is equally clear that much is not and impairs the competitive process. He seems to have a rather low opinion of consumers who are prey to 'persuasive bamboozlement' and who may, because of advertising, become 'irrationally' bound to particular brands (Meade, 1975; pp. 49–50). A feeling that he may at this point have allowed his own value judgements to cloud his economic analysis is reinforced by his proposal for a return in the UK 'to a system of broadcasting which is not based upon commercial advertisement' (Meade, 1975). The restoration of a monopoly may be a high price to pay for correcting an alleged effect of advertising in oligopoly, especially when, as we argued in chapter 4, the empirical evidence is by no means clear on this point. On the other hand for reasons already given, we would support another of his proposals for the dissemination through semi-public bodies of information about the actual qualities and performance of consumer products.

Finally we can mention a policy in which some writers (especially Shepherd) appear to place much greater faith than recent experience warrants, namely the use of countervailing power by public purchasing agencies in their dealings with large firms. In principle where such an agency (in the UK, for example, a nationalized industry or public service like the National Health Service) apparently has monopsony power it should be able to ensure purchases at low prices,[43] the benefits of which can then be passed on to the public. In practice, however, it seems more likely that private firms, for a variety of reasons connected with their objectives and experience, can get the better of their public customers. Thus the Roche Company was eventually required to pay back nearly £4 millions to the National Health Service which it had apparently overcharged for a number of years. The major electrical companies agreed to repay some £7 millions to the Post Office which was almost their sole customer for telecommunications cable and which they had overcharged systematically through a secret market sharing agreement. On the whole the British precedents for public authorities acting as effective counterweights to private market power in this way are not encouraging.

CONCLUSIONS

Anyone expecting conventional antitrust policies, vigorously applied, to produce spectacular results is bound to be disappointed. Although powers, for example, to break-up giant companies have been included in British legislation, these are likely to remain dormant as long as the disruption costs that any dismemberment is likely to bring are considered greater than the eventual benefits from a re-invigorated competition. The once for all gains that probably accompanied the abolition of the multitude of cartels in the 1960s in Britain are unlikely to be repeated. Nevertheless, emphasis by the Monopolies and Mergers Commission in its enquiries on exclusionary tactics by dominant firms and especially some tightening of the controls on horizontal mergers could, judging by recent American experience, help to slow down the rate of increase in aggregate concentration and prevent sudden and dramatic increases in market concentration.

The suggestion made by some writers of supplementing antitrust policies by launching publicly owned enterprises into the oligopolistic struggle seems likely to raise more problems than it solves, especially in an economy like Britain's where public enterprises have rarely had convivial relations with the government. On the other hand, an imaginative use of taxation policies seems in principle to offer a much more positive supplement to antitrust policy. A combination of tax measures designed first to make it easier for giant firms to hive off unwanted divisions and less attractive for them to acquire other firms, and secondly to make it easier for smaller firms to grow, could have a profound effect on the overall size distribution of firms. In the long-run a combination of various policies is likely to produce a more efficient result than one which simple attacks large firms in the private sector.

8

Social Responsibility and Corporatism

INTRODUCTION

Up to this point we have discussed a number of policies that governments can adopt to control and regulate the conduct and performance of large companies. A common characteristic of these policies is that they are imposed by government on the companies through the legal or administrative system or through direct intervention and control. In the second section of this chapter we discuss a quite different approach. In order to keep governmentally imposed policies to a minimum, the central proposal of this school is that large, prominent companies should voluntarily decide to act in a 'socially responsible' way. According to its advocates, if the companies are successful they will not only improve their own performance but also deflect much of the vehement criticism which large companies have aroused, especially in the USA, in recent years.

The apparent worthiness of the ideal is unfortunately matched by a profound difficulty in pinning down in any precise way what 'socially responsible' means. The diligent seeker after 'social responsibility' may be doomed to a similar frustration as that of the thirsty man in the desert who continually seems on the threshold of an oasis, only for it to vanish before his eyes. He is not helped as much as he might be in his enquiry by the voluminous writing on the subject. One recent critic was driven to ask 'Why is this literature so bad?' (Preston, 1975; p. 446). Different writers have emphasized different activities they would include in the category of socially responsible behaviour. Many, for example, feel that once companies become aware that their production process or products cause externalities, especially pollution or damage to the environment, then without waiting for some imposed government policy, they should tackle the problem

148

themselves by changing production methods or installing control devices and so on. Similarly they should take action to diminish racial and sexual discrimination by their recruitment and training policies. Other writers have emphasized the initiatives that large companies should take in ensuring employee participation in decision making, at all levels. In their investment decisions it has been frequently stressed that they should pay special attention to the local development and employment needs of the regions in which they wish to operate. Then, if they have any energy and resources left after these commitments, they should play a prominent role in fostering the artistic, cultural and sporting activities not just of their own employees but also of the local communities of which they are part.

The list is not intended to be exhaustive (we have said nothing, for example, of large companies responsibilities to consumers or to regional and national planning agencies) but it probably includes sufficient items to give the reader a general idea of what is involved. The discussion is aimed especially at the top end of the corporate sector (perhaps the largest hundred enterprises in an economy like the UK) where management is clearly divorced from ownership, where enterprise life is eternal (even though its form may change via merger) and, in particular, where surplus profits are more or less assured. The last is a necessary condition if management is to have sufficient elbow room to introduce the kinds of social behaviour that the above agenda implies. Companies that are closely constrained in their pricing behaviour by competitors are unlikely to have either the inclination or the income to pursue anything other than what they see as their own private interest. Central to the whole issue, therefore, is the notion of market power which generates surplus profits over which management has discretionary authority. Part of the surplus retained can then be devoted either to a new plant which would increase the firm's profitability, or, say, to the installation of control and monitoring devices which improve the 'cleanliness' of the production process or again to the sponsorship of an exhibition of priceless South American arts and crafts.

Supporters of the idea argue that companies must determine the correct balance between their private and social responsibilities if they are to survive in anything like their present form. To opponents the whole concept is anathema not to say subversive of the whole enterprise system. In Britain there has been for some time considerable interest in a rather special form of 'social responsibility'. It is best characterized as Corporatism and also embodies the ideal that enterprises (and trades unions) should be self regulating. In particular this self regulation should be channelled through a series of committees, consisting of representatives of government, trades unions and private enterprise. Just as 'social responsibility' at the individual enterprise level involves in effect the supersession of the market by the discretionary use of corporate resources to meet a social objective, so at the industry or sector level Corporatism entails joint action by a number of enterprises in co-operation with trades unions and government to resolve the country's economic problems. We discuss this notion briefly in the third section.

THE SOCIAL RESPONSIBILITY OF THE PRIVATE ENTERPRISE

The point of departure for many writers of what, for convenience, we shall call the social responsibility school, is a critique of market mechanisms as adequate or efficient regulators of economic activity in the age of the giant, private company. The 'invisible hand' which in an earlier period may have been a reasonable instrument for providing a certain degree of economic and social harmony has, according to this school, now become at times all too visible and at other times palsied or arthritic.

Part of the criticism amounts to a recognition of the limited ability of antitrust policy to modify or change the growth and profitability of the largest companies. Thus it is argued that such firms, far from merely responding to market forces which under certain circumstances lead to an economic optimum, can in fact subvert and mould these pressures to their own ends. As a result they may ensure that the economy persistently stays some way from an efficient resource allocation. Preston and Post (1975, p. 40), for example, conclude: 'it can scarcely be argued that large and powerful firms are subject to the discipline of the market with either the intensity or the speed necessary for effective operation of the market contract mechanism'.

Equally important in their view are the implications of the existing highly skewed distributions of individual and corporate income and wealth. If all participants in the process of market contracting start on more or less equal terms, everyone's preferences can play a full part. But with highly unequal income some preferences may not be catered for at all by the market, simply because of a lack of effective demand. As a result, the overall performance of the market economy can only be regarded as socially optimal if the preferences of the excluded are ignored or treated as irrelevant.

Furthermore, it is now widely recognized that over wide areas of the economy the market mechanism cannot be relied upon to supply the correct quantities and qualities of goods or services. As a result they are collectively produced and used. In this category can be included the public utilities and more recently environmental quality (clean air and water, noise control and waste disposal) and social amenities (such as equality of opportunity, absence of arbitrary discrimination and special provisions for the disadvantaged). To the extent that the collective provision of these and similar goods and services becomes increasingly important in advanced industrial countries, then the pure market mechanisms clearly diminish in importance and what Preston and Post term the 'fundamentalist' criticism of social responsibility weakened.

In effect most of the criticisms of the market mechanism made by members of the social responsibility school are the standard fare of many intermediate microeconomics texts. It by no means follows, however, that acceptance of the shortcomings of the market automatically wins converts to the school. This would imply that no other alternatives are available. It is precisely in order to avoid one of these alternatives, government intervention, that Andrews argues forcefully in favour of companies themselves taking the initiative. In his view government regulation 'is neither a subtle instrument for reconciling private and public interests nor an effective substitute for knowledgeable self-restraint' (Andrews, 1972; p. 138).

Given that the size of the largest companies places them in a unique position in the economy, with the indirect effects of their actions spreading far beyond their initial transactions in factor and product markets, the crucial question then becomes one of defining the boundaries of their concern. It is one thing to accept that the largest enterprises of the 1980s have to recognize wider extra-legal responsibilities than their counterparts of a hundred years ago, quite another to define what they should be and how they should be monitored. Even those generally sympathetic have found a good deal to criticize in a doctrine which 'remains vague and ill-defined' (Preston and Post, 1975; p. 52).

In order to set out the difficulties involved we will concentrate on a specific example which occurs frequently in the literature: pollution and congestion from motor vehicles. We have already noted the seriousness of the atmospheric and environmental pollution caused by the use of road vehicles. The exhaust fumes cause discomfort and disease and destroy vegetation, while the noise and dirt created often makes urban life all but unbearable for many people. Under the impact of heavy vehicles, ancient buildings and possibly whole neighbourhoods are threatened with destruction. The external effects created by the use of motor vehicles clearly dwarf those generated by their production. The traditional or 'fundamentalist' view of motor-vehicle manufacturers' responsibilities in this situation is that they cease at the factory gates (assuming, of course, that all existing laws are being obeyed). On this view the firm will best serve the public interest by using efficient production methods and selling at prices kept as low as possible by competitive forces. In contrast the social responsibility school argues strongly that the enterprises should not only recognize the indirect effects that the use of their products involves but take action themselves to correct them. It is at this stage that an almost inevitable vagueness enters the discussion. The effects of motor vehicles are so all-pervasive and fundamental that it is difficult to envisage how a coherent policy could arise from the spontaneous action of independent companies. First, some who attempt to take the broad view of their responsibilities may introduce, for example, modified engines, fuel and exhaust systems and also refuse to build cars and lorries above a certain size because of their environmental dangers. Others of a more 'fundamentalist' disposition may simply confine themselves to operating within the law and also catering for any unsatisfied demand for large vehicles which their competitors have eschewed. The eventual result of this lack of uniformity of response may simply be to frustrate the well-intentioned efforts of the first group of companies. To the extent that their policies involve more costly methods they will lose out to their rivals and have either to revert to their previous techniques or withdraw from the market altogether. Secondly, it is clear from the example we have chosen (although it applies equally well to a number of other issues) that the production companies themselves are not the suitable instruments for correcting some of the indirect and yet most fundamental externalities that their products create. Many of the problems of congestion and deterioration to the fabric of buildings arise not from the use by an individual of one vehicle but by the attempt by many individuals at particular times and spreading over many years, to use the limited capacity of existing roads. Hence the demand for by-passes, underpasses, road-widening, motorways and traffic-control systems. In many discussions it is not clear whether or not the writer considers that vehicle manufacturers should extend the scope of their social responsibilities to include such projects. The logic of the argument points to that conclusion but it is seldom spelt out.

Preston and Post recognize the second problem – that is defining the boundary of corporate responsibility – and propose the principle of 'primary and secondary involvement' as the correct guide to action. The primary involvement of the firm includes all of the traditional activities associated with its participation in factor and product markets in its pursuit of profits. 'Secondary involvement impacts include the *use* (by others) of merchandise and services sold, the consequences of production and sales activities themselves, the impact of procurement and employment, the neighbourhood effects of physical plant occupancy, and so on' (Preston and Post, 1975; p. 96; italics in the original). They then develop the idea using the example of a major automobile producer. Although they list a number of different 'secondary involvement' impacts, we will note only those relating to our example.[1] They specifically mention 'environmental pollution and the land-use implications of an expanding road-highway network . . . [the] impact of production facilities on their physical environments (pollution, congestion, visual acceptability)' (Preston and Post, 1975). They anticipate that the notion of 'secondary involvement' will meet the frequent criticism that social responsibility has no apparent limits, by giving clear guidelines to management about the legitimate scope of their activities. 'Management responsibility, in our view, extends as far as the limits of secondary involvement, but *no farther* (Preston and Post, 1975: italics in the original). The reader may rightly ask whether Preston and Post have achieved their purpose. As a result of their introduction of the notion of 'secondary involvement' does, for example, the management of an automobile company know better how far his social responsibilities extend? What is he to make of the idea that he should take account of the land-use implications of an expanding road highway network? Should he reason that if he is successful in expanding his sales by 10 per cent in the next three years this would so overload an already crowded urban road system as to make substantial expansion schemes necessary (but which for a number of reasons he considers undesirable) and that therefore he should instead diversify into, say, bicycle manufacturing? Although Preston and Post use an automobile example to explain which social concerns clearly lie outside managerial responsibility (namely water quality, housing standards and general public health) they do not spell out in any more detail how precisely the 'secondary involvement' idea can be made operational by a manufacturing enterprise. We are therefore unfortunately left with the impression that the vagueness about social responsibility that the authors wished to dispel, has, like a phantom, simply changed its shape.

In any case 'secondary involvement' does not meet the first problem raised above: the lack of uniformity in response by firms operating in the same industry. It is perhaps symptomatic of a general over-estimation of the extent to which the largest firms can tame market forces, that this problem has been frequently neglected in the social responsibility literature.

A clear exception in this respect is Arrow (1973) who concentrates on two areas where private profit maximizing behaviour by firms may not lead to socially efficient results. One we have already emphasized, pollution and congestion, and the second occurs where there is great disparity in knowledge about processes or products between buyer and seller and where safety (for workers and consumers) is a major consideration. He does not agree, however, that we can rely solely on the spontaneous action of firms:

> In these situations it is clearly desirable to have some idea of social responsibility, that is, to experience an obligation, whether ethical, moral, or legal. Now we cannot expect such an obligation to be created out of thin air. To be meaningful, any obligation of this kind, any feeling or rule of behaviour has to be embodied in some definite social institution. (Arrow, 1973; p. 309)

As well as informing firms of the standards of behaviour that society expects of them he points out that institutionalization of social responsibility provides some assurance to firms that the same conditions apply to all. No one competitor can then gain an advantage unless he infringes the code laid down from outside. Firms are thus more likely to undertake the additional expenses that socially responsible behaviour is likely to entail. Arrow then lists four kinds of institutions that might embody the social responsibilities of firms. Taken together they seem to provide a much firmer guide to action than either the amorphous notion of 'social responsibility' or the elusive idea of 'secondary involvement'. The four institutions are, (i) legal regulation, which for example, may be used to control vehicle emissions, (ii) taxation, applied say, on chemical wastes released into the atmosphere, (iii) civil liability: attempts (so far with only limited success) have been made, for example, to sue petroleum companies for selling products that can lead to brain damage in children, (iv) ethical codes that lead to restraints on individual conduct by having some generally agreed standard of company behaviour. In the UK, for example, the advertising industry has for some time had an independent body, The Advertising Standards Authority, established by the industry itself, to monitor advertising.

The complexity of some of the issues involved make the varied 'institutions' appropriate in different cases. Thus, for example, Arrow argues that a combination of legal regulation and taxation may be appropriate for dealing with pollution. Regulation may be most appropriate where the pollutant and its effects are known and clearly defined, and where, therefore, easily enforceable standards can be maintained. It is likely to prove too clumsy an instrument where products or processes are changing rapidly and where the legislative response may be too late and inflexible. In some cases of this kind taxation may provide a more efficient solution. The main advantage of taxation is that it allows the individual enterprise to make its own decision on the problem of pollution by adopting what it regards as the least costly adjustment. (Taxation is, of course, the classical solution to the general problem of externalities.)

In cases of product safety a combination of legal regulation and civil liability is likely to be more appropriate. As Arrow indicates, the law in liability cases is still in the process of evolution and it is difficult at the moment to see how much reliance can be placed on this as a mechanism for ensuring socially responsible behaviour. Courts have, however, been loath to assign liability where it cannot be clearly established that the executives of a company involved could reasonably have foreseen that there was a high probability of risk in using products or employing certain processes. Clearly if they knew that a product was liable to certain defects and yet still sold it without warning they would be found liable. But in practice it may be very difficult to distinguish one case from another, and determine probabilities and risks.

Arrow has a more serious reservation about the use of civil liability as a significant means of enforcing social responsibility on profit making firms. It is likely to be extremely costly to any litigant and while the total burden suffered by society from pollution or product defect may in the aggregate be substantial, the burden imposed on any individual may be quite small. As a result, individuals will not be keen to sue. In any case, for a continuing problem like pollution, even a successful outcome for a litigant awarded damages, may reduce but does not solve the problem. A long queue of litigants waiting to establish yet again a well-known set of facts about pollution is a highly inefficient way of solving the problem. In such a case taxation would obviously be preferable.

Previous writers of the social responsibility school may claim that Arrow is talking about something quite different from what they had in mind. They might argue that the three institutions mentioned so far (regulation, taxation and civil liability) were taken for granted as part of the normal framework within which all companies have to operate, and that they were only concerned with those *additional* responsibilities imposed neither by law nor the market but which, nevertheless, the largest companies had a duty to take on. But as we have already mentioned, it is precisely Arrow's insistence that social responsibility must be institutionalized rather than, as he says, 'created out of thin air' that gives his analysis more authority. There may, however, be a good deal of common ground over his fourth social institution, namely ethical codes. He emphasizes that their development may be especially important in the case where there is a great disparity in information between the parties and this probably has most relevance to the question of safety both for employees in their working conditions and customers in the use of products. Such codes already exist in the professions, the best example being in medicine where they provide the vital basis of mutual trust between doctor and patient. The essence of an effective code, according to Arrow, is that both parties should benefit: the client from the knowledge that the seller is bound to use all of his specialized skill on the client's behalf; while the seller himself has the assurance that all competing firms will behave in a similar fashion.[2] Once the code is established all participants will have an interest in ensuring that its precepts are kept, for while *all* benefit from the stability and maintenance of the code, there is the constant temptation for an individual to seek a private advantage by infringing the code. In this respect there is a close analogy between the monitoring by its participants of a cartel and of an ethical code.

Although such codes are far more highly developed and formalized in the professions than in business and have often evolved only over a very long period, Arrow is quite optimistic about their development. First, detailed scrutiny of many economic transactions reveal that they inevitably involve a good deal of mutual trust and restraint. If every possible contingency and condition had to be stipulated in advance most contracts would become impossibly complex. Many transactions have to depend largely on verbal assurances that they will be carried out in accordance with 'common practice'. Similarly in many exchanges one party gives up his goods or services some time before he is paid or vice versa. In other words, the groundwork for more formal ethical codes is already present in the widespread acceptance of these informal rules that nearly all market transactions require. Secondly, the predominance of the corporate giants, frequently a drawback, may in this context be an advantage. Amongst the great number of executives that such companies must employ are bound to be many who recognize the social impact of their organization and want to accept the challenge that this poses. Andrews goes further: 'corporate executives of the integrity, intelligence, and humanity required to run substantial companies cannot be expected to confine themselves to narrow economic activity and ignore its social consequences' (Andrews, 1972; p. 138).

Despite these factors working in their favour, however, Arrow emphasizes that ethical codes cannot be expected to spring up over night or have anything like universal scope.

> They may develop as a consensus out of lengthy public discussion of obligations, discussion which will take place in legislatures, lecture halls, business journals, and other public forums. . . . A more formal alternative would be to have some highly prestigious group discuss ethical codes for safety standards. (Arrow, 1973; p. 315)

To ensure that they are accepted and maintained as part of standard managerial procedure he envisages an educational programme backed up by organizations such as government agencies, trade associations and consumer defence groups.[3] Through their joint efforts he concludes that in certain limited areas, especially safety standards, ethical codes could emerge.

The emphasis on the limited nature of the codes and the specific example given – safety of consumers and employees – should be especially noted. Together they meet the main criticisms that can be raised against the idea of relying on the 'professionalization' of management to enforce an ethical code. In their discussion of this issue, for example, Beesley and Evans (1978) raise the following difficulties. First, the practice of management does not generally have a central unifying value that everyone recognizes, unlike medicine where the sanctity of human life does have this acceptance. Clearly though, the identical value does apply in the specific areas of employee and product safety. While companies may vary enormously in their interpretation of their social responsibilities as far as, say, local development is concerned they are nearly all likely to agree on the prime importance of product safety. Secondly, they suggest that once a professional organization has been given the private responsibility of regulating the performance of its members it may be very difficult thereafter to retrieve these powers for public policy determination. Notwithstanding the obvious authority of the British Medical Association, they are probably overstating the case. But in any event, if the code is restricted to safety standards by industry, where in addition government regulation in one form or another has been established for more than a hundred years, this is unlikely to be a serious problem. Thirdly, there is the question of entry barriers. Enforcement of the ethical code through a fully 'professionalized' management may carry with it the danger that a new industrial Business Managers Association (BMA) could develop full control over entry to large sectors of industry, to the general detriment of the enterprise system. But as Friedman points out in his analysis (and general disapproval) of the workings of the American Medical Association, if entry remains open (if necessary by law) abuse can be avoided (Friedman, 1962; chap. 9). Thus in the case of an association of business executives who agree to a common code on safety, as long as the possibility remains for non-member firms also to operate, then the problem does not arise. Employees (probably through their trades unions) and consumers (through their purchases) can indicate their approval or otherwise of the standards of member and non-member firms.

If their scope is limited to a number of well-defined and important areas, therefore, the development of ethical codes could make a genuine contribution to social responsibility, supplementing those external constraints (regulation, taxation and civil liability) imposed by the government or the judiciary. But critics from the more all-embracing social responsibility school may claim that in narrowing the concept in this way Arrow has conceded too much: to make the idea operational he has paid too high a price. What has happened, for example, to social responsibilities of large companies in the fields of local and regional development, employee participation and artistic and cultural activities, not to mention 'planning'? Shorn of these wider duties they may, with some justification, claim that the concept amounts to little more than that companies should be sensitive to the social pressures felt by any prominent organization or group. Furthermore they see a danger in this restricted approach. Unless companies themselves assume these much wider responsibilities, it is argued, the decision will be taken out of their hands by the government. One suggestion recently made by Bower, for example, would undoubtedly have a dramatic effect on the whole future of the private company sector. Individual values must be incorporated, he argues, into organization behaviour and to 'accomplish this objective we must remove the screens that detach social consequences from their origins in individual acts. Individuals must bear the consequences of their actions, and this may mean the necessity of ending the social, political and, in some areas, even the economic aspects of limited liability' (Bower, 1974; p. 210). It is far from clear, however, whether such a dramatic reform would sharpen individual incentives sufficiently to achieve the desirable net benefits in the form of reduced pollution, increased safety, etc., that Bower anticipates.

On the other hand, Arrow's modest suggestions do meet the criticisms of social responsibility made by the 'fundamentalists'. They see a quite different danger in the assumption by private companies of responsibilities going well beyond those to their shareholders to make profits. In their view once companies become responsible for activities which have hitherto been regarded as the province of the government or which have not explicitly been assigned to them by the law, then it is but a short step to their becoming creatures of the government. The danger has been vividly expressed by Hayek:

> if the management is supposed to serve wider public interests, it becomes merely a logical consequence of this conception that the appointed representatives of the public interest should control the management. The argument against specific interference of govern-

ment into the business corporations rests on the assumption that they are constrained to use the resources under their control for a specific purpose. If this assumption becomes invalid, the argument for exemption from specific direction by the representatives of the public interest also lapses. (Hayek, 1967; p. 305–6).

Some observers have regarded recent changes in the UK in relations between government and industry as clear signs of a movement in this direction. It is this development to which we now turn.

'CORPORATISM' AND INDUSTRIAL POLICY

Historically 'Corporatism' and the 'Corporate State' have been most closely associated with the economic theories of the Italian Fascist Party. But Samuel Brittan has recently taken a certain malicious delight in quoting from one of the most celebrated Fascist theoreticians a passage which, as he says, could have come from a discussion paper published by either a Conservative or Labour Government in Britain of the early or mid-1970s (Brittan, 1977). Indeed, with their emphasis on direct state intervention, unity and co-operation as compared to individual decision-making, competition and market processes, they apparently accepted three of the five defining characteristics singled out by Winkler in his recent analysis of Corporatism (Winkler, 1976).[4] Thus at one time or another the government sought greater control over the investment decisions of individual companies (for example through 'Planning Agreements' under the Industry Act, 1975); offered to achieve economic goals through co-operative effort (for example in 1973 the Prime Minister, Mr Heath, offered employers and unions to 'share fully with the Government the benefits and obligations involved in running the national economy', cited in Brittan (1977; p. 121); and attempted to reorganize and administer industries along 'rational' lines (for example through such bodies as the Industrial Reorganization Corporation, the National Enterprise Board and the sector working parties and economic development councils – Little Neddies of the NEDC).

Although in recent years the theoretical underpinning of the corporatist approach has rarely been spelt out, it was originally based on principles of co-operation and order. The first and possibly key element was direct government control over the investment decisions of individual firms. Secondly, it embraced the idea of ordered co-operation between labour, management and owners in contrast to competition which was regarded as wasteful and disorganized. The 'orderly' restructuring of industries and 'orderly' marketing of output through cartels, both initiated by the state, were preferred to the 'disorder' of market forces. This in turn requires a unity of effort by all parties in industry recognizing their proper responsibilities. As a result all strikes have to be prohibited, with all industrial disputes settled by compulsory arbitration. The corollary of these policies at the international level is an emphasis on mercantilism rather than free trade and control over the international flow of investment funds. Fully developed, the corporatist system has been characterized as one of private ownership but with complete public control, compared, for example, with capitalism (private ownership with private control) or socialism (public ownership with public control) (Winkler, 1976; p. 46). We are not suggesting that anything like the full-blooded Corporate State has or is about to emerge in the UK but a number of commentators have noted close similarities between certain policies proposed by various governments in the 1970s and the corporatist principles that we have just sketched.

In addition recent trends in the structure of the UK economy have been seen as hastening the drift to corporatism. According to Winkler, for example, the most important change has been the growth and extent of industrial concentration. He cites the recent increases in both aggregate and market concentration (which we discussed above in chapter 2) and indicates how they might bring corporatism closer. Most relevant to our central concern is his view that with output in the whole of the manufacturing sector now in comparatively few hands it becomes intolerable for a government to allow any of the giants to fail, because of the enormous direct and indirect consequences on employment, output, investment and exports. Certainly there has been ample evidence over the last twenty years that governments fully recognized this position whatever they may have said in opposition. In cases where the government has used public money to assist a 'private' firm, it will clearly want some direct participation in their subsequent affairs. It was no co-incidence, for example, that one of the very few 'Planning Agreement' signed by a privately owned firm was Chrysler UK to which the government became committed to the extent of approximately £150 million in a rescue plan shortly after the passage of the 1975 Industry Act. Private sector firms

held back from signing Planning Agreements and the accompanying Industrial Strategy was quietly dropped. But the temptation
or opportunity remains. While the level of aggregate concentration is so high and possibly increasing, a future government, faced
by an acute crisis may go much further in controlling the major
policies of the largest companies than was accomplished by the
largely abortive Industry Act of 1975. Despite its direct lack of
impact it remains important for the discussion of corporatism and
we refer to it in more detail below.

The second part of Winkler's argument, on *market* concentration, is much less satisfactory both in his analysis of the statistics
and especially in the inference that he draws from them. Instead
of relying on information at the industry or product level of
aggregation which, with some reservations, come closest to the
idea of a 'market' in economic theory and which were available in
great detail when he was writing, he chose instead data which
divide the whole of manufacturing into a mere sixteen groups,
implying that the whole sector consists of a similar number of
markets. In the conventional analysis of market structure, manufacturing is usually classified either into 130 or so 'industries' or
even more validly into twice this amount of 'products'. Manufacturing industry divided into sixteen groups tells us nothing about
the presence or absence of oligopoly in the UK, contrary to what
Winkler quite clearly claims (Winkler, 1976; p. 53). Few observers would deny that many products are now sold under
oligopolistic conditions (as the more detailed data help to show)
but there are as many if not more products sold into markets
which are very loosely oligopolistic or 'atomistic'. Furthermore
even where concentrated oligopoly apparently prevails there is no
guarantee, as we have seen, that firms will make 'excessive' profits. Quoting the highly aggregated data, however, allows Winkler
to proceed to his second point about concentration and corporatism. While the overall size and importance of the corporate giants
means that no government can allow them to fail, so also their
universal market power means that no government can allow
them to succeed. He therefore argues as follows: 'For the state to
tolerate (and in some cases to sponsor) concentration to this level
and still allow profit maximisation would be to licence corporate
plunder, to issue a permit to hold the nation to ransom' (Winkler,
1976). We suggest that this conclusion rests on a misunderstanding of what constitutes a market and of the nature of market

power. Furthermore, as we have seen above (chapter 5), there is little firm evidence to support this apocalyptic view.

The conclusion is even more difficult to understand when Winkler proceeds to argue that the next factor pushing the UK closer to Corporatism is the decline in the rate of profit in manufacturing industry. While on the one hand, therefore, the government cannot stand aside and allow oligopolists to 'hold the nation to ransom', on the other, it will have to step in and provide more and more finance for the hapless 'plunderers'. The reader may find it very difficult to see how both of these influences can be at work simultaneously. He argues, nevertheless, that the most likely policy outcome of these and related developments will be corporatism, if only because it is the easiest to accomplish. Deconcentration may be regarded as too complicated and technologically costly, while wholesale nationalization would administratively be much more difficult. Thus while taking Winkler's point that high aggregate concentration raises the dangers of corporatism we find the remainder of his arguments – used to support the view that the UK will almost inevitably move towards corporatism – unsubstantiated and unconvincing.

Other writers have viewed recent corporatist manifestations as merely the latest phase in the long British flirtation with 'economic planning'. Budd (1978), for example, regards them as essentially a latterday counterpart of the microeconomic planning proposals that were repeatedly debated in the 1930s. For a while after the war, Keynesian demand management seemed sufficient to achieve the main economic objectives, especially full employment, without the needs for detailed intervention and control at the micro-level of the industry or the firm. But successive balance of payments crises and Britain's slower rate of growth than her main rivals persuaded the Conservative Government of the early 1960s and the succeeding Labour Governments (which in any case needed little persuading) that more detailed control was necessary. The process really started in earnest with the establishment of the NEDC and its related specialized staff (NEDO) and offspring ('the little Neddies') in 1961 through which it was hoped to gain that degree of consensus and co-operation for the achievement of economic goals which is central to the corporatist creed. It would have reached its apotheosis in 1975 if the original Labour Party plans had been put into effect. The main provisions of the eventual act and the related 'Industrial Strategy' appear to have had little lasting effect on the structure and outlook of British industry. But as the latest and probably most ambitious formal attempt to organize the economy along corporatist lines it is useful to examine the original proposals in a little more detail.

The target of the proposals was quite specifically the hundred or so largest enterprises in the private sector whose resources were to be harnessed to serve 'the public interest'.[15] The three main instruments for achieving this control were to be Planning Agreements, a National Enterprise Board and an Industry Act which would provide the government with the necessary powers to meets its economic objectives. If the policy had been put fully into effect it would have accomplished one of the key corporatist aims, that is direct control by the state over the investment decisions of private companies. As originally conceived the National Enterprise Boards was 'to introduce public ownership into the strongholds of private industry' (Labour Party, 1973). It was not clear how many companies were actually to be acquired but major emphasis was then put on their use as an instrument of planning and control over those remaining private companies which would either be competing with the state enterprises or buying from and selling to them.[6] 'In this way, the previous gap between the economic plans of the government and the actual policies pursued in the private sector, would be more effectively bridged than in the 1965 National Plan' (Labour Party, 1973). The bridge was to be reinforced by Planning Agreements between the government and the largest private firms, together with all public enterprises.

> Planning Agreements will bring about a closer understanding between companies – workforce as well as management – and the government on the aims to be followed and the plans to be adopted in pursuit of them. They will not only help to ensure that the plans of companies are in harmony with national needs and objectives; they will also provide a securer and more coherent basis than has existed in the past for ensuring that government financial assistance is deployed where it will be most effectively used. A fuller exchange of information will be an essential ingredient in Planning Agreements; the information which companies provide in this context will be used for this purpose only. (Department of Industry, 1974; para. 7)

Although the agreements were not to be compulsory (contrary to the original intention) it was made clear in the White Paper that they were intended to be effective. Thus the crucial point and the one which aroused considerable opposition was the power of the government to disburse discretionary financial aid to companies that were considered worthy of such selective assistance. Brittan was one critic who realized the full import of the innocuous-looking prose of the White Paper and subsequent Industry Bill:

> the fortunes of a company (and the individuals in it) are to depend not on its own luck and skill, or on known and stated rules, but on whether it is able to satisfy a particular Minister (or his representative) acting, ultimately on his own discretion. . . . Companies who have broken no known law will be subject to favour or discrimination according to the whims of politicians and officials' (Brittan, 1975; p. 63).

In the event companies were more jealous of their autonomy than Brittan had envisaged, or perhaps they took his warning to heart. The government itself was too distracted by the more pressing problems of inflation and the balance of payments, to consolidate their new Industrial Policy. Few companies actually signed Planning Agreements and consequently they never became the powerful instruments of planning and control that was originally envisaged. The National Enterprise Board far from thrusting widely into the most successful parts of the private corporate sector found itself, for the most part, used as a device for supporting the halt and the lame.

The new government elected in 1979 deliberately turned its back on the corporatist aspirations of its predecessor. It emphasized the desirability and effectiveness of competition rather than co-operation and quickly introduced a measure designed to strengthen the powers of the Office of Fair Trading in the investigations of the exclusionary tactics of dominant firms which we discussed in the previous chapter. But by its continued financial support for such firms as British Leyland, British Steel, British Shipbuilders and ICL it has given further evidence of the extent to which any modern government is tied to the ailing corporate giants.

While the level of industrial concentration remains high and is matched by a similar concentration amongst trade unions the temptation of a renewal of corporatist policies will persist. Furthermore, opponents see the real danger of such an approach in the UK as much more likely to promote inefficiency and stagnation, rather than the regeneration of the economy that supporters claim. Brittan, for example, has argued as follows:

> The inefficiencies result from what we might call a fair exchange of

restrictive practices: a tariff for one industry, in exchange for quotas for another and a government subsidy for a third; an agreement to restrict recruiting to one occupation in exchange for higher entry qualification in a second and subsidies to maintain labour in a third; tax subsidies to houseowners to balance council house subsidies; and price controls to please organised consumer interest, with ministerial task forces to investigate the resulting shortages. (Brittan, 1977; p. 123)

Underpinning this alarming agenda is the belief, shared as we have seen by the 'social responsibility school' that under modern circumstances not only do markets perform the tasks of registering preferences and allocating resources poorly, rather than relatively well, but in addition, that co-operation through government sponsored bodies provides the best alternative. The White Papers introducing the National Enterprise Board and the Industrial Strategy were extraordinarily vague about what precise mechanism will be used in place of the price mechanism to allocate resources. Whenever the subject is approached it is immediately shrouded in an almost ritual-like incantation of 'the public interest'. Thus the NEB was to acquire and run firms 'in the public interest'; under the Industrial Strategy key industrial sectors were to be examined by working parties to see how their performance might be improved, 'in the public interest'. The unquestioned assumption is thus that with regard to industry X the public interest – as opposed to the interest of the current employees, owners and customers of industry X – can be discovered by an organization or tripartite committee and more efficient decisions can be made about the future commitment of resources to the industry than if such decisions are left to individual firms responding to a multitude of pressures and changes from the side of input supply or final product demand and to the discoveries of their research laboratories. At the very least it can be argued that the amount of information required to make an efficient decision on behalf of the public will almost certainly not be available in advance and in sufficient detail.[7] As a result the corporatist machinery is likely to become the vehicle for the kind of restrictions listed by Brittan, even though couched in terms of promoting the public interest.

We should add that a rejection of the corporatist approach to the problems posed by the presence of the giant companies is not unreservedly to accept the universal beneficence of market forces. The discussion in chapter 7 suggested that often this was quite clearly not the case. But the rejection does imply the approach has not been properly thought out and in particular that more flexible and efficient results may be available through a modified market system.

CONCLUSION

In the first part of this chapter we discussed the concept of 'social responsibility' which is often proposed as the complement to other 'external' policies, like antitrust, used to regulate firms' market behaviour. There was a danger that the concept may become discredited simply because its advocates had often been too ambitious and all-embracing in their definition with the result that it was difficult to see how the idea could be made operational. A central assumption of the school is that discretionary profits are available for large firms to devote to those policies which they regard as socially desirable. We suggested that this assumption depended on the too ready acceptance of the view that such firms could tame and control market forces to their own advantage and consequently the problem of a lack of a unified response to a particular 'social' problem (for example pollution) tended to be overlooked.

Arrow's analysis of the issue in terms of four 'social institutions', broadly interpreted (legal regulation, taxation, civil liability and ethical codes) although perhaps more mundane than some committed advocates of 'social responsibility' would like, did seem to provide a much sounder framework from which effective policies could emerge. Thus, given the problem of non-uniformity of response by competing firms, legal regulation (of, say, effluent discharges) is likely to provide a much more efficient solution than relying on the spontaneous action of the individual firms. On the other hand, where a central unifying value is held by all firms in a particular industry (for example worker safety and health) it may be possible, with substantial publicity and propaganda, to rely on a self-imposed ethical code. By a combination of policies based on these 'social institutions' Arrow at least considered that direct government intervention in the activities of the largest companies might be avoided.

Other observers have been less optimistic, as we saw in the third section. In the trend of aggregate concentration in the UK and the policy approach of successive governments, they have discerned an unhealthy drift towards corporatism with its emphasis on direct control over firms investment, and on co-operation and unity, at the expense of individual decision-making, competition and market processes. The policies reached a post-war climax in the UK with the Industry Act of 1975 which launched 'Planning Agreements' and the National Enterprise Board with the expectation of much greater direct control by government in the affairs of individual firms. In the event the original intentions were defeated by a combination of extreme wariness on the part of the biggest firms and other distracting problems for the government. The seductive plausibility of cor-poratism is likely to persist, however, as long as the organization of industry and labour remain as heavily concentrated as they are in the UK. Apart from the political dangers that such an approach implies, on purely economic grounds the main danger is that such policies, having no clearly articulated alternative mechanism for resource allocation, will degenerate into a system for trading restrictive practices. The outcome is then likely to be greater inefficiency and stagnation rather than the improvements in industrial performance that advocates of the policies envisage.

9

Disengagement by the State

INTRODUCTION

The antitrust and related policies discussed in chapter 7 are derived essentially from the neoclassical economic analysis of markets. The framework of the analysis is essentially static and the decisions of the agents involved are made with full information about prices and products and in the absence of uncertainty. Thus a monopolist (or group of colluding oligopolists) with complete information about demand and cost can set a profit-maximizing price in excess of marginal cost which (*ceteris paribus*) will lead to resource misallocation. A usual corollary is that such market power may well ensure that excessive profits can be persisently earned, given some barrier which prevents the entry of additional competitors. The implicit benchmark against which the monopoly is assessed is that of perfect competition where freedom of entry and complete information will, in equilibrium, bring prices into line with long-run marginal costs and eliminate the possibility of excess profits.

Despite many avowals that the model of perfect competition is simply a convenient analytical device and does not pretend to simulate conditions in actual markets, it is nevertheless, very often the case that policy proposals for the regulation of industry are derived, albeit indirectly, from the norms of perfect competition. It is this kind of inference that lies at the heart of the critique of orthodox analysis and policy proposals that we discuss in this chapter. Many of the criticisms can be most closely identified with the 'Austrian' School of economics in which there has been a recent resurgence of interest but on some points, especially where the interpretation of empirical evidence is concerned, there is some allegiance with the Chicago School.

The 'Austrians' take strong exception particularly to the

analysis of competition in neo-classical theory. They regard it at best as unhelpful and at worst positively misleading. Thus, they argue, that by assuming perfect information and certainty and by emphasizing equilibrium, the main elements of the *process* of competition in markets and the way that this leads to improvements in resource allocation are overlooked or ignored. It is like coming in at the end of act three of a drama rather than when the curtain is rising on act one: all the subtleties of character and plot have been disclosed, all the misunderstanding, mysteries and mistakes have been resolved and all that remains is the final applause of an admiring audience. Their emphasis, in contrast, is on competition as a process of discovery of fresh profit-making opportunities by entrepreneurial activity. The emphasis, therefore, is on change rather than equilibrium; on finding new information rather than knowing everything in advance; on adjusting to mistakes and miscalculations rather than proceeding smoothly like an engine in a frictionless environment.

Since they regard the theoretical underpinning of much anti-trust policy as largely suspect, it is not surprising that proponents of the 'Austrian' view are sceptical of its relevance and effectiveness. Given a correct framework of law, especially on property rights, they argue that markets, on the whole, produce a more satisfactory result than the available alternatives. Furthermore, an enlarged scope for free markets is, on this view, an indispensable part of the freedom of the individual and a bulwark against the dangers of the Corporate State.

We propose in the second section of this chapter to discuss the 'Austrian' analysis of these questions and the grounds on which they reject or modify most of the mainstream conclusions. In the third section we then examine their policy proposals, saving our doubts about their relevance to an economy as concentrated as that of the UK to the conclusion.

COMPETITION AND MONOPOLY: THE CRITIQUE OF THE CONVENTIONAL APPROACH

It is as well to start by making it clear that one of the main themes of this book – the problems posed by the dominance of capitalist economies by a comparatively few giant firms – has never really troubled those writing in the Austrian or Chicago traditions. Indeed they seem to regard it with supreme indifference. The attitude was made quite explicit more than a quarter of a century ago by a leading Chicago writer on industrial economics George Stigler. In a review of a book analysing the record of the 200 largest US industrial companies over a period of fifty years and the growth of aggregate concentration, Stigler criticized the whole enterprise for its 'dramatic irrelevance' (Stigler, 1956; p. 37). Similarly in his evidence before the Senate Subcommittee on Antitrust and Monopoly in 1964, M. A. Adelman anticipated the support of 'most of my fellow economists' in his comprehensive dismissal of absolute size as 'absolutely irrelevant' (Adelman, 1964; p. 228). On this view the only size that might be relevant to the economic analysis of industry, is size in relation to a recognizable market, where, under certain circumstances, a large market share may be associated with monopoly power.

Writers in the Austrian tradition either remain silent on the issue, presumably because they do not recognize its existence, or while raising the question of aggregate concentration, pretend that it has not increased (Jewkes, 1977; Reekie, 1979) and can therefore be ignored. Attention can then be more clearly focused on the central issue which is the nature of the competitive process and the real sources of monopoly power.

Although the two groups of writers draw their inspiration from different sources and disagree quite fundamentally on a number of points,[1] they are perhaps closest in their analysis of enterprise and markets, and especially on the resulting policy conclusions. For convenience in the remainder of this chapter we shall not distinguish the two schools (unless it is of major importance to do so) bearing in mind the recent dictum of undoubtedly the most famous Chicagoan that 'there is no Austrian economics – only good economics and bad economics' (Milton Friedman, quoted in Dolan, 1976: p. 4).

In common with a diverse range of critics of neo-classical economic theory, the current elder statesman of Austrian economics, F. A. Hayek, has for long been highly critical of the dominant role played both in pure analysis and policy by the theory of 'perfect competition' (Hayek, 1948; chaps. 2, 4 and 5: 1978; chap. 12). The core of his argument is that from the outset, the assumptions of the theory ensure that 'competition' in any meaningful and therefore useful sense is precluded. One consequence of this has always been that businessmen, operating in a continually uncertain and changing environment can find nothing in the economists model of 'perfect competition' that they would regard as competition at all. This failure would perhaps be unimportant if economists did not use the results of the theory for making judgements about the actual behaviour and performance of industry which may have a direct influence on policy and so change the conditions in which firms have to work.

The elements of the theory of perfect competition are well enough known not to detain us by detailed elaboration here. The main assumptions are of a homogeneous commodity offered and demanded by a great number of relatively small suppliers and customers, none of whom can therefore exert any control over price; free entry and exit for resources into the market; and *complete knowledge of the relevant factors on the part of all participants in the market* (Hayek, 1948, italics added). The main emphasis of the Austrian critique of the theory is aimed at this last assumption which in their view robs it of any useful content. With these assumptions the theory of perfect competition 'deals almost exclusively with a state of competitive equilibrium in which it is assumed that the data for the different individuals are fully adjusted to each other while the problem which requires explanation is the *nature of the process by which the data are thus adjusted*' (Hayek, 1948, p. 94, italics added). The assumption of perfect knowledge, therefore, far from being merely a useful simplifying device, legitimate in model building, precludes the analysis of the very subject that it is supposed to address. As Hayek goes on to say, competition must by its very nature be a dynamic process and thus is not amenable to comparative statics. The implications of the assumption of perfect knowledge are very far reaching as the following contrast between the theory of 'perfect competition' and the theory of 'market process' attempts to show. With perfect knowledge, for example, of lowest cost production methods amongst producers, and of all prevailing prices amongst consumers, the co-ordination of producers and consumers plans are smoothly achieved. The equilibrium between sellers and buyers will be maintained until some new disturbance occurs, such as a change in tastes or reduction in costs. As a result of the assumption of perfect knowledge exact details of the change are immediately transmitted to all actual or potential market participants who can again readily synchronize their plans and arrive at a new equilibrium.

In contrast, the theory of 'market process' emphasises the lack of information about such factors as the lowest-cost production methods,[2] the precise size and nature of consumer demands for the particular product at particular times and places. Much of the energy of sellers will therefore be expended in attempting to discover precisely the kinds of information which is assumed in the static theory to be already available. By their efforts in modifying production and distribution methods as well as prices, and by the simultaneous searching and experimentation by consumers, their previously unco-ordinated plans move closer together. What starts out as a wide dispersion of market prices may gradually narrow as more information about conditions in the market is used both by producers and consumers. Although in principle the prices (for a homogeneous product) could converge eventually on 'the competitive price', it is important to recognize that this would only happen when no further new information, experiment or change was forthcoming or even conceivable. But under these circumstances, as Hayek suggests, 'if at any moment we knew that all change had stopped and things would forever go on exactly as they are now there would be no more questions of the use of resources to be solved' (Hayek, 1948; p. 101).

The search for fresh information by sellers and buyers which can improve their position in the market is termed 'entrepreneurial' by Austrian writers. Because of their great emphasis on search, experiment and adjustment to change, they place 'entrepreneurial behaviour' at the centre of the economic stage rather than in the wings (or even in a forgotten storeroom where most recent textbook writers are content to leave it). In comparative static analysis and with perfect information there is no scope for entrepreneurial behaviour. Hence in books discussing neoclassical microeconomics the 'entrepreneur' has either disappeared altogether or makes a fleeting appearance as the owner or controller (or both) of the production unit.[3]

The stimulus to entrepreneurial behaviour on the part of sellers is the opportunity that it gives for making profits. By discovering a method of satisfying consumer needs at a lower price than previously or being able to employ resources, hitherto used to satisfy a rather lower valued consumer want, to satisfy a more highly valued consumer want, the entrepreneur is able to make profits. The fact that he is successful in this enterprise indicates that before his action the plans of sellers and buyers were not perfectly co-ordinated. By seizing the hitherto unrealized opportunities for making profits, the entrepreneur has assisted in the synchronization of the plans of buyers and sellers. Only where these plans are already perfectly fulfilled is there no further scope for entrepreneurial activity. But as we have seen above, in such a state there are no problems of resource allocation left to solve. The realization of entrepreneurial profits is likely to be at the expense of other producers whose position is disturbed by a competitor grasping an opportunity that they themselves had not foreseen or discovered. Except under special circumstances that we discuss below, however, the same potential for entrepreneurial profits was available to them had they been sufficiently alert. On the other hand, many entrepreneurial sallies may fail because of a misreading of the existing market information and mistakes in anticipating consumer demands.

The interpretation, by writers in the Austrian tradition, of competition as a dynamic process of discovery and of the role of entrepreneurial profits leads them to take quite a different view from neo-classical writers of monopoly and the symptoms of monopoly power. We noted in chapter 5 that observers using a market-structure, -conduct, and -performance framework for the economic analysis of industry seemed much more ready to find monopoly profits than either their analysis or the evidence perhaps warranted. It is not too much of an exaggeration to suggest that writers in the Austrian tradition tend to the opposite extreme: they are hard-pressed to find any genuine monopoly profits at all. For example, in two recent expositions, although the authors give examples both homely (conkers, shipped to Australia) and dramatic (Rank-Xerox, photocopying equipment) of enterprises that have earned entrepreneurial profits and although monopoly profit as a distinct category is recognized, no examples of the latter breed are given[4] (Littlechild, 1978; Reekie, 1979). A major reason for this is their comparatively restricted view of monopoly. Only in the case where a firm owns the entire stock of some resource necessary for producing a good which other firms would like to produce but are prevented from doing so by the existing firm (not the government) does true monopoly, on this view, exist. Only in such cases, therefore, will monopoly profits be earned. Specifically excluded from this category are cases where a firm appears to have a monopoly because it is the sole seller of a good or service but where other firms do not find it worthwhile to enter the industry, even though there is no restriction. (This category appears to include both the 'natural' monopoly case of substantial economies of scale but where the extent of market demand allows only one firm to operate profitably, and the case of limited demand where the threat of entry keeps the profits of the single seller to a 'modest' level.) Similarly excluded are cases where a firm has, through entrepreneurial insight and energy, captured a market with a new or modified product and is earning high returns, as long as its position does not depend on exclusive ownership of a unique resource. Sooner or later, depending largely on the technology of the industry involved, such a firm's position will be weakened by substitute and imitative products, and also by the further discoveries of other firms.

What further divides the 'mainstream' writers from the 'Austrians' on this issue of monopoly profit seems largely to turn on their different interpretations of 'free entry' and 'entry barriers'. Although, as Littlechild (1978; p. 33) admits 'Austrian views on markets with few producers – oligopoly – are somewhat ambiguous and not treated at much length', yet their definition of the lack of free entry in the monopoly case seems equally applicable to the more intractable but probably more common, oligopoly. Thus, as we have seen, entry barriers will only exist either where the state has granted some special privilege which excludes newcomers or where existing firms own some unique resource which they deny to others. This interpretation is very close to that of the classical writers but stands in sharp contrast to the modern view which owes much to the work of Bain.[5] In his most widely known work Bain identified three main sources of entry barrier: product differentiation, economies of scale, and a more general category that he called 'absolute cost advantages'. Later writers have elaborated his analysis and sometimes changed the emphasis but essentially his original conception remains intact. Now, while the 'absolute cost' category, if interpreted broadly enough, can include both state-granted privileges and exclusive control of a unique resource and thus fall within the Austrian definition of entry barriers, it is immediately evident that the other categories cannot be so included. Scale economies are quite explicitly ruled out. Product differentiation, which we discussed at some length in chapter 4, is not recognized as an entry barrier by Austrian (or Chicago) writers on the grounds that as long as access to the resources necessary to differentiate products remains open, then it cannot be argued that entry to the industry is prevented by established firms. The argument has been forcefully put by Demsetz who concentrates on advertising expenditures (the source of product differentiation that has probably received most attention):

> It is said that existing firms have created a preference for their products through the use of advertising and, therefore, that new competitors need to advertise even more intensely if they are to attract customers. But the firms now in the industry once needed to attract customers away from the established products of other industries, to an unknown new product, so it is not at all clear that new entrants suffer a disadvantage as compared with those who showed the way. (Demsetz, 1974; p. 174)

In short, most sources of entry barriers in conventional textbook discussions are rejected as such by writers in the Austrian–Chicago tradition.

More important for our purpose in this chapter, they also reject the policy implications that seem to flow readily from the orthodox view. This proceeds briefly as follows. In the presence of entry barriers, as conventionally defined, and with 'moderate' or 'high' concentration, collusion between existing firms will tend to be the rule rather than the exception. The existing firms will thus jointly be able to earn a monopoly return and possibly allow themselves to become slack without their position being undermined by an undisciplined competitor. Resources will, therefore, be misallocated. To prevent these results or at least to minimize their occurrence there should be strong antitrust policies including strict control of mergers, prosecution of 'parallel action' and even the dismemberment of companies deemed guilty of abusing a position of market power.

We have already discussed in chapter 5 this over pessimistic view of the ease with which oligopolists can achieve a stable joint-profit-maximizing position. We might add that the apparent lack of direct-price competition in oligopoly may mask first, intense competition in discounts from list prices and secondly, the more profound effect of competition from new products, processes, organizational and distribution methods which may shift the balance of power in a market much more profoundly than a marginal price adjustment.

The main thrust of the critique by Austrians of the orthodox view, however, is aimed at the underlying comparison between what is claimed to happen under oligopoly with what would happen under perfect competition. In view of our earlier remarks on the Austrian rejection of the concept, it is not surprising to find

Hayek amongst the most influential critics even though his views were first published thirty-five years ago. He argues that it is misleading and dangerous to use, however indirectly, the benchmark of perfect competition to draw out policy inferences when such a state is not possible:

> There is no sense in talking of a use of resources 'as if' a perfect market existed if this means that the resources would have to be different from what they are, or in discussing what somebody with perfect knowledge would do if our task must be to make the best use of the knowledge the existing people have. (Hayek, 1948; p. 104)

Despite imperfections, he argues that the market under most circumstances will perform that task better than any of the available alternatives, even if this means that some individuals for some time are selling products in excess of marginal costs and making high profits. A firm which discovers a new way of lowering the cost of production will be in such a position:

> Even if in each instance prices were only just enough to keep out producers which do not enjoy these or other equivalent advantages, so that each commodity were produced as cheaply as possible, though many may be sold at prices considerably above costs, this would probably be a result which could not be achieved by any other method than that of letting competition operate. (Hayek, 1948; p. 101)

A similar view has recently been put by Fisher who argues that if existing firms are forced to reduce their prices to a level that just prevents the entry of new firms, then 'competition is doing its job' (Fisher, 1979; p. 30). Positive profits are thus quite compatible with competition which is delivering the best performance from the feasible choices available. The argument is reminiscent of the reply given by the ninety-year-old man on being asked what he thought about being very aged: 'Well, its better than the alternative.' Unlike the 'perfect' abstraction, real competition involves positive information costs, positive costs of actually mobilizing resources plus 'the heavy hand of chance'. The correct question for policy, therefore, is not 'the degree to which a market descriptively diverges from perfect competition but the degree to which it diverges in either direction from that intensity of competition which takes account of the real social costs of competing' (Demsetz, 1976; p. 374). We can now consider the kind of policy proposals to which the foregoing analysis leads.

178 *Part Three: Policies*

ANTITRUST POLICY AND THE MARKET PROCESS

We are fortunate in having available a recent statement of the policy implications given by a writer inspired by the Austrian tradition (Littlechild, 1978; especially chapters VI and VII). His book was written partly in response to that of Meade (1975) mentioned in chapter 7 and for ease of comparison with that chapter we shall deal with the proposals for monopoly and concentrated oligopoly, mergers and restrictive practices in the same order.

A natural outcome of the somewhat narrow vision of the bases of monopoly and the short-lived nature of high profits, is the suggestion that existing competition policy should be severely curtailed. In a country like the UK where present policy is viewed by many observers as already over modest, this proposal might be very difficult to understand. But it follows logically from the Austrian analysis of monopoly, entrepreneurship and the role of profit. Thus Littlechild proposes that the British Monopolies and Mergers Commission in its enquiries into 'dominant' firms (those with control of one-quarter or more of the market) should confine its attention to the identification of the sources of monopoly power. Unfortunately he does not give any examples from recent reports of the Commission of what would be so considered by a writer of the Austrian School. In recent years the Commission has discovered a rich variety of 'things done' by dominant firms which it considered were attempts to preserve or strengthen the firms' position and which it recommended should be ended. For example, Courtaulds were criticized for giving favourable terms to a subsidiary, Roche for giving drugs away free to the hospital service and armed forces, Unilever and Procter and Gamble for 'excessive' advertising, Birds Eye Foods for giving extra discounts for exclusive contracts, and so on.[6] Although these strategies were clearly intended to strengthen the position of the existing firm *vis-à-vis* rivals or potential entrants, since similar terms or offers could be made to customers by competing companies and since existing firms did not have exclusive control over some essential resource,[7] it is doubtful whether in Austrian eyes any of these practices would constitute 'sources of monopoly power'. Failing their explicit recognition by an Austrian, however, this conclusion must remain tentative.

If the Commission were to confine itself to identifying sources of monopoly power, it would not be able to assess the performance of dominant companies. Yet one of the key points in many recent reports has been an evaluation of the profitability of such companies. As we saw in chapter 7 although the Commission has been quite prepared to recognize the role of exceptionally high profits under some conditions, there have also been a number of cases where very high profits have been condemned as an abuse of monopoly power. With Littlechild's proposal put into effect, this part of the Commission's work would cease. Again, from the analysis of entrepreneurial action and the role of profits in the previous section, it is not difficult to understand why this proposal should be made. What on the conventional view, might be interpreted as excessive profit resulting from market power is seen from an Austrian standpoint as simply the reward for alert entrepreneurship. As long as similar opportunities were and are open to competitors, then no abuse has occurred. Indeed to the extent that a body like the Commission is instrumental in getting profits reduced (and in some cases past profits repaid) it will be stifling future entrepreneurial endeavours and this will imply a misallocation of resources since producer and consumer plans will be less completely harmonized than they would otherwise have been.

Part of the Austrian critique of the profitability analysis of bodies like the Monopolies and Mergers Commission concerns the period of time involved. While the Commission may consider that a period of perhaps 5–10 years is long enough to determine whether profits reflect market power rather than some other temporary influence, the Austrian view is that all profits[8] are in their nature ephemeral and will sooner or later be eroded by the entrepreneurial action of competitors. With the emphasis firmly placed on competition as a dynamic process it is to be expected that profitability and market shares will vary considerably through time. On this view the 'top' in any market will be a slippery place although there is clearly great scope for controversy about what is meant by 'sooner or later'. After all glaciers can be said to slip as well as avalanches. In principle, however, this analysis of competition and its effects on individual firms should be amenable to at least partial verification, Hayek notwithstanding.[9] The fact that this aspect of the competitive process has received comparatively little direct attention is perhaps a partial vindication of the criticism that orthodox theory has concentrated too much on statics at the expense of dynamics. Thus a plethora of statistics on product and industry concentration have been collected in the USA and UK, while little or nothing is

known about the rate of turnover of leading firms. It has frequently been pointed out that the level of seller concentration for
a particular product may have remained 'high' for a number of
years and yet if none of the leading firms in the first year
remained at the top in the last year this would suggest that the
competitive struggle had been very intense even though in any
one year the market leaders had sizeable market shares. Reekie,
writing from an Austrian perspective attempts to illustrate the
point with three recent examples from British manufacturing
industry (Reekie,1979; p. 25). In each case (cigarettes, soap
powders and petrol retailing) although the market leader
remained on top, its market share had diminished by the end of
the period shown.[10] With some digging around in official and
trade publications it may be possible to increase this list by
perhaps a dozen products but in comparison with the 300 or so
concentration ratios recently published,[11] this is obviously a negligible amount. Perhaps some of the ingenuity shown in refining
measures of concentration should be devoted to the task of devis-
ing a summary measure of changes in market shares, in a form
publishable in the official statistics. Such a measure would give a
much clearer indication of the intensity of competition and thus
allow us, to some extent, to gauge the vigour of entrepreneurial
activity in an economy as concentrated as that of the UK.

We lack also systematic evidence on the behaviour of profit
rates earned by different firms in different markets over time. As
we have seen, some case-study material is available from the
reports of the Monopolies and Mergers Commission even though
Austrians may be loath to agree that what the reports have sometimes uncovered are monopoly returns. But profit figures for a
long enough period, for fairly distinct markets and for a large
cross section of industry are not available. Unfortunately a recent
study which purports to address this question by examining the
aggregate profit figures for a sample of the largest US manufacturing firms misses the main point. The finding that profits 'above
the norm' tend to persist through time for these companies really
tells us nothing about whether they face a 'competitive' or
'monopolistic' environment in the individual markets in which they
operate, despite repeated assertions by the author to the contrary
(Mueller, 1977). It is well established not only that the largest
firms tend to be more diversified than others but also that the
extent of their diversification has been increasing recently. Profitable firms in one period may, therefore, retain their position in

subsequent periods through active diversification even though profits in their original lines may be falling due to competition. Persistently high total profits by diversified firms, therefore, are quite consistent with active competition in all their markets. The data that the Monopolies and Mergers Commission extracts, albeit for a comparatively small sample of products showing profits on a narrowly defined basis, are much more suitable for testing this hypothesis than the consolidated information for a broad range of products used by outside researchers.

Clearly existing data leave much to be desired when trying to test the dynamic theory of competition. But the logic of the Austrian theory points to a policy towards monopoly which would restrict enquiries to identifying the sources of monopoly power. That this would be a fairly minimal commitment is also evident from the definition of monopoly and entry barriers which we discussed in the previous section.

The same logic may be carried over to those monopolies legally conferred on companies in the private sector in the form of patents. In many countries the sole right to the use of information on a patented product or process is regarded as a necessary stimulant to invention. For many years, therefore, a company with a patent to a key process may be effectively insulated from effective competition. The monopoly profit, the reward for innovation, remains legally immune from the entrepreneurial efforts of others unless they in turn can outflank the existing patent with new knowledge of their own. The dilemma which confronts mainstream writers on this subject (that is whether the restriction on competition which patents allow pays off in more rapid technical progress) is even more acute for writers in the Austrian tradition. Having defined monopoly purely as the control over some unique resource which prevents any newcomer entering the industry, this should logically include the sole rights conferred by patents. It is interesting that Littlechild, although defending the profits of Rank-Xerox and Roche from the conventional attack that they were abusing their dominant position, does suggest that 'presumably one of the reasons for the high level of profits, and for the lack of actively competing firms, is the existence of patents' (Littlechild, 1978; p. 47). His remedy, consistent with his view of the competitive process, is that all patent protection should be abolished (p. 80). He is confident that the incentives this would give for new entry to fields previously blocked by patent barriers would lead to improved industrial performance and that this would outweigh any adverse consequences on the rate of invention. Without going quite so far other writers have proposed that the value of patented ideas should be assessed and the sum paid out of the public purse in return for free access to the information for whoever wants it, mainly on the grounds that as it can be made available at (practically) zero marginal cost it should therefore have a zero price. A reward for invention would thus remain but without the simultaneous restriction on competition. The problem, of course, which Austrians may be quick to point out, is that the assessment of the value of an invention soon after it is first made will, in most cases, be very difficult to determine, if only because no-one can be sure what other discoveries are about to be made or how a particular discovery may be incorporated into many others not originally foreseen. The drastic step proposed by Littlechild is unlikely to be even approached by a country like the UK which has recently moved in the opposite direction by extending the period of patent protection from sixteen to twenty years. But if most of the genuine monopoly power exercised by some of the largest companies does come from patent protection a reform along the lines of that above may be much more effective in curbing it than some of the 'mainstream' antitrust policies discussed in chapter 7.[12]

An equally clear-cut and brief policy proposal is made by the Austrian writers on mergers: abolish all merger supervision and control (Littlechild, 1978; p. 80). Since the buying and selling of companies or their fusion into a new unit can be regarded simply as another aspect of the competitive process, the reshaping of industrial structure that results will, on this view, bring a more satisfactory co-ordination of economic activity than any available alternative. Thus the frustration of merger plans by antitrust policy on the grounds that it would have led to monopoly or a significant decline in competition, is short sighted and misguided. Short sighted because it sees only the immediate effect of increased concentration in the market and not the longer term effects of either the merged company's greater competitiveness or the process of competition which will erode its market share; misguided because it implies that the antitrust authority has access to more complete and detailed information about the future course of events in the market than those most likely to be directly affected and therefore most ready to respond to the unforeseen changes. Writers of this persuasion are not, therefore, hampered by the niceties of estimating net welfare benefits which, as we saw in chapter 7, has been the main focus of recent orthodox discussion of merger policy. The trade-off between the adverse effects of market power and the beneficial effects of greater economies – even if it is cast in dynamic terms – does not arise. Mergers cannot create monopoly (of the Austrian kind) but they are part of the competitive process and may result in improved efficiency. If the plans of the merging companies fail because of unforeseen circumstances (as some of them undoubtedly will) then 'what the market has put together it can also take apart'. Within this framework, therefore, there is not even a place for a limited fall-back position which broadly speaking has been the UK policy providing for the detailed scrutiny and possible prevention of only those rare merger specimens that would result in such a large market share as to create a strong presumption of future monopoly power.

Although less directly relevant to the position of the largest firms we can also mention briefly the Austrian attitude to cartels. As we might expect by now it conflicts with the orthodox view. Thus although Littlechild mentions a possible dilemma, he concludes nevertheless that 'most Austrians would probably not favour laws against restrictive practices, relying for protection once again on the possibility that new entry would overcome such barriers' (Littlechild, 1978; p. 49). Since the whole rationale of most cartels is to impede entry and the competitive process, the conclusion is, at first glance, a little surprising in view of the crucial role played by competition in the Austrian analysis. Furthermore a defence of many cartels is that by preventing the uncertainties of competition existing firms will feel secure enough to make large investments which otherwise they would regard as too risky. In other industries, as British experience amply demonstrated,[13] the conduct of cartels was specifically designed to make entry by newcomers as difficult as possible. One example was exclusive dealing maintained by aggregated rebates. In such a scheme distributors agree to trade only with manufacturing members of the cartel in return for rebates based on their total purchases from *all* members rather than their purchases from a single firm. An entrant is therefore confronted with the unenviable choice of either trying to match these aggregated rebates which have nothing to do with economies achieved by individual firms, or establishing his own distribution system which his competitors can avoid.

How, then, are such deliberate attempts to impede the competitive process reconciled with a policy view that on the whole favours the abolition of control over cartels?[14] The answer lies in the very great confidence the writers have in the strength of competitive forces reasserting themselves, even where careful steps have been taken to undermine them. On this they can draw on the orthodox analysis which emphasizes the great difficulties that existing firms will have harmonizing their members interests, especially where there are different levels of efficiency and financial strength. Some may want relatively low prices and large output, others may prefer higher prices with a consequently lower output. The compromise price level will almost certainly run the risk that some firms will 'cheat' to increase their profits. As this becomes known recriminations will start and more and more sales will be made below the 'official' price level. In other words cartels are inherently unstable and will periodically collapse due to conflicts of interest. But in addition to these internal forces Austrian writers also stress the perpetual pressures from outside: from new products, or processes, new sources of supply (for example imports) new methods of organization (for example direct selling to customers) as well as changes in consumer tastes. Thus although they are perhaps slightly less wholehearted in their recommendation for the complete abandonment of control over restrictive practices than over mergers, they place much greater emphasis on the spontaneous 'controls' provided by the market.

Before concluding this section it is appropriate to add a few words on the attitude these writers take to the nationalized industries. Although our main concern is with policies towards very large private-sector companies we have already discussed in chapter 7 the proposal for the state to act as an entrepreneur and have its own companies competing with private-sector firms in markets where competitive forces appear weak. A mirror image of this proposal is made by writers in the Austrian tradition. In view of their definition of monopoly it is not surprizing that they are strongly opposed to the state granting legal monopolies to the nationalized industries. They are very sceptical of the effectiveness of government controls on the performance of these enterprises and their policy proposals are therefore intended to re-establish competition wherever possible. Thus for some profitable industries like telecommunications, intra-city postal services and even gas and electricity supply the repeal of the statutory monopoly to allow new entry is recommended. The corollary of this proposal is that if a nationalized enterprise sees a profitable opportunity in another field then it should be free to invest in it. In those cases where, as Littlechild puts it, competition *within* the market is not feasible, competition *for* the market could be developed. One possibility, for example, is to auction short-term franchises for local power and gas supplies just as independent television and local radio are organized in the UK at present.

For all nationalized enterprises the objectives should be set out clearly and in terms which are both operational and easy to monitor. Thus Littlechild favours targets such as a specified level of net revenue or self financing as against marginal cost pricing and the use of a test rate of discount. Since these criteria would apply to those industries currently making losses (and where presumably no new entrants would appear even if allowed) they would have to trim their scale of activities so as to meet their performance criteria. The precise extent and method of finance of any 'social obligations' should be made explicit and subject to the control of Parliament, as essentially a political question rather than one of economics. With this exception, the nationalized industries should be completely free of governmental control.

Littlechild recognizes that under present circumstances this last proposal in particular is very unlikely to be adopted,[15] especially as he argues that the real motive behind much British nationalization is not to promote the efficient allocation of resources but to prevent it (Littlechild, 1978; p. 58). Largely for this reason other writers in this tradition have volunteered more fundamental suggestions for improving the performance of nationalized enterprises. Thus Friedman (1977) has proposed giving them away, via an issue of shares in a 'mutual fund' to all citizens of the UK who after all, as he argues, are supposed to be their real owners in any case. Thereafter a market in the shares would arise similar to those that already operate for shares in private sector companies. Clearly this is a much more radical proposal than simply opening up the nationalized industries to more competition but Friedman envisaged it as part of a larger programme of 'unwinding' government involvement in the economy.[16] For the nationalized industries this would obviously be the disengagement *par excellence*, the ultimate solution to a perennial problem.

CONCLUSION

Perhaps the most important part of the contribution of Austrian writers to the debate about policy towards the private sector, even one dominated by a few giants, is the stress they place on competition as a dynamic process, worked out against a background of ignorance and uncertainty. It provides a useful counterweight to the more extreme recommendations made by some other observers who base their conclusions on a different analytical framework. Calls for the break-up of large companies, for example, seem largely based on a static rather than a dynamic view of competition. Furthermore, the point stressed originally by Hayek and recently re-emphasized by Demsetz and Fisher is that the performance of industry, especially in heavily concentrated markets, should be assessed not according to some unattainable ideal but according to what the next best alternative would offer. This is likely to provide a much more salutary guide to the policy maker than recommendations stemming, however obliquely, from the theory of perfect competition with its crucial assumption of full information.

There are, therefore, definite gains to be made from a study of Austrian and related ideas. However, it is when we come to examine some of the detailed conclusions and recommendations (especially when these are put into a particular context such as UK manufacturing industry in the last quarter of the twentieth century) that doubts arise. For example, whether one appeals by way of explanation to the predictions of Marx or simply to the central limit theorem, the facts show at least to most observers, that capitalist economies tend over time and with some interruptions to become more and more heavily concentrated. One possible consequence of this which in view of the analysis should be of central importance, is that entrepreneurial incentives might become increasingly weakened. A number of writers have argued that managers of very large enterprises may be much less willing to take risks, especially those associated with innovation and change, than the (owner) managers of smaller firms. One reason may be the asymmetry between 'punishment' and rewards. Thus while the manager of a large enterprise may suffer as a result of a risky new project which turns out badly, either by being shunted into the equivalent of a career-siding or even by being unseated following a successful takeover bid, he is unlikely to gain fully from projects that turn out successfully. His salary may increase but nothing like in proportion to the increase in profitability and value of the assets he administers. Thus if the people involved in making entrepreneurial decisions about new products, processes, organizational methods and so on are not necessarily the main beneficiaries from any resulting profits, they are likely to prefer less hazardous and nerve-racking policies. For this reason it has been argued that an economy dominated by a comparatively small number of giant firms may be less dynamic than one consisting of a much greater number of medium-sized and smaller firms, each a centre of individual initiative.

Surprisingly little, however, has been written by recent writers in the Austrian tradition on this and related points. The impression created is that so long as impediments to entrepreneurial behaviour are minimized it is immaterial whether the economy has one-hundred firms or one-million: entrepreneurial endeavours are likely to be as intense now as they were a century ago. If industry is open to new competition then, in this view, that is a sufficient condition for industrial performance in the long-run to be the best attainable. For this reason Reekie feels able to apply the above argument, on asymmetric rewards, to nationalized enterprises but not to their private sector counterparts. But many would argue that the largest private-sector enterprises show many of the characteristics of nationalized enterprises and are just as likely to suffer from bureaucratic timidity.

A second and related point concerns the time taken for the competitive process to come into full play. It may take many years (even in the absence of effective patents) for new entrants[17] to erode the profits of a single enterprise or small group of enterprises which have attained a dominant position in a market, albeit originally due to entrepreneurial far-sightedness. It is not unreasonable from their point of view that they should use some of their high profits simply to maintain their position. One way may be through bribery, political lobbying and special advertising campaigns. On other occasions the best option may be to acquire any rivals which show signs of challenging their position. Many may feel, therefore, that in such cases it is quite compatible with most of the Austrian analysis for the state to have available the machinery to prevent such acquisitions. Similarly except in a few instances there is a good case for making it as difficult as possible for firms to collude in order to frustrate the competitive process. At the very least, therefore, the onus of proof should lie with those wishing to maintain a cartel, rather than with those objecting to their presence.

The attitude of the 'disengagement' school on all three issues would probably be that there are good reasons to suppose that the performance of industry would be no better with the policies than without them. They would be similarly opposed to the kinds of discriminatory tax policies in favour of small firms that we discussed in chapter 7. According to their analysis the spontaneous adjustment of the market will inevitably produce a superior performance because it is based on a fuller use of all of the information disbursed amongst suppliers and customers than could possibly be achieved by an administrative or legal agency, however well intentioned. The conclusion applies so long as the basic legal framework is appropriate, regardless of the present and probable future size distribution of firms. Put in this way the power of the market becomes practically an article of faith because it is not possible to test the validity of the analysis. Whatever the performance of an unrestricted market yields 'must', on this view, be for the best, for although we obviously cannot know what would have happened had, say, certain large mergers been prevented, we do know (because theoretical analysis tells us) that the alternative would have been inferior. It is ironic that writers in the Austrian tradition who have been highly critical of 'historicists' for accepting the inevitability of certain trends in economic development have themselves apparently fallen prey to a similar species of mystical belief.

10

The Left and 'Monopoly Capitalism'

INTRODUCTION

In the last chapter we argued that, if anything, members of the Austrian school placed no special significance on the growth of the largest companies and their position in the modern economy. Since many of them had never relied on the theory of *perfect* competition but had emphasized imperfect information and competition as a dynamic process, they saw no fundamental difference between an economy where the largest private enterprises produced a negligible proportion of total output and one where they accounted for a major part of the whole and employed directly and indirectly hundreds of thousands of people. As long as the possibilities for entry and innovation were kept open and the incentives for entrepreneurial profits maintained, then markets, by and large, would deliver the best available performance regardless of the somewhat incidental size of the individual firms concerned.

For writers of the 'Left' this view has, of course, always been untenable. Members of what, for convenience, we will call the 'Old Left'[1] have always viewed the growth of the corporate giants as confirmation of the Marxian prediction of the increasing concentration of capital. In this respect the work of Baran and Sweezy is especially important. In *Monopoly Capital* (Baran and Sweezy, 1977) they attempt to reconcile the main thrust of Marx's analysis of the development of capitalism with the emergence of giant enterprises and the implications that this had for competition between them and their ability to gain an *increasing* amount of monopoly profit. They thus put the largest enterprises (or monopolies as they prefer to call them) 'at the very centre of the analytical effort' (p. 20). We discuss their central thesis on pp. 190–194 below. Writers of the 'New Left' who came to prominence in the latter part of the 1960s and early 1970s while fully recognizing the dominant role played by such enterprises in modern capitalism, placed particular emphasis on what they saw as possibly the most pernicious and all-pervading consequence of this development, namely the 'alienation' and false consciousness of the working class. The implications of this analysis are also considered in the second section.

It is when we turn from the diagnosis of the ills of capitalism, in which the corporate giants have a leading role, to the solutions offered by the Left for change, that the real difficulties start. For with few exceptions the cupboard is bare. Most writers who have drawn their main inspiration from Marx seem to feel that having analysed thoroughly and often with great ingenuity the inconsistencies of capitalism and its fairly imminent demise that the task is done, and historical inevitability can be relied on to do the rest. Baran and Sweezy make it clear from the sub-title of their book that they are writing 'an essay on the American Economic and Social Order'. Hence they may feel absolved from any responsibility for explaining in detail how economic problems would be solved in the era following monopoly capitalism. The same point can be made about those from the 'New Left' who are long on diagnosis and critique and short on prescription and remedy. Some proposals that have been made, including worker-managed firms, we discuss in the third section.

MONOPOLY CAPITALISM AND THE GROWING SURPLUS

The main task that Baran and Sweezy tackled was to explain why in the era of monopoly capitalism there is a chronic tendency for the giant enterprises to generate a greater and greater economic surplus which has to be absorbed in some way or another if the system is to survive. It is thus a bold attempt to bring Marxian analysis to bear on the type of economy that exists in the US (which they regard as the most highly developed capitalist economy) in the second half of the twentieth century. The predominant place in that economy is taken by a comparatively small number of giant enterprises which clearly have enormous economic and social power. In such an economy instead of the rate of profit dwindling, as Marx, starting from a different microeconomic structure predicted, the central problem becomes one of ensuring that the growing economic surplus that the market power of the giant enterprises allows, can be absorbed and thus avoid the collapse of the whole system under the weight of its internal contradictions.

Overshadowing the economy, like a vast albatross, is thus the economic surplus ('the difference between total social output and the socially necessary cost of producing it' (Baran and Sweezy, 1977; p. 117)) which grows with the increasing dominance of the monopoly enterprises and requires more and more ingenious methods for its absorption. To sustain their thesis the authors have first to explain how the surplus arises and grows under monopoly capitalism and then how it is maintained, partly by the efforts of the giant enterprises themselves through their sales efforts and partly by their interaction or symbiosis with the political and military complex. In the space available we concentrate our attention on the first part of their analysis (how the surplus arises) and part of the second (its absorption through the sales effort) because this is most directly relevant to our main theme.

In order to explain monopoly capitalism's chronic tendency to produce a surplus, Baran and Sweezy use a comparatively naive model of price determination under oligopoly. They make it plain that oligopoly amongst the giant enterprises is their central concern rather than single-firm monopoly because 'today there are probably fewer genuine monopolies than there were at the turn of the century, but there is also infinitely less cut-throat competition' (Baran and Sweezy, 1977; p. 61). This admission is a bit puzzling because genuine monopolists are likely to have an easier time raising their price and restricting their output than oligopolists who have to reach a common understanding. The surplus might then tend to be higher under monopoly than under oligopoly. However, according to Baran and Sweezy while there has been no diminution in the desire of the largest enterprises to maximize profits, despite the 'managerial revolution', there has been apparently a fundamental change in the extent to which they can control the external, market environment in which they work. Profit maximization thus makes them ruthless in the pursuit of minimum cost, but the avoidance of damaging price competition makes them equally keen to establish a *modus vivendi* with their immediate rivals in the market. The most common form of price determination that Baran and Sweezy suggest is price leadership of the collusive type, that is the kind that allows stable joint-profit maximization. The operation of these twin forces thus allows joint profits to approach the monopoly level.

On this view of oligopoly there is little scope for looser, less successful forms of collusion where price leadership tends to be of the 'barometric' kind. Nor is there much attempt by the corporate giants to enter each other's markets as this might prove disruptive of the status quo. Firms grow to respect their mutual self-interest in not behaving aggressively to one another for fear of being worsted in another market where they may be more vulnerable.[2] It is largely on this ground that Baran and Sweezy also reject the Schumpeterian view of competition amongst oligopolists. Schumpeter argued that by focusing much of their attention of price competition economists missed the really profound aspect of competition through innovation of process, product or new method of organization (as we noted above in chapter 3). This process of 'creative destruction' was what really mattered rather than marginal adjustments of price. Baran and Sweezy dismiss this view as irrelevant to the behaviour of the giants because of their 'co-respectiveness' for each other. The authors cannot allow this form of active competition to have much impact because its force would be to destroy previous positions of monopoly and monopoly surplus. They therefore argue that 'there is a strong positive incentive for the large corporation in an oligopolistic industry not only to seek continuously to cut costs but to do so faster than its rivals' (Baran and Sweezy, 1977; p. 77) and also that this involves a relentless quest for new methods. But the fruits of this endeavour will not be used against their rivals because of their mutual respect for each other's market power. They conclude: 'the kinds of non-price competition which they do engage in are in no sense incompatible with the permanence of monopoly profits and their steady increase over time' (p. 82). There is thus no scope at all for X-inefficiency of the kind which Leibenstein has argued afflicts many enterprises with market power, for this also would erode monopoly profits. On the other hand, there seems to be no incompatibility between the Baran and Sweezy thesis and the view that much of what would otherwise be monopoly profit is absorbed in the acquisition and maintenance of market power. They do not directly argue that the surplus will be absorbed in this way but having discussed as insignificant three conventional explanations for surplus absorption (population growth, innovation and foreign investment) they can offer their own explanation of how monopoly capitalism deals with the problem.

The part of their analysis which has the most direct bearing on the present discussion is that which is concerned with the sales effort. For Baran and Sweezy (1967) 'advertising constitutes as much an integral part of the system as the giant corporation itself' (p. 126). The naive price leadership model which they employ to explain price determination in monopoly capitalism means that price competition is very infrequent but this leaves the way clear for most of the competitive energies to be devoted to advertising. Those who may have considered that the abandonment of price competition and the mutual respect that the giants had for each other's market positions meant an end to competition and an enjoyment of monopoly returns were, apparently, very much mistaken. For under monopoly capitalism, competition is as fierce and relentless as ever but is channelled into advertising and sales promotion and all the paraphernalia that goes with it (such as product variation and style changes, packaging and presentation and 'planned obsolescence', Baran and Sweezy, 1967; p. 120). They see the role of sales promotion as crucial to the survival of monopoly capitalism not because it causes demand to shift between the sales of different products but because it is indispensable to bolster total demand in a system which has a chronic tendency to under-consumption, under-investment and under-employment. To think in terms of its removal or reduction on the grounds that resources thus employed are misallocated and/or unproductive is to misunderstand this fundamental point, because any success in such a 'reform' would merely contribute to the destruction of the system.[3] Although the resources devoted to the sales effort (including much of what is confusingly called research and development but what is merely part of the drive to differentiate products) and much of the output which it supports are 'socially necessary' within the framework of monopoly capitalism, in any other context they must be regarded as misused and wasted.

> What is certain is the negative statement which, notwithstanding its negativity, constitutes one of the most important insights to be gained from political economy: an output the volume and composition of which are determined by the profit maximisation policies of oligopolistic corporations neither corresponds to human needs nor costs the minimum possible amount of human toil and human suffering. (Baran and Sweezy, 1967; p. 142)

It is interesting to note in this respect that we have already encountered a similar argument used by Cowling and Mueller in their estimates of social costs of monopoly power.[4] They explicitly assume that most, if not all, of the sales effort, especially advertising, is expense incurred to maintain monopoly power, and therefore should be treated as part of the social costs involved. Although they appear in the firms' accounts as costs, advertising expenses, on this view, are treated as part of the monopoly surplus.

The New Left accept and extend this interpretation of the role of advertising and sales promotion under monopoly capitalism. In particular they emphasize their role in reinforcing the false consciousness amongst workers who are thus led simultaneously to accept both their position as consumers who recognize the desirability of even greater consumption and also their 'alienated' place in the work environment. The latter concept of alienation is especially important since it can be linked directly to one kind of fundamental change in the organization of production – labour-managed firms – which we consider in the next section.

Adam Smith recognized the danger that great increases in the division of labour might bring by condemning a man in his work to the continued repetition of 'a few simple operations' which give him 'no occasion to exert his understanding or to exercise his invention in finding out expedients for removing difficulties which never occur' (Smith, 1977; Book V). Whereas he considered that the worst effects could be overcome by education and that the increases in wealth that resulted from increases in the division of labour more than outweighed the negative effects, members of the New Left, drawing on the early writings of Marx, see alienation as endemic to capitalism, reaching its climax in the monopoly stage. Thus under monopoly capitalism alienation is inevitable because workers neither own the means of production nor have any say in how production should be organized or what products should be produced. The highly developed division of labour where each individual belongs to a mechanical or functional group ensures that no-one can act as a spontaneous, free and human individual. To the feeling of isolation that this produces is added one of self estrangement because the organization of production robs the work process of any idea of individually purposeful activity. Thus workers become 'dehumanized' and alienated from their inner selves. They are forced into such jobs in order to earn an income but the corporate giants then ensure by their sales effort that this is for the most part spent on an endless round of frivolity and waste, since it is not in their interests to cater for the genuine 'needs' of workers.

As far as the New Left is concerned this view of the workers place in monopoly capitalism has the great advantage that it is apparently impregnable against empirical or analytical criticism. Thus it is not admissible to point to evidence that suggests that many workers are apparently quite satisfied with their jobs, as for example, Domar does, because this is simply a reflection of the false consciousness that the capitalist mode of production engenders. The workers have been conditioned through the whole cultural and social environment to see no real alternative (except perhaps unemployment) and therefore their response is bound to be positive. For the same reason the fact that trade unionists apparently place 'improved work environment' low down on their list of priorities cannot be taken as evidence that 'alienation' is relatively unimportant. Secondly, it is not accepted that under monopoly capitalism those workers who prefer an enriched work environment and lower money wages can find such jobs. The reason is that improvements in the work environment are inimical to profits and hence, given the ownership of the means of production, the former will always give way to the latter. Consequently the quality of the work environment is bound to remain suboptimal as far as workers are concerned under monopoly capitalism (Edwards *et al.*, 1970). It is just not possible for those with a very strong preference for a rich work environment to find the appropriate job opportunities because they will not be on offer. Evidence of wage differentials between plants and firms of different sizes in similar industries adduced to support the view that capitalism caters for different work preferences and monetary–non monetary reward mixes, simply misses the point. Thirdly, because the sales effort of the giant enterprises shapes consumer preferences and conditions demand it is not legitimate to point to the pattern of expenditure as revealing anything about *genuine* consumer needs. The latter could only be expressed under an entirely different system of production and organization of society. Under monopoly capitalism all that it reveals is the effectiveness of advertising and the poverty of consumerism with its numbing effect on the finer senses.[5]

In these circumstances it therefore becomes impossible to frame a test of any hypothesis about this aspect of monopoly capitalism which, if rejected by the empirical evidence, may lead to a tentative modification of the underlying analysis. Evidence of considerable covert price competition in oligopoly, or the failure of many products despite heavy advertising and promotion would do nothing to change the analysis.

Writers of both the Old and New Left aim, of course, at a comprehensive and fundamental critique of the political, social and economic organization of capitalism. In the space available we have only been able to sketch briefly three features of this critique (the nature of competition under oligopoly, the role of advertising, and worker alienation) which are directly relevant to our main theme. But we have probably said enough to show that at the heart of the critique are the giant enterprises which, it is claimed, through their enormous power do so much to direct and control the conditions of most peoples' lives. For writers of the Left capitalism is an 'evil and destructive system which maims, oppresses and dishonours those who live under it' (Baran and Sweezy, 1977). Given the total rejection of the system as it stands, it is logical to ask how writers in this tradition envisage that these organizations can be changed so as to become the servants rather than the masters of society.

PLANNING OR MARKETS AND WORKERS CONTROL

Those who sympathize with some or all of the indictments made against the giant companies may anticipate that the severity of the critique will be matched by an equally detailed and systematic programme setting out the organization of production and the mechanism of resource and product allocations that would follow in the wake of fundamental changes that are seen as inevitable. Unfortunately their optimism is largely misplaced. With few exceptions writers in this tradition have been loath to spell out in any detail how the basic economic problems that confront any society would be solved after monopoly capitalism.

Sweezy at least is quite clear that one thing that most writers in the tradition have in common is 'a profound lack of interest in schemes or efforts to reform (the whole capitalist-imperialist system) except as they may be related to revolutionary tactics (Sweezy, 1972; p. 658). He adds later for good measure: 'To speak of reforming capitalism is either naivete or deception' (p. 660). Thus the break with the past would be complete and fundamental. Tinkering with antitrust policies, piecemeal nationalization, 'planning agreements' and similar policies to contain the corporate giants are clearly ruled out. Under these circumstances, it is legitimate to ask what methods the Left propose for handling the following five problems, neatly summarized by Lindbeck:

> 1) obtaining *information* about preferences; 2) *allocating* resources to different sectors in accordance with these preferences; 3) deciding which *production techniques* to use; 4) creating *incentives* to econom-ise in the use of resources, to invest and to develop new technologies; and finally 5) *co-ordinating* the decisions of millions of individual firms and households to make them consistent. (Lindbeck, 1971; p. 33)

Baran and Sweezy were writing an essay on the American economic and social order and therefore give little attention to what they regard as the superior system that will succeed it. But there are scattered throughout the book a number of references to 'a rational economic order'[6] which suggests that industry would be owned by the state and micro-economic questions would be solved by 'planning' of some kind. Thus:

> If a socialist society, for example, should find that through some planning error more consumer goods were being produced than could be sold, given the existing structure of prices and incomes, the simp-lest and most direct remedy would clearly be to cut prices. This would reduce the amount of surplus at the disposal of the planning authorities and correspondingly raise the purchasing power of con-sumers. The threatened glut could be quickly and painlessly adjusted: everyone would be better off, no-one worse off. (Baran and Sweezy, 1977; p. 115)

Presumably the rise in consumer's purchasing power would cause them to increase their demand for other items which may then cause a shortage and require some other price adjustment and so on. In fact the evidence from Eastern Europe where such methods have been used now for many years suggests precisely that these co-ordination problems cannot be 'quickly and pain-lessly' solved which is why some have tried to re-introduce the market as an allocative device. Here, however, we have to tread carefully. In their 1966 book Baran and Sweezy seem to accept the USSR as the leader of a world-wide socialist challenge to the monopoly capitalism of the USA.[7] Indeed they develop part of their explanation of why the USA has vastly increased its military expenditure (which thereby assists in the process of surplus absorption) in terms of a response to the rise of the socialist systems. In other words in 1966 when monopoly capitalism was first published the USSR was considered socialist. By 1972, however, Sweezy not only rejected any idea that the USSR was 'socialist' but claimed that it was 'once again' naivete or deception to cite the Soviet Union to prove anything about socialism: it is not a socialist society and even more important, it is not moving towards socialism but away from it' (Sweezy, 1972; p. 660).[8]

At one point Baran and Sweezy explain, in effect, that the details of the system that will replace monopoly capitalism have not been worked out and that indeed there is no reason why they should be:

> The concrete structure of a rational social output and the optimal conditions for its production can only be established in the fullness of time – by a process of groping, of trial and error – in a socialist society where economic activity is no longer dominated by profits and sales but instead directed to the creation of the abundance which is indispensable to the welfare and all-round development of man. (Baran and Sweezy, 1977; p. 142)

If resource allocation under socialism is to be in the hands of a bureaucracy, however well intentioned, we are confronted by another apparent contradiction. As a number of commentators have observed one of the central criticisms of monopoly capitalism made by writers of the Left has been the inordinate power wielded by irresponsible private companies. Yet as George Orwell with characteristic candour was prepared to admit many years ago: 'collectivism is not inherently democratic, but on the contrary, gives to a tyrannical minority such powers as the Spanish Inquisitors never dreamed of' (Orwell, 1970; p. 143) or, one might add, as a multinational conglomerate never dreamed of. Instead of eliminating 'excessive' power there is thus the danger that it may simply be transferred into different hands and very much enhanced in the name of socialism. It is largely on this ground that, in contrast to the Old Left, more recent writers have mostly rejected central planning and the bureaucratic controls that accompany it. Unfortunately, as Lindbeck has pointed out, they also, for the most part, reject markets as an allocative and co-ordinating mechanism. In many ways markets are seen as instrumental in prolonging the evils of monopoly capitalism. By reducing everything to money values they debase human relationships and assist in the exploitation of workers by capital. They serve the purpose of production for profit and not for need. Their existence is rationalized by bourgeois economists in terms of free exchange from which both parties benefit when in fact most market transactions are the equivalent of zero-sum games: what one gains the other loses, an inevitable outcome given the organization of production under capitalism.

If, however, both planning and markets are rejected as the means of coping with the basic economic problems that any society faces, the Left like the king in the fable, has no clothes at all as Sherman, to his credit, explains: 'it is simply a chimera to think that an advanced economic system can operate with *neither* a market *nor* a central planning bureaucracy. No third way of economic decision-making has been invented. One must choose some combination of these evils' (Sherman, 1972; p. 332). The failure of many on the Left to accept this basic point seems to be due to the belief (that pervades Monopoly Capital for example) that the problem of scarcity no longer really exists. The fact that many live in relative poverty and wretched conditions in capitalist societies is, on this view, due to the enforced scarcity engineered by the giant corporations with the connivance of government. Once society is changed and capitalist production and organization has been superseded by the socialist alternative the 'correct' composition of goods and services will be produced and ensure that everyone's genuine needs are catered for. Clearly if this is believed then it follows that no special mechanism will be required for handling the five problems mentioned above, just as there is no need to 'administer' in any way the supply of air.

One concept that has met with a generally favourable response and been given special attention by a number of New Left writers has been workers' control, not simply in the general sense of the ownership of the means of production in their name by the state (which in practice may mean by a privileged elite) but in the specific sense of complete control of the organization and running of enterprises by the people who work in them and share whatever returns they may make. The importance that is attached to this method of operating enterprises springs naturally from the analysis of alienation under monopoly capitalism. This implies that as soon as the worker accepts employment in a capitalist enterprise he gives up any control over what is produced and, perhaps more important, the methods used in production. He therefore becomes alienated in his place of work and this has repercussions in practically every other aspect of his life (Gintis, 1972). Consequently if this divorce is ended the most important source of alienation will also be removed.

Supporters of labour-managed firms have argued that most if not all of the conflict of interests shown by capitalist enterprises can be resolved by this fundamental organizational change. In addition the sense of alienation that is likely to accompany the bureaucratic controls of enterprise in a centrally planned system can also be avoided. Where workers not only own but also have responsibility for all of the policy decisions of the enterprise, the result, it is suggested, will be harmony and efficiency because those most directly involved will be choosing democratically the methods and organization of production, the duties and rewards of participants and the future plans for investment. Thus Vanek, for example, concludes:

> Without any doubt, labour-management is among all existing forms of enterprise organisations the optimal arrangement when it comes to the finding of the utility-maximising effort, i.e. the proper quality, duration and intensity of work, by the working collective. Not only is there no situation of conflict between management and the workers that might hinder the finding of the optimum, but the process of self-management itself can be viewed as a highly efficient device for communication, collusion control and enforcement among the participants. (Vanek, 1969; p. 1011)

In view of the apparent efficiency gains that can be made by organizational changes of the kind which gives workers much more direct control over the work environment it is worth enquiring whether capitalist firms cannot seize this opportunity to improve their own performance. We argued earlier,[9] for example, that an *organizational* innovation amongst the very largest enterprises has probably been of great importance for their continued vitality. There has been a lot of evidence from industrial psychologists at least since the famous Hawthorne experiments in the 1920s that direct involvement by workers in the decisions that affect the detail of their work can have dramatic and positive effects on their performance (Mayo, 1933). The New Left has cited similar, more recent evidence in their discussions of alienation (see for example Gintis, 1972; pp. 280–1). In view of the pre-eminence of the profit motive and the relentless drive to reduce costs which governs the activities of the largest enterprises under monopoly capitalism[10] why have they not introduced, perhaps in a modified form, measures to take advantage of this potential for efficiency gains?

At its simplest the answer given is that with a capitalist organization of production, changes which improve the work environment can only be made at the expense of profits and therefore will not be introduced. But this implies that the 'improvement', taking the form perhaps of a less detailed division of labour in the production process or less capital intensive methods which might be preferred by workers, will in fact produce a lower level of output and hence not only lower profits but also lower wages. In other words, the level of efficiency would be lower. For if the change could be made without affecting profits but giving workers a different 'package' of monetary and non-monetary income (that is wages plus an enhanced work environment) there is no reason why some capitalist firms would not use such methods. Indeed some would argue that one of the advantages of capitalism is that it does allow workers to choose between different firms offering different mixtures of monetary and non-monetary rewards. There are some writers on the New Left who would accept that in effect under a system of workers control the total physical product would be smaller but its composition would be quite different and the change in work environment would more than outweigh the reduction in output. In any case, as we have seen, they argue that consumption of most existing output yields little or no genuine satisfaction for workers and therefore the change would undoubtedly be an improvement. An extension of these ideas to encompass small self-sufficient organizations prompted Lindbeck to retort 'that most adherents of these "commune models" show no signs of establishing such organisations for themselves; they instead seem to argue that *all of us* should live in that way' (Lindbeck, 1972; p. 678).

A different answer is given by those who maintain that worker control will bring *greater* efficiency not less. In this case there is scope for increases in profits, wages and work environment if workers directly participate in the organization of production. To illustrate this point Gintis (1972, p. 258) quotes the following conclusion from a survey of the empirical evidence of industrial psychologists: 'There is scarcely a study in the entire literature which fails to demonstrate that satisfaction in work is enhanced or ... productivity increases accrue from a genuine increase in worker's decision-making power' (Blumberg, 1969). So capitalist firms can, apparently, modify their operations and improve both their efficiency and work environment. Those which are slow to adapt will find their profitability suffering compared to their rivals and will find it increasingly difficult to hire the right kinds of workers. But this conclusion is erroneous according to

Gintis. The 'entire literature' refers to moderate worker control instituted

> only in marginal areas and in isolated firms fighting for survival. When the threat is over, there is a return to 'normal operating procedure'. The threat of worker escalation of demand for control is simply too great, and usurpation of the prerogatives of hierarchial authority is quickly quashed. Hence, efficiency in the broader sense is subordinated to the needs of bureaucratic control. (Blumberg, 1969; p. 281)

In other words, even profits which under monopoly capitalism might be though to override all other considerations, are sacrificed to preserve the rights of the managerial class. On this view, as long as capitalist organization persists, however modified to increase worker participation, then some work environments which might end alienation are ruled out because they pose a threat to the ruling elite. The argument thus depends on the complete absence of competition from maverick firms at home and abroad which have less interest in their caste feelings and more in making greater wealth for themselves (and incidentally for their workers). It also depends on a much greater recognition of class interest on the part of managers, prepared to sacrifice possibly large amounts, than either reason or observation will support. While such behaviour may be characteristic of a feudal aristocracy, it fits ill with the ideas of a modern business community, as Furubotn (1976; p. 216) has observed.

For the New Left, however, an economy consisting of worker owned and managed enterprises with their desirable non-alienating properties, is one which has a great deal of attraction, at least superficially. The qualification seems necessary because it is not clear that the New Left writers have either thought through or accepted the full implications of what the principle of workers control for all enterprises would mean in practice. The five economic problems would remain, even if the economy had been reconstituted in this way. A combination of market and planning mechanisms would have to be used to allocate resources and distribute goods. Thus the workers' co-operatives would in many industries have to compete with each other: some would flourish and others would fail; periodically unemployment would emerge in the transition from one enterprise to another; in some activities the enterprises would wish to advertise their products, unless this was regulated by a central planning agency which in effect supervised demand; as some enterprises were more successful than others and grew faster and wealthier, so an unequal distribution of incomes would emerge unless corrected by the kind of taxation and redistribution policies already attempted by many capitalist governments. None of this is meant to deny that worker-owned and -controlled enterprises may not yield the positive benefits that many writers have claimed. It is simply to illustrate that the basic economic problems do not disappear with the change of organization even if it is a profound change. The dislike of the New Left for both markets and bureaucratic planning severely weakens the effect of their attack on the numerous problems of capitalism.

In the case of worker-managed firms this weakness is unfortunate because by being associated with the writings of the New Left the concept may be condemned as 'utopian' when in fact it deserves more serious consideration. There is no reason why the institutions of the last hundred or so years should be regarded as definitive. Nor is it adequate to argue that workers' co-operatives would have grown spontaneously and flourished if they were inherently superior or equal to joint stock companies. It took the passage of the 1856 Companies Act to ensure that the latter had a significant impact on the UK economy. Before this they had been few in number, unstable and usually short-lived. From the perspective of the late eighteenth century they were regarded as the 'enemies of good management' (Smith, 1977). But if workers' co-operatives are to emerge as an important supplement to conventional 'capitalist' companies their potential weaknesses have to be appreciated as well as their strengths. It seems likely, for example, that their internal organizational problems may be more serious than a superficial examination might indicate. Two examples can briefly illustrate the point. First, if all important decisions for the enterprise are taken by simple majority vote then the original majority is likely to take steps to ensure that its established position and policies are not threatened. This may have important implications for the efficiency and employment policy of the enterprise. As each new member is not merely an employee but also a full participant in decision-making, the established majority may be over cautious in the number of new members they admit, since too great an influx of new members may undermine their own position. Under these circumstances they may not increase employment up to the point where the marginal product of labour is equal to the maximum attainable average wage, in other words, the capital–labour ratio of the enterprise may remain suboptimal because of the 'political' considerations of the ruling group.[11] Secondly, if all members participate in the residual or profit of the enterprise, unless special precautions are taken they may become X-inefficient because of the lack of incentive afforded to the 'managers' or what Alchian and Demsetz more neutrally term the 'monitors' (Alchian and Demsetz, 1972). As the latter do not have control over the disposal of the entire surplus they may not exert themselves to ensure that it is positive. The same weakness may afflict managerially run capitalist enterprises, of course, and is only modified by the possibility of dismissal (by existing shareholders) or takeover. In a similar fashion worker-managed firms may have to institute a system whereby the 'monitors' can be dismissed by a majority of members. But in view of the first point made above this may be more difficult in practice than it seems.

Thus like most complex organizations developed to solve difficult problems, worker-managed firms have a collection of advantages and pitfalls. It is important to remember also that they should be compared with the actual structure and running of modern enterprises rather than with the idealized textbook construct. The difficulties just mentioned may be regarded as trivial when considered alongside the problems created by the corporate giants.

The difficulty is, however, that while worker-managed firms may, under certain circumstances, successfully compete with or even supersede capitalist enterprises of *medium* size they are probably ill-suited to the task of replacing the core of monopoly capitalism, that is the hundred or so largest enterprises which are individually very large and jointly control a substantial fraction of the entire economy.[12] The point is explained in some detail by Jay (1977) in the course of a paper, *The Workers Co-operative Economy*, where he discusses the feasibility of almost the entire UK economy being re-organized by law into one of worker-managed enterprises. In his judgement 'there is no question that experience and *a priori* reasoning both suggest that workers' co-operatives work best when they are small – up to maybe 1000 members – and that their supposed advantages tend to evaporate as size rises much above that level' (Jay, 1977; p. 23).[13] Leaving aside the people employed in nationalized industries and in central and local government, about seven million were employed in the UK in 1973 in enterprises with over 2000 employees. On the face of it, therefore, there appears to be an unbridgeable gulf between the practical size of reasonably efficient workers' co-operatives and the actual size now found in a wide range of manufacturing industry. Even if it is allowed on the one hand that the upper limit for co-operatives could feasibly be extended by, for example, confederations of separate units and on the other that the largest capitalist enterprises realize few social economies to justify their present size, the gap remains very considerable. The irony may therefore be that whereas alienation and related problems are probably most acute in the very largest enterprises, workers control which may seem the most appropriate means of remedying the situation may not be practical in these cases.

At the level of the plant rather than the enterprise there is already some indirect evidence that institutional and market forces may provide their own corrective to the most obvious effects of alienation. First, there is a marked and perhaps unsurprising direct relationship between plant size in manufacturing and 'strike proneness'. The full details are discussed in Prais (1978) and we mention only one or two points here. For example, over the period 1971–73 the percentage of plants in manufacturing with 100–199 employees suffering a strike was 3 per cent compared with 76 per cent of plants employing over 5000 and there was a constant increase in the degree of 'strike proneness' throughout the size distribution of plants. To the extent, therefore, that alienation is connected with remoteness from control by workers over the details of the work process, which seems more likely in larger rather than smaller plants, this may be reflected in the above figures. Although it was not possible to classify the strike figures by industry there was some suggestion that the heavy industries (like metal manufacture, mechanical engineering and vehicles) were more vulnerable to strikes than the light industries (food manufacture, textiles and clothing, and furniture). This brings us to the second point. In a comparison of plant sizes for light and heavy manufacturing industries in the UK, Germany and the USA Prais has also found that in those industries where technology apparently requires large-sized plants, the biggest UK plants are 'too small' by international standards whereas in those cases where technological factors are much less important, UK plants may be too large (Prais, 1982). Unfortunately comparable evidence on 'strike-proneness' for Germany and the USA is not available and therefore any inference must be tentative. But there is the possibility that the costly effects of alienation, as manifested in the level of strikes in the largest plants, may constrain the expansion of UK plants in some key industries to a size which by international standards are too small.[14] Carried to the limit this explanation would imply that unless firms adjusted their plants (and thus their organization of production) to sizes that UK workers were prepared to accept, costs will rise to such an extent as to make their operation unprofitable. The problem for some British industries would then be that if other countries, because of social or cultural differences, *can* successfully operate larger plants where technological economies of scale are significant, they would eventually lose their foreign and domestic market shares in any case. This in turn implies that whatever comparative advantage the UK may once have had in such industries would have much diminished, and this may have important implications for the future size distribution of firms. If the heavy manufacturing industries play a smaller part in the economy in the future this may also mean a levelling off or even a reversal of the trend of increasing aggregate concentration which the UK experienced between the end of the Second World War and the mid-1970s.

CONCLUSION

The Baran and Sweezy analysis of what they termed monopoly capitalism focuses on the behaviour and performance of the corporate giants. These are seen as in complete control of their economic environment, fervently seeking to minimize costs and earn the maximum return that respect for their competitors will allow. The competitive struggle is as intense as ever but takes the non-price forms of advertising and style changes which also have the function of absorbing a large amount of the economic surplus to which all such economies are chronically prone. The position of the worker-consumers is, if anything, worse than that envisaged by Thomas Hobbes for man in a state of nature. Alienated in his place of work by meaningless tasks over which he has no control, he gains little or no 'real' satisfaction from the goods his income will buy because he has been conditioned by the relentless and sophisticated sales effort of the giant enterprises into a state of false consciousness.

Under such circumstances to speak of reforms of the corporate sector as we have done in the last three chapters by a combination of tougher antitrust, discriminatory taxes, and other piecemeal legislative changes, is a complete waste of time. Only revolutionary change will eradicate the evils of monopoly capitalism.

It is at this point, however, that the writers of both the Old and New Left falter and probably lose a lot of support that some aspects of their critique may have gained. While New Left writers in particular seem especially in favour of worker-owned and -managed enterprises as most likely to minimize the 'alienation' which they see as a fundamental sickness of monopoly capitalism there is little sign that they have accepted the full implications of how such an economy would solve the basic problems that face any society. The apparent acceptance of central planning by the Old Left implies that the post-revolutionary economy is likely to run into the same economic (let alone political) problems as Eastern Europe, the USSR, and Cuba. On the other hand, the rejection by many New Left writers of both planning and markets to co-ordinate economic activity leaves them, as Domar scathingly remarks, with 'just another utopia' (Domar, 1974; p. 1313), and not an especially imaginative utopia at that.

The rejection is a pity because it has meant that in the UK at least the possibility of an economy of worker-manager co-operative enterprises as an alternative to the present system has received less systematic attention than it merits. The discussion by Jay touches on many of the issues but he was writing from a different perspective and with a view to solving the problem in the UK not of over-powerful giant enterprises but, as he saw it, trade unions which frustrated the twin objectives of full employment and stable prices. But past experience of worker co-operatives suggests that their advantages are likely to peter out at a size far below that to which the largest capitalist enterprises have grown. So although they may find a place in the middle ranks of manufacturing concerns under more favourable circumstances than the political environment of the UK in the 1980s provides, they are unlikely to supersede the corporate giants.[15]

Part Four: Conclusion

11

Halting the Trend

In a review of the economic literature on the modern corporation, Marris and Mueller (1980) concluded that there are now three major alternatives for industrial policy available to a country like the United States. First, the preservation of the existing form of 'managerial capitalism' with its emphasis on growth (especially through merger) and non-price competition; secondly, further moves towards democratic socialism or a government–business partnership; and thirdly, an attempt to reverse the growth of industrial concentration by the break-up of large corporations, and restrictions on mergers and some forms of non-price competition (like advertising). Broadly speaking these options correspond to the policies discussed respectively in chapters 9, 8 and 7 above. They apparently reject (or at least do not include) the option considered in chapter 10 as being too far removed from present democratic institutions. They argue that the choice among the three options is not obvious and cannot be left to the evolutionary process of corporate capitalism on Darwinian grounds because there is no guarantee that this evolution would produce the most efficient result. They thus reject the non-interventionist approach of the Austrian school. Indeed they predict that on recent past trends the corporate economy is more likely to converge into a system resembling the USSR if this option is continued, rather than into the decentralized competitive economy that writers of the non-interventionist school seem to have in mind. Failure to face up to the strong concentration-increasing forces of capitalist economies robs this approach of much credibility once we move from the *theory* of the competitive process to the *facts* of modern enterprises. For the reasons offered in chapter 10 we reject the iconclastic proposals of the Left, without necessarily concluding that worker-managed enterprises may not offer a feasible alternative to capitalist enterprises in a variety of circumstances. We therefore agree with Marris and Mueller that this narrows the possibilities to some variant of options two and three.

For the reasons developed in chapter 8 we are suspicious of the likely efficiency of a solution in which 'some hundreds of competing planned economies (i.e. giant corporations) operat[e] in close partnership with government' (Marris and Mueller, 1980; p. 59). In practice the close partnership may boil down to little more than a trade in restrictive practices and special privileges at the expense initially of consumers and eventually of everyone, due to general uncompetitiveness. In other words the corporatist approach which is what a government–business partnership amounts to is, in our judgement, not the best approach available. It is noticeable that neither Marris and Mueller nor Galbraith whom they cite, have explained in any detail just how this partnership would work. The five basic economic problems which Lindbeck accused the New Left of not facing in their suggestions for reconstruction, would equally have to be solved by the proposed 'partnership' but the precise mechanism remains discreetly hidden. It is not clear what would prevent this association also from 'converging into a Soviet-type system'. Indeed it seems plausible to argue that the convergence is just as likely to be hastened as impeded by such an alliance, especially in time of crisis.

We are left, therefore, with the third alternative, extended in a number of ways explained in chapter 7. This approach recognizes the economic and political dangers of increasing concentration by a small group of giant enterprises and seeks to redress the balance by a combination of antitrust and taxation policies which as far as possible will be certain and uniform in their incidence. The circumstances under which the policies would operate would thus be known in advance to all parties concerned and all would be aware that they would be applied to every company without special treatment for a favoured few. The implications of this policy approach could be quite far reaching as we pointed out in chapter 7.

It could mean, for example, making all cartels illegal and any infringement subject both to criminal and civil proceedings for damages. Although this would not make parallel behaviour impossible it would make it more difficult and help to confine price leadership to the less damaging 'barometric' variety. In merger cases, while the existing machinery which allows for the investigation by the Monopolies and Mergers Commission of important proposals, could continue, those involving a market share of, say, 50 per cent or more could be subject to automatic High Court injunction, following an application by the Director General of Fair Trading. The companies involved would not be allowed to offer conjectural post-merger economies as a defence. We need to emphasize, however, that in any one year the number of merger proposals caught by the new procedure would be very small. Most mergers would proceed as at present, unhampered.

The achievement of 'monopoly' by internal growth remains problematical. The break-up of large firms by the courts which some writers have recommended is not only likely to be costly because they may include some of the more efficient and dynamic firms but is also unlikely to achieve any dramatic increase in the competitiveness of the economy. To suggest that the internal expansion of independent companies beyond a certain market should be prohibited by the Courts (Rowley and Peacock, 1975; p. 181) is likely to produce the worst of both worlds: efficient companies would be inhibited (and probably forced into a series of second-best diversifications) while the administration of the revised antitrust policy would fall into disrepute because of the impossible task placed upon it of, in effect, monitoring market shares. To the extent that the large market share rests on an artificial impediment to entry like a patent, then it may be more feasible to encourage competition by making licensing compulsory wherever the patent holder has achieved more than a specified market share. In this case the court would have to decide first, the size of the market share and then, if it was above the threshold, the terms on which licensing of competitors would take place. Clearly this is a compromise between providing sufficient incentives for innovation on the one hand, and encouraging the entry of new competition on the other. It also leaves the courts with the difficult problem of having to decide the level of licence payments. But this kind of approach seems much less likely to disrupt the efficient than large scale dismemberment.

The corollary of an even-handed approach in antitrust policy when every company knows in advance what to expect, must be a similar attitude to other interventions by the government. We argued in chapter 7 that there were good grounds for rejecting selective intervention by a state-owned enterprise into some oligopolies as a means of increasing competition. There are good reasons also why governments should resist the temptation of giving *selective* assistance to some firms or some industries which are either in short-run difficulties or alternatively considered by a ministry to be an area of future potential growth. Recent British experience with the former category may have given even the most ardent interventionist second thoughts on this issue. In future if the government is to give assistance to firms (and the precise rationale for this has never adequately been explained apart from a general recoil from the idea that a very large enterprise could actually go bankrupt)[1] this should be open to all on the same terms. Not only would this ensure that no firm gains a competitive advantage over others by receiving grants or 'soft' loans but it would have the added benefit of avoiding conflict between antitrust policy (especially where mergers are concerned) and other 'intervention' policy as practised in recent years in the UK by bodies like the Industrial Reorganization Corporation and the National Enterprise Board.

The second category (industries considered ripe for future growth) should similarly be non-selective and for the same reason. There must be serious doubts about the comparative efficiency of government departments as opposed to private sector enterprises assessing future growth and profit prospects and investing accordingly. There is a good deal in the Austrian view that there is little reason to expect that the quality and detail of information for making commercial judgements available to a government agency will be superior to that of an enterprise that will bear the risks of its decision.

The suggestions made so far apply to monopoly rather than large size *per se*. For the reasons given in chapter 7 it seems unwise to extend merger control to cases where a large market share is not at issue but where a large amount of assets are likely to change hands. The threat of such takeovers may provide a useful incentive against X-inefficiency while any subsequent market power effects are likely to be negligible if the companies operate in different industries. Suppose, however, that two of the largest enterprises in the UK which were also very large by EEC standards decided to merge and that their major activities were in different markets and hence the merger fell outside the scope of the 50 per cent rule. Should there be some form of surveillance and control of such sudden large increases in overall size even though no 'monopoly' is created? The purely economic arguments (discussed in the second part of chapter 5) are not very persuasive and seem in the last analysis to depend on an extension of the concept of monopoly into situations where it cannot be sustained. It has probably not improved the reputation of anti-trust policy either in the UK or elsewhere to try to justify on economic grounds alone control or prohibition of such mergers. Nevertheless this should not detract from the general feeling amongst many observers that accompany mergers of this importance (cf. Dewey, 1974; pp. 12–13). The unease stems from a dislike of the discretionary authority which very large conglomerate mergers may deliver into the hands of the management of a private-sector enterprise. In other words the real objection to such mergers is political: they may be incompatible with a decentralized, mixed economy and even with parliamentary democracy. British merger policy already has a precedent for controlling some mergers on other than narrow economic criteria. All acquisitions of newspapers by a newspaper proprietor *have* to be referred to the Monopolies and Mergers Commission, unless they have a circulation of under 25 000 copies or they are not economically viable. The reason for giving no discretion about references in such cases was that in a parliamentary democracy it was thought undesirable that control over newspapers should become concentrated into fewer hands unless there were very compelling reasons for the change. It can be similarly argued that the control over resources and the discretionary authority that, say, a merger between Imperial Chemical Industries and the General Electric Company would produce is politically unacceptable, even though no 'monopoly' question is involved. In such a case arguments about whether the merger increases the scope for cross subsidization, predatory pricing or reciprocal dealing are of negligible importance. On these grounds, therefore, it is reasonable to extend the new scope of merger policy to cover, for example, the largest 50 enterprises.[2] The Court could be empowered to issue an injunction against any proposed merger between such companies even though the 50 per cent 'monopoly' criterion was not met. The injunction would be automatic once the court had established the status of the companies involved. By placing the political considerations in the forefront of the issue much, rather weak, economic argument would be avoided and in addition, companies would know in advance what the antitrust attitude to such mergers would be. Conglomerate mergers outside this very select group would remain free of control, for the reasons already given.

Other proposals mentioned at the end of chapter 7 also aim to control the *overall* growth of the largest enterprises while encouraging the development of small and medium-sized firms. It was suggested there, following Meade and Prais, that perhaps the most feasible way of achieving this objective was by changes in the tax system which discriminated in favour of smaller firms and against the largest. Just as those with the smallest incomes were exempt or paid very little income tax while those with the largest incomes paid higher than the standard rate, so small firms would make little or no contribution to a company tax which would become progressively steeper, the larger the overall size of the firm. If this was coupled with provisions making it easier and financially attractive to hive off subsidiaries into independent companies, the expected slowdown in the growth of the giants might be achieved with the companies themselves making the crucial decisions about the future shape of the enterprise, rather than having a remedy forced upon them by an outside agency. Furthermore, if for tax purposes size was measured by assets, thus raising the private cost of capital to large firms and lowering it for small firms, this might go some way to offset the capital market's present bias in favour of large firms (Prais, 1981; p. 169) which we considered in chapter 3. So that the ultimate objective of such policies was not frustrated by devices such as interlocking directorships additional safeguards would be required. Evidently a giant company may hive off a subsidiary because the tax advantage under the above suggestion outweighs the prospective net return if it is retained, yet keep effective control through a number of key directorships. Truly independent new companies, therefore, would have to have independent directors. Those in charge of the new companies would have to relinquish (for a specified period) any office in the former parent company.

Part of the hostility that the largest companies generate amongst the public stems from a feeling of helplessness and ignorance in the face of what are regarded as their ability to manipulate and control. The feeling can be considered as part of a more general problem of the asymmetrical distribution of information. While there is considerable evidence (as we observed in chapter 5) that the recent increases in aggregate concentration in the UK have been accompanied by an equally rapid growth of diversification amongst the corporate giants, the amount of information they are required to publish in their annual accounts has remained largely unchanged since the 1949 Companies Act.[3] Most of the information that is published in the accounts is either consolidated over all of the enterprises activities or is disaggregated in a form which the directors may find convenient but which is unhelpful to the outsider. Since in the UK the largest companies are now both relatively bigger and more diversified, consolidated accounting means that *less* information is available to outside observers, whether potential shareholders, consumers or entrepreneurs, about the performance of a larger section of the economy than was the case, say, thirty years ago. The giant enterprise remains to all intents and purposes like a sealed black box which annually releases the barest facts about its recent functioning. Inside the black box, however, a great deal of careful measuring takes place. With the change in their internal organization that accompanied their growth and diversification (chapter 3) came divisional reporting of sales, costs and profits which could be used by management to assess the performance of the separate parts of the enterprise. While the information available inside the enterprise was increasing both in scope and detail, that available on the outside was diminishing. The argument for retaining profits for re-investment rather than distributing them to shareholders who can then judge how they should be spent can thus be made almost irresistible: the directors have much more knowledge about prospective profitabilities than actual or potential shareholders and therefore can act more efficiently than the capital market. The bigger and more diversified the largest companies become the greater, on this view, will be the lack of information in the capital market and hence the greater incentive to retain rather than distribute profits and so on.

To restore at least partially the balance of information available to top managements compared to shareholders and the capital market there could be a number of useful additions to the information published in company accounts. For example, since companies monitor the internal performance of their divisions using profits, sales, employment and capital figures, it should impose no great extra burden on them for these to be published in their accounts. What is especially important, however, is that they appear in a way that make them consistent not only with previous years but also with other companies operating in the same industries.[4] It would then be possible for outsiders to assess the comparative performance of different companies in a much more detailed way than is presently possible.

A second aspect of information which has aroused a great deal of opposition is advertising. We observed in chapter 4 that although the evidence on the effects of advertising was, to say the

least, conflicting, there was nevertheless highly distinguished
support for regulation and control over the above that provided
by the law (such as, for example, in the Trade Descriptions Act).
We also noted, however, that unless controls were designed in a
more imaginative way than hitherto in the UK they may produce
almost exactly the opposite effect from that intended. Cigarette
advertising, banned from television in one form emerged in
another, with possibly more damaging effects.[5] A policy which
recognizes the asymmetry in information between producers and
consumers for complex products and also its public-good characteristics, is one where publically funded agencies increase the
amount of independent knowledge available. The findings of
their analysis of the performance of different brands would then
be published in the same way as, for example, reports from the
existing Consumer Affairs section of the Office of Fair Trading
are published at present. Advertising would thus not be controlled but advertised products would be subjected to detailed technical tests on a more extensive scale than, for example, the Consumers Association can presently afford. If after the results of the
tests of advertised products brand X is shown to be technically
superior to brand Y but many consumers still prefer to buy brand
Y then on the grounds of consumer sovereignty they should be
allowed that choice.

The above policy may go some way to meet the unequal information argument but it does not deal with the view that advertising, especially in oligopoly where it may simply counter that of a
rival, generates a waste of resources. As we suggested in chapter
4 although it has many adherents this view is almost impossible to
substantiate empirically and yet many proposals have been made
for direct policies to reduce or control the volume of advertising.
The difficulty with general controls is that they may inhibit the
very firms which on other grounds should be encouraged. A newcomer may erode the market share of existing firms by advertising. On the other hand if advertising does not create entry barriers a control on *future* levels is likely to freeze market shares
into their established mould. Even a lump-sum tax on all advertisers above a certain limit is likely to have as its main effect a
comparable increase in other forms of non-price competition
which critics would similarly condemn as a waste of resources.
For this reason we prefer for most products an indirect approach
which leaves firms free to choose their own competitive strategy.
The feasible alternatives to the present system of regulating the

content of and to some extent the media for advertisements through the law, seem unlikely to produce a more efficient result. Indeed since additional regulations would have to be enforced the volume of resources devoted to 'non-price competition plus enforcement' may well be greater than the saving achieved through any reduction in advertising.

A number of observers have seen advertising as merely one way in which enterprises invest in monopoly. But they have noted that other less obvious means of pursuing or maintaining monopoly such as lobbying, public relations, political contributions and bribery will be available especially to the largest firms and that this also leads to waste. Resources devoted to these activities have a positive opportunity cost and therefore the total product is lower than it would otherwise be. The appropriate policy response on this issue is clearly very difficult to frame because the scope for such activity seems to depend very much on the workings of the political system. For example it is probably true that the UK system of tight political party discipline for voting on all important measures lends itself much less to these kinds of activities than the American system where representatives at federal and state levels may vote on individual issues across party lines. Nevertheless with the kind of discretionary anti-trust policy that we have at present in the UK the system is potentially open to abuse. Whether or not a merger, for example, meeting one of two criteria is referred to the Monopolies and Mergers Commission rests entirely in the hands of the minister. Many of the mergers involved are highly controversial and in some cases individuals stand to make enormous gains if the merger is completed. The minister and his immediate advisers may thus be open to very strong pressures from the interested parties. Under a non-discretionary anti-trust policy of the kind suggested above this possibility is eliminated since if the courts decided that the market share criterion was met, the merger would automatically be prohibited. Although investment of resources to acquire or maintain a monopoly position can never be eliminated while competition is imperfect, they are probably minimized by the even-handed and non-discretionary policy approaches to industry that we have outlined.

We need to consider one further aspect of information and this concerns the development of an efficient policy towards the environment. In the discussion of social responsibility (chapter 8) there seemed few grounds for expecting coherent controls on environmental pollution to emerge if firms were expected to behave spontaneously in a 'socially responsible' manner, partly because the concept itself was by no means clear and partly because a non-uniform response would threaten the competitive position of the more dedicated firms which would eventually have to abandon the attempt. The problem of pollution is so complex that a variety of measures are probably required to meet different parts of the problem but three frequently discussed are charges (for effluent emissions) regulation (by setting standards for emissions) and prohibition (where highly toxic pollutants concentrate rather than disperse in the environment). There is broad agreement that a system of charges imposed on the polluter in line with the incremental damage caused will lead to the most efficient adjustment. In effect the system provides an incentive for the firm itself to make whatever adjustment is in its own interest but providing the charges are set at the correct level this will coincide with the social interest and the external diseconomy will be internalized. The problem is to discover what the 'correct' charges for the optimum control of the emission should be. A number of different approaches to this problem have been suggested but all imply a considerable two-way flow of information between government and firms. If the policy is to succeed firms must know what are its objectives, how precisely it affects them and how they are expected to respond. Similarly the government will require considerable information about the technology of emission control, waste recycling and the forms of pollution damage. In his review of these problems Rothenberg concluded that

> an appropriate framework and business self-interest do not guarantee a successful programme [of environmental protection]. If businesses see in the various rigors of compliance an arbitrary government interference or competitive disadvantage, their response could be defensive, evasive or legally obstructive. (Rothenberg, 1974; p. 215)

The difference between success and failure of the policies may thus depend on the companies following the spirit as well as the letter of the law. A positive response from the largest enterprises could result if they interpret this as part of the informal ethical code on which Arrow (1973) laid emphasis. More cynically, it could be argued that failure to co-operate fully in a more efficient but less directly interventionist policy would merely ensure their subsequent replacement by more direct (and probably less efficient) controls.

The policy response outlined in this chapter has been based on the recognition that there are strong concentration-increasing forces in capitalist economies. The trend, however, is not inevitable. With a sufficiently imaginative and consistent set of policies it is quite possible to halt and even reverse it without at the same time seriously damaging either the efficiency or flexibility of the corporate sector. Left to itself past experience suggests that the sector would come under the control of fewer and fewer boards of management which eventually no democratically elected government would be prepared to see operate free of direct political control. The underlying objective of policies towards big business should, in our judgement, be to avoid this unappealing prospect.

Notes

Chapter 1: The Ambiguities of Size

1   The companies are 'private' in the sense that their shares are owned by individuals or other private institutions, rather than the state but 'public' in the sense that their shares are quoted on a stock exchange.

Chapter 2: The Anatomy of the Corporate Giants

1   See Feinstein, 1972, Table 17.
2   At least for a period in the 1960s it did seem as though the Labour Government in Britain favoured policies of this kind. For example in paras. 2 and 3 of the White Paper introducing the Industrial Reorganization Corporation (Cmnd. 2889 HMSO, 1966) we read:

> The need for more concentration and rationalisation to promote the greater efficiency and international competitiveness of British industry . . . is now widely recognised . . . many of the production units in this country are small by comparison with the most successful companies in international trade whose operations are often based on a much larger market.

3   For a full discussion of these difficulties see (Prais, 1981) chapter 6 and Appendix F.
4   Prais did attempt to compare the share of the hundred largest German enterprises in manufacturing with that of their British counterparts. The comparison had to be made using quite different data from those quoted on p. 21 above and should be treated as approximate. In 1968 the share of the hundred largest German enterprises in sales of the manufacturing sector was 43 per cent compared with 62 per cent for the UK (Prais, 1981; p. 159). Aggregate concentration is thus half as high again in Britain as in Germany.
5   This is based on the index using manufacturing employment rather

223

than total population. Given the very high labour productivity in the USA with a comparatively small manufacturing work force, the comparison in the text is probably more appropriate.

6 The limits of the index are 1 for an enterprise operating in only one industry and 120 for an enterprise operating equally in every manufacturing industry.

7 The 'product' or 'group of products' as defined in the Census of Production probably comes reasonably close to the idea of at least part of a 'market', the concept used in microeconomics for analysing oligopoly and monopoly. Nevertheless, it is important to remember that the Census statistics are only a partial approximation to the theoretical concept and should be treated with caution. Detailed discussions of the shortcomings of Census data are readily available. See for example, Devine *et al.*, 1979; chapter 2.

8 This is on the assumption that co-ordination is maintained by indirect and tacit means as most forms of overt collusion run into legal problems. In the UK although most overt agreements in manufacturing have been abandoned since the early 1960s following the early decisions of the Restrictive Practices Court, it is clear that various forms of tacit agreement have taken their place. Indeed the sanctions under present law are so feeble that some firms prefer to flout the law and maintain secret market-sharing agreements—see for example, *The Economist*, 27 August 1977; p. 75 and the Monopolies and Mergers Commission (1978) *Electric Cables*, HMSO, para. 363.

9 For a much more detailed series of estimates of concentration in other sectors see, Aaronovitch and Sawyer, 1975; chapter 5.

10 Since the oil crisis the situation has, if anything, become even more bizarre. A citizen in the south of England may have just been deafened by the Concorde aircraft which is the most extravagant of all in fuel use and has been financed by public rather than private enterprise. He may just have seen a commercial urging him to buy more electrical appliances and this may have been followed by a Government commercial exhorting him to save fuel. Clearly we need a Swift to do full justice to this situation.

11 The number is taken from the *Times 1000*, 1976–77.

12 It is difficult to be precise because of the ambiguity surrounding some companies (for example Boots is both manufacturer and retailer, Texaco distributes petroleum but is part of a large integrated oil company).

13 Most of our attention will be focussed on the ownership of the equity capital of the largest companies as this usually carries with it the right to vote at shareholders meetings.

14 This literature generally recognizes the need for some minimum level of profit to offer as a sop to shareholders who might otherwise sell out. The value of the company on the Stock Exchange might

then fall to a sufficiently low level to make it vulnerable to a takeover bid. New owners may well sack the existing managers, so clearly this was a situation to avoid. For an excellent survey see Hay and Morris (1979; chapters 8 and 9).

15 This group includes breweries and distilleries but excludes property and finance companies.

16 The figures should be taken as estimates because of the difficulties of avoiding a number of technical problems. But the order of magnitude of the increase is not in doubt (Prais, 1981; pp. 119, 271).

17 To quote one extreme example: the Prudential Assurance Company had a holding of more than 7 per cent in thirty-four of the fifty largest industrial companies in the *Times 1000* list for 1976–7. The average holding was 3.1 per cent.

18 This point is taken up in chapter 3 below.

19 The largest companies in each sector were taken from *The Times 1000*, 1976–7.

20 *De facto* rather than *de jure*. Restrictive agreements have to be registered and then justified before the Restrictive Practices Court. The onus of proof is clearly on members of the agreement. Since the early decisions of the Court usually went against the agreements most have been abandoned or modified (see chapter 7).

21 This issue is taken up in chapters 8 and 10.

Chapter 3: Efficiency, Technology and Size

1 See chapter 5 pp. 99–105

2 Indeed, as we shall see below the radical critique goes much further than this and argues that 'efficiency' of this kind makes no sense because if the 'correct' values and changed institutions that go with them were present, current output would not be produced at all.

3 There are a number of different methods of estimating plant economies of scale and all are subject to a great many technical problems. For a general discussion see Needham (1978).

4 It may be the case, for example, that production costs are lower when several production plants are serviced by a common tooling shop than when either they each have their own tool room or they purchase the service across the market cf. Prais (1981; p. 46).

5 The published concentration ratios do not include certain industries shown in Table 3.1

6 It is usually the case for example, that the largest firms in an industry to operate the largest plants, see Pratten, 1971; Appendix A.

7 This is not to say, of course, that the absolute size of the largest plants remained unchanged. On the contrary their average size about doubled between the mid 1930s and 1968 (Prais, 1981; p. 51).

8   In many industries transport costs in relation to product unit value may lead to firms with a number of plants in different locations in order to serve the whole market at a lower cost than would be achieved by a single or few very large plants.

9   Discussions of this point usually mention the case where profits can be completely stabilized if a firm produces two products whose profits are perfectly inversely correlated. It is usually not extended to show how special this case is. For if the firm wanted to diversify further, it is bound to upset the profit stability. Clearly it is logically impossible to find three (or more) products whose profits are perfectly and negatively correlated. If A is inversely correlated with B, and B with C then C and A must be perfectly and *positively* correlated.

10 In 1968, the last year for which comprehensive data are available, advertising was equal to an average of 3 per cent of net output for 186 manufacturing industries. For nine product groups the figure was more than 10 per cent.

11 This conclusion may actually understate small-firm participation in 'research' simply because what for them may be part of their normal business practice in maintaining their sales, may in larger, more rigidly structured organizations be labelled as 'research' or 'development'.

12 These examples and many more are described in Jewkes *et al.* (1969).

13 Unfortunately Freeman does not give a separate size grouping for enterprises with 5000 or more employees which would have allowed direct comparisons with similar data for the US. More recent information covering the period 1970–80 indicates that companies with 10,000 or more employees have increased their share of innovations to 66 per cent, see *Science and Technology Indicators for the U.K.: Innovations in Britain since 1945* by J. Townsend *et al.*, Science Policy Research Unit, University of Sussex, mimeo December 1981.

14 They were responsible for 40 per cent of net output in 1958 compared with 33 per cent in 1970. The Census of Production from which the net output figures are taken did not include *enterprise* statistics until 1958.

15 Many examples of developments by individuals and small firms are painstakingly analysed by Jewkes *et al.* (1969). In view of evidence they present, their exasperation with Galbraith is fully justified, cf. their footnote on p. 227.

16 Other references are given in his 1969 article which is especially relevant in the present context as it was specifically concerned with the welfare losses of X-inefficiency.

17 See for example, Edwards (1957).

18 We may note that the argument really depends on a reversal of the

case considered on p. 56 above where the monopoly had *lower* costs than the competitively organized industry. Here Leibenstein is arguing that the monopolist has higher costs as a result of *X*-inefficiency.

19 Scherer (1970; p. 408). The figure in the text is that labelled 'inefficiencies due to deficient cost control by market sector enterprises insulated from competition'. If we also included the item 'inefficiencies due to deficient cost control by defence and space contractors' the figure would rise to 2.6 per cent of GNP. He was so alarmed at the misuse of these rough and ready estimates given in the first edition of his book that he removed them from the second edition cf. Scherer, 1980; p. 470.

20 We take up in the next chapter the subject of selling costs, especially advertising, and economic welfare. Some writers have recently argued that most (if not all) advertising expenditure should be counted as detracting from welfare.

21 We appreciate that there may also be external *economies* which are also 'externalities'. But in the present context we wish to focus exclusively on external 'bads' rather than 'goods'.

22 Hannah and Kay (1977).

23 As sufferers from its air and environmental (not to mention stratospheric) pollution, French and British citizens may rejoice that other airlines have so far declined the delights it has to offer. But as taxpayers they may be less than happy.

24 In order to keep the diagram simple we assume not only constant private costs but also constant external costs. It is probable in many cases that the latter increase at an increasing rate as output is increased as, for example, the chemical reaction among pollutants accelerates.

25 For a fuller discussion of these issues see Burrows (1979) and Rothenberg (1974).

Chapter 4: Advertising and Consumer choice

1 Unfortunately for those who would like to see a beautiful simplicity between corporate size and heavy advertising two groups of consumer products that are perhaps the most heavily advertised—pharmaceuticals and cosmetics stubbornly refuse to be dominated by the largest companies. In 1975 the five largest firms selling pharmaceutical preparations accountd for 39 per cent of sales while those selling cosmetics accounted for 42 per cent of sales.

2 Bain here relies on Chamberlin's contribution to the theory of oligopoly which he believed was one of the most important aspects of the Theory of Monopolistic Competition. See Bain (1967) and chapter 5.

3 A useful survey and critique of both sides of this argument are given in Goldschmid *et al*. (1974), part 3.

4 Some preliminary results were published in 1967. These were considerably extended in their monograph published in 1974.

5 We might note in passing that the whole subject of advertising and product differentiation can give rise to the most acute linguistic and even metaphysical problems. Thus E. H. Chamberlin:

> The issue with which we are concerned (definition of selling costs) may be illustrated by the well-worn example of the 'fins' on American automobiles. Are they a part of producing an automobile with fins, or are they a cost of *selling* an automobile which is conceived as being without fins? (Chamberlin, 1962; p. 275)

6 Perhaps taking their cue from this case study, the British Price Commission suggested that the UK opticians trade association should drop its agreement to restrict advertising as this probably tends to increase consumer ignorance of products and hence may allow higher prices to persist (Price Commission, 1976).

7 Co-ordination of price changes may take a variety of forms where overt cartels are frowned on by the law. We argue in chapter 5 below that this may frequently take the form of 'barometric' price leadership. The present method apparently favoured by the major oil companies in the UK is for managing directors to point out in speeches or press releases that there will have to be an increase in oil prices in the near future for a number of reasons. Early May 1978 was an example. Incidentally the reason given on that occasion was high overheads caused by persistent below capacity working in refineries planned and built on forecasts of oil-demand growth made redundant by the steep rise in oil prices. While the price increase may raise oil company revenues it will certainly make the over-capacity problem worse.

8 These two components plus the dead-weight loss in allocative efficiency (less than $\frac{1}{2}$ of 1 per cent of value added) make up what Comanor and Wilson term 'total costs to society'. If the monopoly transfer of income is included either on grounds of equity or those offered by Tullock that they represent resources expended in *maintaining* monopoly power – we arrive at the 'total cost to consumers' which Comanor and Wilson estimate at between 5 and 6 per cent of value added.

9 The circulation of *Which* was approximately 630 000 in 1979, according to Swann (1979; p. 289).

10 Although the thesis received its full development in *The Affluent Society* first published in 1958, the views have been re-endorsed by Professor Galbraith in the revised edition (1969) and the theme can also be found in two of his other works (1967) and (1975).

11   He has developed his ideas in a number of papers but they are treated at length in his important work *The Joyless Economy* (1976).

12   Scitovksy points out that this may be exactly the opposite case to that of making certain activities involving drugs, alcohol, and tobacco either very difficult or very expensive by taxation. In these cases the sequence is exactly opposite–pleasure or euphoria followed in cases of over indulgence by nausea, illness or even death. If the consumer had full prior knowledge of the whole sequence he would probably modify his behaviour. As he cannot initially have such knowledge the learning process may be long and painful. In some cases, of course, the information may only be acquired when it is too late and addiction has occurred (Scitovsky, 1971; chapter 11).

13   In view of our criticisms of the tobacco companies' sponsorships of sporting events (p. 80) we should add that these companies have also played a leading role in assisting the arts. Imperial Tobacco, for example, as part sponsors of the Pompeii Exhibition in London contributed £1½ millions.

Chapter 5: Competition and Conglomeration

1   He also identified other important characteristics such as the number and size distribution of buyers, the degree of vertical integration, the rate of growth of demand, but the three mentioned in the text have probably received the greatest amount of attention.

2   That is, the share of sales made by the five largest firms was equal or greater than 70 per cent.

3   Also the difference between price and marginal cost if average costs are assumed to be constant over the relevant output range.

4   The results given by Bain both in 1956, (chapter 7) and 1959 (chapter 11) are, of course, much more detailed than the very brief summary given in the text.

5   The largest eight firms had 70 per cent or more of sales. Bain did not assume a continuous relationship between profit rates and concentration but in line with Chamberlin's theory argued that at very high concentration levels effective collusion would be much more likely.

6   The actual extent of their market power will, of course, depend upon a number of other structural features which we discussed on pp. 91–92.

7   We will use the terms interchangeably, although 'conglomerate' is frequently reserved for companies that have grown very fast by acquisitions in many industries. It is also, perhaps because of its ugliness, often used as a term of abuse.

8 This allows them to rearrange their portfolios speedily without disturbing prevailing share prices. A similar transaction involving shares of a smaller company is likely to have a much more depressing effect on the market price.

9 The dichotomy between 'conglomerate' and 'specialist' is, of course, a gross over-simplification. Most firms in many size groups produce a variety of products.

10 For a fuller discussion of these and other cases see Utton (1979; chapter 5.) None of the cases mentioned in the text dealt either mainly or exclusively with 'predatory practices'. Ironically the only report so far made specifically on this issue concluded that pricing policies had been unobjectionable–see Monopolies Commission, (1963) *Electrical Wiring Harnesses for Motor Vehicles*, HMSO.

11 The same is true of the USA; see Backman (1970).

12 Results for a similar exercise for the UK were inconclusive. The sample of industries included was rather small because of data problems, and although the relationship between concentration change and entry by diversification seemed to be negative, the result was not statistically significant (Utton, 1979, chapter 3). The result of a third study, by the Federal Trade Commission into the effect of aggregate concentration (that is the share held in industries by the largest 200 manufacturing firms) on the change in concentration in those individual industries is probably misleading because of the specification of the relationship estimated.

13 For example, it has only been possible so far to measure the variables in one year because of data problems and therefore the 'entry' effect may be blurred.

Chapter 7: Antitrust and Related Policies

1 For historical reasons the term 'antitrust' is used in the USA whereas Europe tends to favour 'competition policy'. We shall use the terms interchangeably.

2 Some of these were reviewed in chapter 2 above.

3 Since its creation in 1948 the title, size and scope of the Commission has changed a number of times. For a detailed discussion of the constitution and the work of the Commission up to the mid 1960s see Rowley (1966). For a critical survey of some of its later works see Sutherland (1969).

4 It can also be given a 'general reference' on a particular type of market conduct, for example refusal to supply, recommended resale prices, parallel pricing or on a particular practice by an individual company. We take up the question of parallel pricing below, pp. 123–124.

5 As we shall see below in merger enquiries, the definition of what

constitutes the market in horizontal cases has caused more difficulty.

6   For an excellent brief review of the development of antitrust laws see Scherer (1980; chapters 19–21).

7   As we shall see below there is a school of thought that holds that the greatest impediment to the dynamic efficiency of markets lies not in the restrictions imposed by firms, which are bound to be short-lived but in the clumsy interventions of all kinds by governments (cf. chapter 9).

8   See for example Goldschmid *et al.* (1974; chapter 7).

9   In sixteen reports made either by the Monopolies and Mergers Commission or the Price Commission and in some cases both, the leading firms were judged technically efficient in fourteen. Only two cases were criticized for their lack of progressiveness although the evidence on this aspect of performance was less fully developed. All cases involved products where seller concentration had been very heavy for some time and where import competition was minimal (Utton, 1981b).

10   Although mergers can be challenged under the Sherman Act if they 'tend to reduce competition or create a monopoly', special provisions were thought necessary, following the dramatic wave of mergers at the turn of the century. Unfortunately the wording of the 1914 Celler Act and subsequent interpretations by the Supreme Court made the provision almost totally useless in merger cases. The act was amended in 1950 so effective antitrust policy dates from that year.

11   The qualification is important because antitrust policy both in the USA and the UK only affects the most important of all mergers that actually take place. According to Scherer only about 1–2 per cent of all mergers have been challenged. In the UK the percentage is much smaller than this, although if only those sizeable mergers which come within the scope of the legislation are considered the percentage is roughly the same as for the USA.

12   In this partial equilibrium framework the net social benefit of a particular price–cost configuration is defined as the total revenue plus consumers' surplus, minus social cost (where private and social costs are assumed to be identical).

13   If all monopoly profit is removed to the 'cost' side of the equation then, of course, we are back with the existing American antitrust position.

14   In principle, of course, it is possible that post merger costs may actually rise above AC_c. In this case competitive pressures are probably so moribund as to make all hopes of an efficient private sector vain.

15   At present most merger enquiries by the Monopolies and Mergers Commission have to be completed within six months of the reference.

16 For much more detailed assessment of how Williamson's approach might work out in practice see Utton (1975).

17 When the narrower definition of the 'market' was used the share in both cases was about 90 per cent. The Commission was satisfied that the narrower definition was justified.

18 The Commission was satisfied that 'the bargaining power of the buyers in this case is sufficient to ensure that the merged company will always be under the strongest pressure to keep its costs and profit margins as low as possible'. (Monopolies Commission, 1967a; para. 13).

19 In the DuPont case which was brought under the Sherman Act rather than under the Celler-Kefauver Act, General Motors was required to sell off its 23 per cent holdings in DuPont. The holding was acquired in 1917, the initial proceedings started in 1949 and the final Supreme Court decision was made in 1957. Divestiture was finally completed in 1962 and involved a special Act of Congress. (Scherer, 1980; p. 549).

20 Members of the Panel include staff from the Monopolies and Mergers Commission and the Director General of Fair Trading.

21 This comment is based on Appendix Table 7 of the review (p. 111). At the time, spring 1978, forty-three references had been made (since 1965) fifteen had been abandoned without a report; thirteen had been found against the public interest, and fifteen not likely to operate against the public interest.

22 In the NEDO volume, *Competition Policy*, any change which might make mergers more difficult or reduce their volume was opposed on the grounds that it might hamper the 'rationalization' of British industry (NEDO, 1978).

23 For a summary of the evidence see *Review of Monopolies and Mergers Policy* (HMSO, 1978, annex D) and on the effects of mergers Cowling *et al*. (1981) and Meeks and Meeks (1981).

24 The argument that sizeable mergers will allow small-scale plant to be closed and larger, lower-cost plant to take its place should be treated sceptically. The implication is that market power is required before the reorganization becomes profitable, otherwise the companies could proceed to achieve the economies by internal expansion.

25 Prais (1981; p. 162) suggested that the relatively tough antimerger policy of the USA probably helped to stabilize the level of aggregate concentration in recent years while in the UK it continued to rise rapidly.

26 If pre-merger market power exists at one stage of production it may subsequently be used to change the market structure of the other production stage (up or down stream). But here the problem is the existing market power rather than the vertical integration itself.

27 For a detailed antagonistic view of this development see Blair (1972).

28 The phrase is Manne's (1965).
29 Although as is usual in economics there are strong dissenting voices, cf. below chapter 9.
30 For example if discounts to retailers are made to depend on aggregate purchases from all cartel members or if they all threaten to boycott retailers who wish to buy from firms outside the cartel, it may be much more difficult for entrants to make any headway in the industry. For a detailed discussion and other harrowing examples see Monopolies Commission (1955).
31 Restrictive Trading Agreements, Report of Registrar, July 1969–June 1972, Cmnd 5195, HMSO (1973).
32 We appreciate that however strong the antitrust policy information exchanges between firms cannot be eliminated. The smaller the number of firms the greater the probability that a co-ordinated response to some market change can be made if necessary simply by using the telephone.
33 Again British experience both in some nationalized industries and more recently with the National Enterprise Board suggests that this is likely to be the fate of public enterprises introduced into oligopolistic industries.
34 For a brief review of these tribulations see Maunder (1979; chapter 5).
35 For present purposes we are assuming that a state enterprise with general management experience already exists, inspired perhaps by the example of the IRI. We are thus avoiding the problems associated with setting up a new organization from scratch.
36 If other firms have been kept out, despite high profits, by the size of scale economies in relation to market demand, entry on a sufficient scale by new building is not possible without causing prices to fall for all firms (including the public enterprise) below long-run average costs. In other words, all will make losses. This amounts to the 'natural monopoly' case which is unlikely to occur in manufacturing industry where imports can compete with domestic production. In the main text we therefore concentrate on other sources of entry barriers.
37 Cf. Chapter 4 above.
38 There is also the problem that we are not tackling here of deciding which company the public enterprise should take over. Given the size of the UK economy and the level of concentration in the markets affected there is likely to be little choice but to acquire the market leader which is likely to be very large.
39 In the seven cases examined in Utton (1979) where predatory pricing had been used the average market share of the dominant firm was more than 90 per cent.
40 Cf. Chapter 5, pp. 97–98. Shepherd was apparently aware of this evidence but found it, rather conveniently, 'ineffectual' (p. 129 fn).

41   More recently this has in effect meant 'not levied' since many com-
     panies have escaped all Corporation Tax by taking advantage of
     generous inflation accounting provisions (cf. Kay and King, 1978;
     chapters 11 and 12).
42   The 1969 Tax Reform Act in the US made interest not allowable as
     a deduction for tax purposes when it related to large convertible
     debenture issues made in connection with a merger (Prais, 1981;
     p. 296).
43   Formally in the bilateral monopoly model which may be the most
     appropriate for the analysis of such cases price is indeterminate
     between the 'high' level which the seller may wish to receive and
     the 'low' level which the buyer would like to pay. Supporters of the
     policy clearly expect the public buyer to be able to force prices
     down to the 'lower' level.

Chapter 8: Social Responsibility and Corporatism

1   In addition to pollution their list includes: safety; employment
    related issues such as the human impact of assembly line work,
    training opportunities for disadvantaged workers and hours and
    overtime requirements; relationships with dealers and suppliers.
2   Just as in other areas of economic or social behaviour the assurance
    will work most of the time. It does not guarantee that some indivi-
    duals will not deliberately try to break the code for their own
    advantage.
3   It is interesting to note in this connection that the 1973 Companies
    Bill had a provision that in the directors part of the company account
    arrangements for promoting the safety and health of the public
    should be published. The Bill was not taken up by the new Labour
    Government of 1974 and therefore never became law.
4   Perhaps not surprisingly there is also in the UK considerable support
    for economically nationalist policies–especially import controls–the
    fourth characteristic. The fifth, labelled 'success' by Winkler,
    emphasizes goal achievement rather fastidious adherence to due
    processes of law. We leave to the reader the task of deciding whether
    this feature is discernable in the UK.
5   The proposals were set out in a number of documents published
    while the Labour Party was in opposition and soon after it came to
    office in 1974. For a detailed account see Budd (1978; chapter 7).
6   If this is reminiscent of the kind of role envisaged for state enterprise
    in oligopoly discussed in the previous chapter it should occasion no
    surprise. The editor of the book which we referred to there was also
    a major influence on the Labour Party proposals at this time, both
    through another book (Holland, 1975) and as a member of the
    Study Group which produced the Opposition Green Paper.
7   Some observers, of course, claim that it is in the nature of the prob-

lem that such information cannot be available to such a committee in advance. See chapter 9 and Hayek (1948; especially chapters 2 and 4).

Chapter 9: Disengagement by the State

1 Especially over methodology (Dolan, 1976; chap. 3).
2 Even if the physical production methods are widely known, some firms may have discovered cheaper sources of input supplies, for example, which make their costs lower than that of others.
3 Students new to the subject must often be puzzled as to why the rather cumbersome, foreign word is introduced into the discussion at all since, under static assumptions, the 'entrepreneur' is called upon to perform nothing more than routine, day to day functions. They could at least be told that he is really a ghost from the classical past of economics, for as McNulty has shown the classical view was much closer to the Austrian view than to modern abstractions (McNulty, 1967).
4 This comment is correct while we confine our attention to the private sector of industry. As we can see on pp. 184–185 a major contention of the Austrian writers is that the granting of special privileges to state-owned enterprises generates monopoly profits.
5 Cf. chapter 5.
6 For a detailed discussion of some of these cases see Utton (1979; chapter 7).
7 The question of patents which arose in the Roche case is discussed on pp. 121–122.
8 The one exception is pure monopoly profit defined in the way discussed on pp. 174–175.
9 'The necessary consequence of the reason why we use competition is that *in those cases in which it is interesting*, the validity of the theory can never be tested empirically' (Hayek, 1948; p. 180: italics in the original)
10 Although in one case the decline (of the Imperial Group's share of the UK cigarette market) was fairly marginal.
11 *Statistics of Product Concentration of UK Manufacturers for 1963, 1968, and 1975*, Business Monitor, PO 1006, HMSO (1979).
12 A main conclusion of a recent comprehensive enquiry was that except for a rather narrow range of products (which included pharmaceuticals) the impact of patents was slight (Taylor and Silberston, 1973).
13 See in particular the report on *Collective Discrimination* (1955).
14 We should note that although Littlechild says most Austrian writers would probably *not* favour control of restrictive practices, in his concluding list of policy suggestions, he does give the option of

either dissolving the Restrictive Practices Court, or allowing access to it by private plaintiffs (Littlechild, 1978; p. 80).

15   Even the Conservative Government elected in 1979 and committed to more competition for nationalized enterprises used a rise in gas prices as a means of reducing the overall level of the public sector borrowing requirement.

16   His answer to those who might argue that this solution would be politically unacceptable to the Trade Unions was simple: 'If the trade unions object, then give the nationalised industries to the unions' (Friedman, 1977; p. 53).

17   It should be clear from chapter 5 that 'entrants' may either be new firms or the subsidiary of an existing giant.

Chapter 10: The Left and 'Monopoly Capitalism'

1   We should perhaps apologise in advance for using labels which one eminent authority regards as at best irrelevant and at worst ludicrous (Sweezy, 1972). In distinguishing between the 'Old Left' and the 'New' we wish merely to indicate a change of emphasis. While the 'Old' Left drew their inspiration from the whole corpus of Marx's works but emphasized his mature view expressed in *Capital*, the 'New' Left has tended to reach back to his earlier work and especially the notion of 'alienation' for its particular critique of modern capitalist enterprise.

2   This part of the argument is thus very similar to the 'mutual forbearance' hypothesis that we encountered in chapter 5.

3   Baran and Sweezy take 'bourgeois' economists to task for not recognizing the key role played by advertising whereas it has been fully acknowledged by businessmen and marketing experts. To support their argument they quote a prominent New York investment banker who raised the spectre of under-consumption in the absence of sales effort thus: 'clothing could be purchased for its utility value; food would be bought on the basis of economy and nutritional value; automobiles would be stripped to essentials and held by the same owner for the full ten to fifteen years of their useful lives' (p. 128). Presumably, therefore, there is a vast untapped demand for these and other products which the authors know about but apparently are unknown to any profit-seeking company. It does not occur either to the author quoted or to Baran and Sweezy themselves that profit maximizing firms would take advantage of these opportunities if they really existed. Failure to recognize this point seems to rest ultimately on a rather low opinion of consumers who can have their 'true' wishes so easily frustrated by advertising campaigns, an opinion not uncommon on the Left as others have recognized (Domar, 1974; pp. 1305–6).

4 Cf. chapter 4.

5 Several writers have pointed to the apparent contradiction in much New Left writing between an emphasis on the need for much greater equality of income on the one hand and a great contempt for nearly all forms of material objects purchased by consumers and which cannot lead to fulfilment and happiness. If consumption is unimportant why stress income redistribution as a primary objective? Its achievement might, on this view, actually reduce the happiness of the recipients (Cf. Domar, 1974; and Lindbeck, 1971.)

6 It is evident that they can have no inkling of what a chill sound that phrase has to Europeans who throughout the past sixty years have been frequently promised 'new' and 'rational' economic orders only to see the promises turn to tyranny.

7 See in particular Baran and Sweezy (1977; chapter 7).

8 Domar's comment is particularly apt:

> If existing socialist countries are not really socialist, could not the proponents of 'real' capitalism declare all existing capitalist countries not capitalist? After all none of them have perfect competition and complete *laissez-faire*. . .Then we would be comparing completely imaginery systems! (Domar, 1974; p. 1303)

9 Chapter 3.

10 Baran and Sweezy (1977; especially chapter 3).

11 If majorities did coalesce in this way the implication is that there might be a considerable number of minorities for whom the labour-managed firm was no solution to the problem of alienation. For fuller development of this and the points mentioned in the text see Furubotn (1976; pp. 218–224).

12 See above chapter 2.

13 The starting point of his discussion was not the problems posed by the corporate giants and alienation, but those created by the conflict between democratically elected governments committed to full employment and stable prices on the one hand and free association in trade unions on the other. In his view in many Western economies but especially the UK, trade-union growth and power now make it impossible for these institutions to co-exist with the achievement of the economic objectives. He argues that an economy where all firms above one hundred employees have legally to be workers co-operatives may give a more acceptable solution than the one presently on offer.

14 The Left would argue that since all three economies in the comparison are capitalist 'alienation' in their sense must be as widespread in all of them, so there must be some other explanation for the difference in plant sizes.

15 The development of worker-managed firms within the conventional capitalist economy is, as we have indicated, anathema to the

New Left. Also, given the problem that he was addressing, Jay argued that it would only be solved by a complete adoption of worker-managed firms throughout the economy. Half measures or piecemeal introduction would not succeed, in his view.

Chapter 11: Halting the Trend

1   Given the recent size of selective subsidies to ailing companies, it can be argued that a new motive for growth was to become so large as to qualify for subsidies if the company showed signs of failure. Since the larger the company the less the likelihood of takeover and the greater the chance of subsidy perhaps it is now true in the UK that the giants have insulated themselves almost completely from death.

2   The number of companies mentioned is merely illustrative. It might be extended according to developments in the EEC and the trend of aggregate concentration in the UK.

3   It is true that the 1967 Companies Act increased the requirement to publish certain information for example on sales, directors salaries and contributions, but the detailed form in which this information was published was left largely to the discretion of directors.

4   The additional information that had to be published after the 1967 Act has proved to be of limited use since each company can choose how it is to be presented. It is not generally possible, therefore, to compare one company with another.

5   In this case, of course, the controls were instituted on health grounds not because advertising was seen as a waste of resources. Contraceptive advertisers have similarly been denied a place in television commercials and have therefore sponsored motor racing with what effects we leave the reader to decide.

References

AARONOVITCH, S. and SAWYER, M.C. (1975), *Big Business*, Macmillan, London.

ADELMAN, M.A. (1964), Testimony before the Senate Subcommittee on Antitrust and Monopoly, *Economic Concentration, Overall and Conglomerate Aspects*, Washington.

ALCHIAN, A.A. and DEMSETZ, H. (1972), Production, information costs and economic organisation, *American Economic Review*, vol. 62, 5, pp. 777–795.

ANDREWS, K.R. (1972), Public responsibility in the private corporation, *Journal of Industrial Economies*, vol 20, 2, pp. 135–145.

ARROW, K.J. (1973), Social responsibility and economic efficiency, *Public Policy*, vol. 21, 3, pp. 303–317.

BACKMAN, J. (1970), Conglomerate mergers and competition, in *Conglomerate Mergers and Acquisitions, St. John's Law Review*, vol. 44, Special Edition, pp. 90–132.

BAIN, J.S. (1951), Relation of profit rate to industry concentration: American manufacturing, 1936–40, *Quarterly Journal of Economics*, vol. 65, 3, pp. 293–324.

BAIN, J.S. (1956), *Barriers to New Competition*, Harvard University Press, Cambridge, Mass.

BAIN, J.S. (1959), *Industrial Organisation*, Wiley, Chichester.

BAIN, J.S. (1967), Chamberlin's impact on microeconomic theory, in Kuenne, R. (ed.) *Theory of Monopolistic Competition in Retrospect*, Wiley, Chichester.

BARAN, P.A. and SWEEZY, P. M. (1977), *Monopoly Capital*, Penguin Books, Harmondsworth.

BEESLEY, M. and EVANS, T. (1978), *Corporate Social Responsibility*, Croom Helm, London.

BENHAM, L. (1972), The effect of advertising on the price of eyeglasses, *Journal of Law and Economics*, vol. 15, 2, pp. 337–352.

BERRY, C.H. (1975), *Corporate Growth and Diversification*, Princeton University Press.

BLAIR, J.M. (1972), *Economic Concentration*, Harcourt Brace Jovanovich, London.

239

BLUMBERG, P. (1969), *Industrial Democracy*, Schocken Books, New York.

BOWER, J. (1974), On the amoral organisation, in Marris, R. (ed.) *The Corporate Society*, Macmillan, London.

BRITTAN, S. (1975), Towards a Corporate State, *Encounter*, vol. 44, 6, pp. 58–63.

BRITTAN, S. (1977), *The Economic Consequences of Democracy*, Temple Smith, London.

BRITTAN, S. (1978), How British is the British Sickness, *Journal of Law and Economics*, vol. 21, 2, pp. 245–268.

BROZEN, Y. (1971), Bain's concentration and rates of return revisited, *Journal of Law and Economics*, vol. 14, 2, pp. 351–369.

BUCHANAN, J.M. (1969), External diseconomies, corrective taxes and market structure, *American Economic Review*, vol. 59, 1, pp. 174–177.

BUDD, A. (1978), *The Politics of Economic Planning*, Fontana, London.

BURROWS, P. (1979), *The Economic Theory of Pollution Control*. Martin Robertson, Oxford.

BUTTERS, G.R. (1976), A survey of advertising and market structure, *American Economic Review, Papers and Proceedings*, vol. 66, 2, pp. 392–397.

CAVES, R.E. (ed.) (1968), *Britain's Economic Prospects*, George Allen and Unwin, London.

CHAMBERLIN, E.H. (1962), *The Theory of Monopolistic Competition* (eighth edition), Oxford University Press, London.

CHANNON, D.F. (1973), *The Strategy and Structure of British Enterprise*, Macmillan, London.

COMANOR, W.S. and LEIBENSTEIN, H. (1969), Allocative efficiency, *X*-efficiency and the measurement of welfare losses, *Economica*, vol. 36, 143, pp. 304–309.

COMANOR, W.S. and WILSON, T.A. (1974), *Advertising and Market Power*, Harvard University Press, Cambridge, Mass.

COMANOR, W.S. and WILSON, T.A. (1979), The effects of advertising on competition: A survey, *Journal of Economic Literature*, vol. 17, 2, pp. 453–476.

COWLING, K. and MUELLER, D. (1978), Social costs of monopoly power, *Economic Journal*, vol. 88, 352, pp. 724–748.

COWLING, K., STONEMAN, P., CUBBIN, J., CABLE, J., HALL, G., DOMBERGER, S. and DUTTON, P. (1981), *Mergers and Economic Performance*, Cambridge University Press, Cambridge.

COWLING, K. and WATERSON, M. (1976), Price-cost margins and market structure, *Economica*, vol. 43, 171, pp. 267–274.

DEMSETZ, H. (1974), Two systems of belief about monopoly, in Goldschmid, H.J. Mann, H.M. and Weston, J.F. (eds.) *Industrial*

Concentration: The New Learning, Little, Brown & Co., Boston, Mass.

DEMSETZ, H. (1976), Economics as a guide to antitrust regulation, *Journal of Law and Economics*, vol. 19, 2, pp. 371–384.

DEPARTMENT OF INDUSTRY (1974), *The Regeneration of British Industry* Cmnd. 5710, HMSO.

DEVINE, P.J., LEE, N. JONES, R.M., and TYSON, W.J. (1979), *An Introduction to Industrial Economics*, Allen and Unwin, London.

DEWEY, D.J. (1968), *Imperfect Competition: A Radical Reconstruction*, Columbia University Press, New York.

DEWEY, D.J. (1974), The new learning: One man's view, in Goldschmid, H.J., Mann, H.M. and Weston, J.F. (eds.) *Industrial Concentration: The New Learning*, Little, Brown & Co., Boston, Mass.

DIXIT, A. and NORMAN, V. (1978), Advertising and welfare, *The Bell Journal of Economics*, vol. 9, 1, pp. 1–17.

DOLAN, E.G. (ed.) (1976), *The Foundations of Modern Austrian Economics* Sheed and Ward Inc., London.

DOMAR, E.D. (1974), Poor old capitalism: A review article, *Journal of Political Economy*, vol. 82, 6, pp. 1301–1313.

EDWARDS, C.D. (1955), Conglomerate bigness as a source of power, in *Business Concentration and Price Policy*, National Bureau of Economic Research, Princeton University Press.

EDWARDS, C.D. (1964), Hearings before the Subcommittee on Antitrust and Monopoly of the Committee of the Judiciary of the US Senate, part 1, *Overall and Conglomerate Aspects*, Washington DC.

EDWARDS, R.C., MacEWAN, A. and the Staff of Social Sciences 125 (1970), A radical approach to economics: Basis for a new curriculum, *American Economic Review, Papers and Proceedings*, vol. 60, 2, pp. 352–363.

EDWARDS, R.S. (1957), *Competition in the British Soap Industry*, Oxford University Press, London.

FEDERAL TRADE COMMISSION (1969), *Economic Report on Corporate Mergers*, Washington DC.

FEDERAL TRADE COMMISSION (1972), *Conglomerate Merger Performance*, Washington DC.

FEINSTEIN, C.H. (1972), National Income, Expenditure and Output of the United Kingdom 1855–1965, Cambridge University Press, Cambridge.

FISHER, F.M. (1979), Diagnosing monopoly, *Quarterly Review of Economics and Business*, vol. 19, 2, pp. 7–33.

FRIEDMAN, M. (1962), *Capitalism and Freedom*, The University of Chicago Press, Illinois.

FRIEDMAN, M. (1977), *From Galbraith to Economic Freedom*, Occasional Paper 49, Institute of Economic Affairs, London.

242 *References*

FURUBOTN, E.G. (1976), Worker alienation and the structure of the firm, in Pejovich, S. (ed.) *Government Controls and the Free Market*, Texas A and M University Press, Texas.

GALBRAITH, J.K. (1967), *The New Industrial State*, Penguin Books, Harmondsworth.

GALBRAITH, J.K. (1975), *Economics and the Public Purpose*, Penguin Books, Harmondsworth.

GALBRAITH, J.K. (1976), *The Affluent Society* (second edition), Penguin Books, Harmondsworth.

GINTIS, H. (1972), Alienation in capitalist society, in Edwards, R.C. Reich, M. and Weisskopf, T.E. (eds) *The Capitalist System*, Prentice-Hall, Englewood Cliffs, New Jersey.

GOLDBERG, L. (1973), The effects of conglomerate mergers on competition, *Journal of Law and Economics*, vol. 16, 1, pp. 137–158.

GOLDSCHMID, H.J., MANN, H.M. and WESTON, J.F. (eds) (1974), *Industrial Concentration: The New Learning*, Little, Brown & Co., Boston, Mass.

HART, P.E. and MORGAN, E. (1977), Market structure and economic performance in the United Kingdom, *Journal of Industrial Economics*, vol. 25, 3, pp. 177–193.

HART, P.E. and CLARKE, R. (1980), *Concentration in British Industry, 1935–75*, Cambridge University Press, Cambridge.

HANNAH, L. and KAY, J.A. (1977), *Concentration in Modern Industry*, Macmillan, London.

HARBERGER, A.C. (1971), Monopoly and resource allocation, reprinted in Archibald, G.C. (ed.) *Readings in the Theory of the Firm*, Penguin Books, Harmondsworth.

HAY, D. and MORRIS, D. (1979), *Industrial Economics*, Oxford University Press, London.

HAYEK, F.A. (1948), *Individualism and Economic Order*, University of Chicago Press, Illinois.

HAYEK, F.A. (1967), *Studies in Philosophy, Politics and Economics*, Routledge and Kegan Paul, London.

HAYEK, F.A. (1978), *New Studies in Philosophy, Politics, Economics and the History of Ideas*, Routledge and Kegan Paul, London.

HAYEK, F.A. (1979), The non-sequitur of the 'Dependence Effect', reprinted in Mansfield, E. *Readings in Microeconomics*.

HICKS, J.R. (1953), Annual survey of economic theory: The theory of monopoly, reprinted in Stigler, G.J. and Boulding, K.E. (eds.) *Readings in Price Theory*, Allen and Unwin, London.

HOLLAND, S. (1972), *The State as Entrepreneur*, Weidenfeld and Nicolson, London.

HOLLAND, S. (1975), *The Socialist Challenge*, Quartet Books, London.

HMSO (1978), *Review of Monopolies and Mergers Policy*, HMSO, London.

JAY, P. (1977), *The Workers Co-operative Economy*, Manchester Statistical Society, Manchester.

JEWKES, J. (1977), *Delusions of Dominance*, Institute of Economic Affairs.

JEWKES, J., SAWERS, D. and STILLERMAN, R. (1969), *The Sources of Invention* (second edition), Macmillan, London.

JOHNSON, H.G., (1970), The economics of advertising, in Needham, D. *Readings in the Economics of Industrial Organisation*, Holt, Rinehart, and Winston, New York.

KAY, J.A. and KING, M.A. (1978), *The British Tax System*, Oxford University Press, London.

KRISTOL, I. (1975), On corporate capitalism in America, *The Public Interest*, no. 41, Fall, pp. 124–141.

LABOUR PARTY (1973), *National Enterprise Board*, Opposition Green Paper.

LEIBENSTEIN, H. (1978), X-inefficiency Xists – Reply to an Xorcist, *American Economic Review*, vol. 68, 1, pp. 203–211.

LINDBECK, A. (1971), *The Political Economy of the New Left*, Harper and Row, New York.

LINDBECK, A. (1972), Rejoinder, in Symposium: Economics of the New Left, *Quarterly Journal of Economics*, vol. 86, 4, pp. 665–683.

LITTLECHILD, S.C. (1978), *The Fallacy of the Mixed Economy*, Institute of Economic Affairs, London.

McNULTY, P.J. (1967), A note on the history of perfect competition, *Journal of Political Economy*, vol. 75, 4, pp. 395–399.

MANN, H.M. (1974), Advertising, concentration and profitability, in Goldschmid, H.J., Mann, H.M. and Weston, J.K. (eds) *Industrial Concentration: The New Learning*, Little, Brown & Co., Boston, Mass.

MANN, H.M., HENNING, J.A. and MEEHAN, J.W. (1967), Advertising and concentration: An empirical investigation, *Journal of Industrial Economics*, vol. 16, 2, pp. 34–45.

MANNE, H.G. (1965), Mergers and the market for corporate control, *Journal of Political Economy*, vol. 73, 2, pp. 110–120.

MARKHAM, J. (1973), *Conglomerate Enterprise and Public Policy*, Harvard University Press, Cambridge, Mass.

MARRIS, R. and MUELLER, D.C. (1980), The corporation, competition and the invisible hand, *Journal of Economic Literature*, vol. 18, 1, pp. 32–63.

MARSHALL, A. (1961), *Principles of Economics* (eighth edition), Macmillan, London.

MASON, E.S. (1957), *Economic Concentration and the Monopoly Problem*, Harvard University Press, Cambridge, Mass.

MAUNDER, P. (ed.) (1979), *Government Intervention in the Developed Economy*, Croom Helm, London.

244   *References*

MAYO, E. (1933), *The Human Problems of an Industrial Civilisation*, New Macmillan, London.

MEADE, J.E. (1975), *The Intelligent Radical's Guide to Economic Policy*, Allen and Unwin, London.

MEEKS, G. and MEEKS, J.G. (1981), Profitability measures as indicators of post-merger efficiency, *Journal of Industrial Economics*, vol. 29, 4, pp. 335–344.

MISHAN, E.J. (1971), On making the future safe for mankind, *The Public Interest*, no. 24, Summer, pp. 33–61.

MONOPOLIES COMMISSION (1955), *Collective Discrimination*, HMSO, London.

MONOPOLIES COMMISSION (1966), *Report on the Supply of Synthetic Detergents*, HMSO, London.

MONOPOLIES COMMISSION (1967a), *Guest, Keen and Nettlefolds Ltd. and Birfield Ltd., A Report on the Merger*, HMSO, London.

MONOPOLIES COMMISSION (1967b), *British Insulated Callenders Cables and Pyrotenax, Report on the Merger*, HMSO, London.

MONOPOLIES COMMISSION (1967c), *Ross Group Ltd. and Associated Fisheries Ltd. A Report on the Proposed Merger*, HMSO, London.

MONOPOLIES COMMISSION (1968), *Thorn Electrical Industries Ltd. and Radio Rentals Ltd., A Report on the Proposed Merger*, HMSO, London.

MONOPOLIES COMMISSION (1973a), *Report on the Supply of Chlordiazepoxide and Diazepam*, HMSO, London.

MONOPOLIES COMMISSION (1973b), *Parallel Pricing*, HMSO, London.

MONOPOLIES AND MERGERS COMMISSION (1978), *Report on the Supply of Electric Cables*, HMSO, London.

MUELLER, D.C. (1977), The persistence of profits above the norm, *Economica*, vol. 44, 176, pp. 369–80.

NATIONAL ECONOMIC DEVELOPMENT OFFICE (1978), *Competition Policy*, HMSO, London.

NEEDHAM, D. (1978), *The Economics of Industrial Structure, Conduct and Performance*, Holt, Rinehart and Winston, London.

ORNSTEIN, S. (1972), Concentration and profits, *Journal of Business*, vol. 45, 4, pp. 519–541.

ORWELL, G. (1970), *Collected Essays, Journalism and Letters*, Vol. 3. Penguin Books, Harmondsworth.

PEACOCK, A. (1976), Some economic aspects of the arts, in Blaug, M. (ed.) *Economics of the Arts*, Martin Robertson, Oxford.

POLANYI, G. and POLANYI, P. (1974), Parallel pricing: A harmful practice? *Moorgate and Wall Street*, Spring, pp. 39–62.

POSNER, R.A. (1975), The social costs of monopoly and regulation, *Journal of Political Economy*, vol. 83, 4, pp. 807–827.

PRAIS, S.J. (1978), The strike proneness of large plants in Britain,

Journal of the Royal Statistical Society, series A, vol. 141, 3, pp. 368–384.

PRAIS, S.J. (1981), *The Evolution of Giant Firms in Britain* (second impression), Cambridge University Press.

PRAIS, S.J. (1982), *Productivity and Industrial Structure*, Cambridge University Press.

PRATTEN, C.F. (1971), *Economies of Scale in Manufacturing Industry*, Cambridge University Press.

PRESTON, L.E. (1975), Corporation and society: The search for a paradigm, *Journal of Economic Literature*, vol. 13, 2, pp. 434–453.

PRESTON, L.E. and POST, J.E. (1975), *Private Management and Public Policy*, Prentice Hall, Englewood Cliffs, New Jersey.

PRICE COMMISSION (1976), *Prices of Private Spectacles and Contact Lenses*, HMSO, London.

PRICE COMMISSION (1979), *BOC Limited–Compressed Permanent Gases and Dissolved Acetylene Sold in Cylinders, Cylinder Rentals and Fixed Charges*, HMSO, London.

REEKIE, W.D. (1979), *Industry, Prices and Markets*, Phillip Allan, Deddington, Oxon.

RHOADES, S.A. (1973), The effect of diversification on industry profit performance in 241 manufacturing industries, 1963, *Review of Economics and Statistics*, vol. 55, 2, pp. 146–155.

ROTHENBERG, J. (1974), The physical environment in McKie, J.W. (ed.) *Social Responsibility and the Business Predicament*, The Brookings Institution, Washington.

ROTHSCHILD, K.W. (1953), Price Theory and Oligopoly, reprinted in Stigler, G.J. and Boulding, K.E. (eds.) *Readings in Price Theory* Allen and Unwin, London.

ROTHSCHILD, K.W. (1971), Introduction, in *Power in Economics*, Penguin Books, Harmondsworth.

ROWLEY, C.K. (1966), *The British Monopolies Commission*, Allen and Unwin, London.

ROWLEY, C.K. and PEACOCK, A.T. (1975), *Welfare Economics: A Liberal Restatement*, Martin Robertson, Oxford.

SCHERER, F.M. (1970), *Industrial Market Structure and Economic Performance*, Rand McNally, Chicago.

SCHERER, F.M. (1974), Economies of scale as a determinant, in Goldschmid, H.J., Mann, H.M. and Weston, J.F. (eds) *Industrial Concentration: The New Learning*, Little Brown & Co., Boston, Mass.

SCHERER, F.M. (1980), *Industrial Market Structure and Economic Performance*, Rand McNally, Chicago.

SCHMALENSEE, R. (1974), Brand loyalty and barriers to entry, *Southern Economic Journal*, vol. 40, 4, pp. 579–588.

SCHUMPETER, J.A. (1965), *Capitalism, Socialism and Democracy*, Allen and Unwin, London.

SCHWARTZMAN, D. (1960), The burden of monopoly, *Journal of Political Economy*, vol. 58, 6, pp. 627–630.

SCITOVSKY, T. (1964), *Papers on Welfare and Growth*, Allen and Unwin, London.

SCITOVSKY, T. (1971), *Welfare and Competition* (second edition), Allen and Unwin, London.

SCITOVSKY, T. (1976), *The Joyless Economy*, Oxford University Press, London.

SHEPHERD, W.G. (1975), *The Treatment of Market Power*, Columbia University Press, New York.

SHERMAN, H. (1972), *Radical Political Economy*, Basic Books, London.

SMITH, A. (1977), *The Wealth of Nations*, Everyman Edition, London.

STANWORTH, P. and GIDDENS, A. (1975), The modern corporate economy: Interlocking directorships in Britain, 1906–70, *Sociological Review*, vol. 23, 1, pp. 5–28.

STIGLER, G.J. (1947), The kinky oligopoly demand curve and rigid prices, *Journal of Political Economy*, vol. 55, 5, pp. 432–449.

STIGLER, G.J. (1956), The statistics of monopoly and merger, *Journal of Political Economy*, vol. 64, 1, pp. 33–40.

STIGLER, G.J. (1968), Barriers to entry, economies of scale and firm size, in *The Organisation of Industry*, Irwin.

STIGLER, G.J. (1970), Reciprocity, in *Report of Stigler Task Force on Productivity and Competition*, reprinted in *Economic Concentration*, Part 8, Washington DC.

STIGLER, G.J. (1976), The Xistence of X-Efficiency, *American Economic Review*, vol. 66, 1, pp. 213–216.

SUTHERLAND, A. (1969), *The Monopolies Commission in Action*, Cambridge University Press, Cambridge.

SWANN, D. (1979), *Competition and Consumer Protection*, Penguin Books, Harmondsworth.

SWANN, D., O'BRIEN, D.P., MAUNDER, W.P.J. and HOWE, W.S. (1974), *Competition in British Industry*, Allen and Unwin, London.

SWEEZY, P.M. (1972), Comment, in Symposium: Economics of the New Left, *Quarterly Journal of Economics*, vol. 86, 4, pp. 658–664.

TAYLOR, C.T. and SILBERSTON, A. (1973), *The Economic Impact of the Patent System*, Cambridge University Press.

TELSER, L.G. (1964), Advertising and competition, *Journal of Political Economy*, vol. 72, 6, pp. 537–562.

TULLOCK, G. (1967), The welfare costs of tariffs, monopolies and theft, *Western Economic Journal*, vol. 5, 2, pp. 224–232.

UTTON, M.A. (1975), British merger policy, in George, K.D. and Joll, C. (eds.) *Competition Policy in the UK and EEC*, Cambridge University Press, Cambridge.

UTTON, M.A. (1979), *Diversification and Competition*, Cambridge University Press, Cambridge.

UTTON, M.A. (1981a), *Domestic Concentration and International Trade*, Discussion Paper 42, National Institute of Economic and Social Research.

UTTON, M.A. (1981b), *Persistent Concentration, Import Competition and Industrial Performance*, mimeo.

WEISS, L. (1969), Advertising, profits and corporate taxes, *Review of Economics and Statistics*, vol. 51, 4, pp. 421–430.

WEISS, L.W. (1974), The concentration–profits relationship and anti-trust, in Goldschmid, H.J., Mann, H.M. and Weston, J.F. (eds) *Industrial Concentration: the New Learning*, Little, Brown & Co., Boston, Mass.

WILLIAMSON, O.E. (1971), Managerial discretion, organisational form and the multidivisional hypothesis, in Marris, R. and Wood, A. (eds) *The Corporate Economy*, Macmillan, London.

WILLIAMSON, O.E. (1972), Economies as an antitrust defense: The welfare trade-offs, reprinted with amendments in Rowley, C.K. (ed.) *Readings in Industrial Economics*, Vol. 2. Macmillan, London.

WINKLER, J.T. (1976), Corporatism, *European Journal of Sociology*, vol. 17, 1, pp. 100–136.

VANEK, J. (1969), Decentralisation under workers management: A theoretical appraisal, *American Economic Review*, vol. 59, 5, pp. 1006–1014.

Index